A Glass Half Full

SOUTH ASIA DEVELOPMENT FORUM

A Glass Half Full

The Promise of Regional Trade in South Asia

SANJAY KATHURIA, EDITOR

South Asia Development Forum

Home to a fifth of mankind, and to almost half of the people living in poverty, South Asia is also a region of marked contrasts: from conflict-affected areas to vibrant democracies, from demographic bulges to aging societies, from energy crises to global companies. This series explores the challenges faced by a region whose fate is critical to the success of global development in the early 21st century, and that can also make a difference for global peace. The volumes in it organize in an accessible way findings from recent research and lessons of experience, across a range of development topics. The series is intended to present new ideas and to stimulate debate among practitioners, researchers, and all those interested in public policies. In doing so, it exposes the options faced by decision makers in the region and highlights the enormous potential of this fast-changing part of the world.

Contents

    Sanjay Kathuria and Priya Mathur

    Introduction   27

    Establishing the Context for Intraregional Trade in
    South Asia   32

    The Untapped Trade Potential   35

    Barriers to Intraregional Trade and Investment   39

    The Benefits of Current Trade Patterns   53

    Conclusions   64

    Annex 1A: Tables   65

    Notes   77

    References   81

2 **Border Tax Distortions in South Asia: The Impact on
    Regional Integration**   87
    Sanjay Kathuria and Guillermo Arenas

    Introduction   87

    Trade Protection in South Asia   88

    Tariff-Related Constraints on SAFTA's Effectiveness   97

    Conclusions and Directions for Reform   100

    Notes   102

    References   104

3 **A Granular Approach to Addressing Nontariff
    Barriers: India's Trade with Bangladesh and Nepal**   105
    Nisha Taneja

    Introduction   105

    Approach of the Chapter   106

    Institutional Framework and Regulations Governing NTMs   109

    NTM Restrictiveness, Regulations, and Procedural Obstacles   117

    Conclusion and Policy Recommendations   138

    Annex 3A: Classification of Nontariff Measures by Chapter   141

    Annex 3B: Sanitary and Phytosanitary Measures and
    Technical Barriers to Trade   142

    Annex 3C: Classification of Procedural Obstacles   143

    Annex 3D: Harmonized System Codes, Selected Items   144

    Annex 3E: Questionnaire for the NTM Survey:
    India and Nepal   145

4 Reducing Connectivity Costs: Air Travel Liberalization between India and Sri Lanka

Sanjay Kathuria, Mauro Boffa, Nadeem Rizwan, Raveen Ekanayake,
Visvanathan Subramaniam, and Janaka Wijayasiri

5 Bangladesh–India Border Markets: Borders as Meeting Points

Mohini Datt, Prithviraj Nath, Indranil Bose, and
Sayandeep Chattopadhyay

Boxes

Figures

Foreword

I am delighted to have in my hand a book that asks how we can turn proximity from a burden to an advantage. *A Glass Half Full: The Promise of Regional Trade in South Asia* advocates an approach of open regionalism, using intraregional trade as complementary to, and as a stepping stone for, deeper global integration. This book, written by Sanjay Kathuria and a team of South Asian researchers, stands out for its effort to bring together in a single tome theoretical knowledge and ground realities of trade in South Asia.

This is a much-needed book. I have long been acutely aware of the huge potential of regional trade and exchange in South Asia, which can power the entire region to grow faster and improve standards of living. To leave this untapped is a wastefulness that has little justification in a region that still has so much poverty and malnutrition. It is sobering to recall that South Asia still accounts for 33 percent of the world's poor and 40 percent of the world's stunted children. I have for long argued that the right way to evaluate a society is in terms of the well-being of its bottom segment.

The immense value of this book lies in the fact that it does not just make a case for greater regional trade and cooperation; rather, it shores it up with detailed data and surveys conducted specially for this project. All policy makers of the region would be well-served to read this book, which shows that had South Asia not created artificial barriers, our countries would be trading three times as much among themselves as they currently do.

Recent growth in most major South Asian economies has been the subject of global interest and analysis. Take the case of Bangladesh. Once a basket case, Bangladesh has become one of Asia's unexpected success stories in recent years, in terms of growth and also in terms of many social indicators. But there is no room for complacency. This is where Bangladesh can harness the fruits of deeper cooperation between itself and its neighbors on trade, investment, connectivity, and energy—efforts that will be critical for sustainability and overall development.

This is true for all South Asian countries, large or small. Even India, the largest country in the region, will benefit. Deeper regional trade and connectivity can, for example, reduce the isolation of northeast India, give India better access to markets in East Asia, and allow it to substitute fossil fuels by cleaner hydropower from Nepal and Bhutan. Trade between India and Pakistan is a paltry US$2 billion. The book shows that without artificial barriers, this should be US$37 billion. My hope is that such interaction will go beyond economic gains and help promote trust and peace, as the book illustrates so well.

One learns an immense amount from this monograph, such as the role of haats on the edge of India and Bangladesh. These local border markets enable small volume trading for local communities on both sides of the border. An initiative by the governments of Bangladesh and India aimed at recapturing the once thriving economic and cultural relationships is now changing cross-border relations, reducing incentives for smuggling. Moreover, the interaction across the border has bolstered trust and cooperation among Indians and Bangladeshis.

Another interesting case is India-Sri Lanka air services liberalization. Today, Indians and Sri Lankans enjoy direct connections from Colombo to 14 Indian cities, with a total of about 147 flights per week, resulting in India becoming the largest source of foreign tourists in Sri Lanka. Overall, however, connectivity among South Asian countries, even for capital cities, is still very limited. This deters trade.

Despite the existence of the South Asian Free Trade Area (SAFTA) since 2006, we are far from achieving the goal of tariff-free trade. This report brings to light fresh evidence on rather opaque "paratariffs" levied by some countries in the region. Such tariffs are basically import duties in disguise, and imply that, in practice, there are very substantial duties on a wide range of products traded within South Asia, despite SAFTA.

When I joined the World Bank, one of my first projects was to initiate a report on mind, society, and behavior—about the role of psychology and social norms in promoting development. When we think of development and growth, we focus on getting our fiscal policy right, monetary policy right, and taxation system right, and indeed these are extremely important. But a society's development also depends on the social norms and mindsets of the people. Cross-country studies show that nations in which there is a lot of trust among people do well economically. One message that emerges from this multicountry study strongly reinforces this. Trust promotes trade; and trade fosters trust, interdependency, and constituencies for peace. Bad history can still result in positive outcomes, provided our countries take incremental yet concrete steps to tap the potential of deeper integration in the region.

As economists, our primary function is to encourage an informed debate, so that policy makers have solid foundations on which to build their actions. This report more than fulfills its share of the bargain. There is a lot for the important stakeholders, especially policy makers and civil society, to now take forward.

Kaushik Basu

Professor of Economics and C. Marks Professor, Cornell University, Ithaca, New York
Former Chief Economist of the World Bank (2012–16)

Acknowledgments

This report was prepared by a core team led by Sanjay Kathuria, and included Priya Mathur, Nadeem Rizwan, Mohini Datt, and (in earlier stages) Sohaib Shahid. Nikita Singla led the outreach and dissemination effort. Grace James supported the team during the entire cycle of production. The primary authors of each chapter were as follows: Overview and Chapter 1 (Sanjay Kathuria and Priya Mathur); Chapter 2 (Sanjay Kathuria and Guillermo Arenas); Chapter 3 (Nisha Taneja); Chapter 4 (Sanjay Kathuria, Mauro Boffa, Nadeem Rizwan, Raveen Ekanayake, Visvanathan Subramaniam, and Janaka Wijayasiri); and Chapter 5 (Mohini Datt, Prithviraj Nath, Indranil Bose, and Sayandeep Chattopadhyay). Prabir De was a key contributor to Chapter 3, leading some of the field work and helping in the design of the questionnaire. The primary surveys for this report were undertaken by the South Asia Watch on Trade, Economics and Environment (SAWTEE) in Kathmandu; the Consumer Unity and Trust Society (CUTS), Jaipur, in collaboration with Unnayan Shamannay in Dhaka; the Bureau of Research on Industry and Economic Fundamentals (BRIEF) in New Delhi; and the Policy Research Institute (PRI) in Dhaka.

Other contributors included Hiau Looi Kee, Marcio Augusto De La Cruz Gomez, Ravindra Yatawara, Sandeep Kohli, Shruti Vijayakumar, and T. G. Srinivasan.

The team thanks the following for very helpful comments and reviews: Aaditya Matoo, Ali Zafar, Anabel Gonzalez, Anushka Wijesinha, Charles Kunaka, Charles Schlumberger, Garry Pursell, Gladys Lopez-Acevedo, Hiau Looi Kee, Jose Daniel Reyes, Jose Guilherme Reis, Manique Gunasekera, Martin Rama, Matías Herrera Dappe, Michael Engman, Michael J. Ferrantino, Michael Friis Jensen, Prabir De, Pritam Banerjee, Nadia Rocha, Philippe H. Le Houerou, Rohan Perera, Sebastian Saez, and Siddharth Sharma.

The report was prepared under the guidance of Manuela Francisco and (earlier) Esperanza Lasagabaster and under the stewardship of Robert Saum and (earlier) Salman Zaheer.

The team thanks the South Asia External Communications team, including Alexander Anthony Ferguson, Dilinika Peiris, Elena Karaban, Joe Qian, Mehreen Saeed, Mehrin Mahbub, Nandita Roy, Rajib Upadhya, Raouf Zia, Sudip Mozumder, and Yann Doignon for its proactive involvement and support.

The team is very grateful to Kaushik Basu for writing the Foreword and to Arvind Subramanian, Indrajit Coomaraswamy, Ishrat Husain, Reema Nanavaty, Swarnim Waglé, and Wahiduddin Mahmud for sharing their thoughts on the book.

The team would like to place on record its sincere appreciation to the Department for International Development for its steadfast support for the preparation of the report and the overall regional trade agenda in South Asia, and to the governments of all South Asian countries for their cooperation.

About the Editor and Authors

About the Editor

Sanjay Kathuria is Lead Economist and Coordinator, South Asia Regional Integration, in the World Bank's Macroeconomics, Trade, and Investment Global Practice, based in Washington, DC. In more than 25 years at the World Bank, he has worked in several regions, including Europe and Central Asia, Latin America and the Caribbean, and South Asia. Prior to joining the World Bank, he was a Fellow at the Indian Council for Research on International Economic Relations in New Delhi. He graduated from St. Stephen's College, and he received his master's at the Delhi School of Economics and his doctorate from Oxford University. His research interests include economic growth, international trade and trade policy, economic integration, competitiveness, technology development, fiscal policy, and financial sector development.

About the Authors

Guillermo Arenas is an economist in the Global Trade and Regional Integration unit at the World Bank. He specializes in the microeconomic analysis of trade and fiscal policies using firm-level data.

Mauro Boffa is a Research Associate at the Robert Schuman Centre for Advanced Studies. His main specialization is international economics, with a particular focus on e-commerce and the impact of trade policies on international trade flows and global value chains.

Indranil Bose is Associate Professor, Department of Political Science, St. Xavier's College, Kolkata, India. His research interests include political economy, public administration, and international relations.

Sayandeep Chattopadhyay is Research Associate, CUTS International, India. His research interests include connectivity, trade facilitation, and grassroots development.

Mohini Datt has worked in development and trade for more than a decade, largely at the World Bank. She currently works at the UK Government's newly formed Department for International Trade as a senior trade policy adviser on UK-South Asia relations.

Raveen Ekanayake was a Research Officer at the Institute of Policy Studies of Sri Lanka, with research interests in trade, foreign direct investment, and private sector development.

Priya Mathur has worked in development as an economist at the World Bank, as well as a strategy consultant in the private sector with the Boston Consulting Group. Currently, she works with the World Bank on international trade and regional integration and on global value chains.

Prithviraj Nath is Associate Director, CUTS International, India. His research interests include connectivity, regional integration, trade facilitation, sustainability, and grass-roots development, with a focus on the Bay of Bengal region.

Nadeem Rizwan is a consultant in the Macroeconomics, Trade, and Investment Global Practice of the World Bank. He works on trade policy, competitiveness, and regional integration issues in South Asia.

Visvanathan Subramaniam is a master's degree candidate in international affairs at the Graduate Institute of International Affairs and Development, Geneva, with a specialization in trade and international finance.

Nisha Taneja is Professor at the Indian Council for Research on International Economic Relations. Her broad areas of interest include World Trade Organization issues, regional trade, industrial economics, and institutional economics.

Janaka Wijayasiri is a Research Fellow at the Institute of Policy Studies of Sri Lanka. His areas of research interest include trade issues at the bilateral, regional, and multilateral levels of policy significance to Sri Lanka.

Abbreviations

ASA	air services agreement
ASEAN	Association of Southeast Asian Nations
BHMC	border haat management committee
BSTI	Bangladesh Standards and Testing Institution
CAGR	compound annual growth rate
CAM	conformity assessment measure
CBEC	Central Board of Excise and Customs (India)
CDIS	Coordinated Direct Investment Survey
cess	Export Development Board Levy (Sri Lanka)
CUTS	Consumer Unity and Trust Society
DDA	Department of Drug Administration (Nepal)
DGDA	Directorate General of Drug Administration (Bangladesh)
DIIO	Data In, Intelligence Out
FDI	foreign direct investment
FSS	food safety standard
FSSAI	Food Safety and Standards Authority of India
FTA	free trade agreement
GDP	gross domestic product
GMP	Good Manufacturing Practice (World Health Organization)
GST	goods and services tax
ICAO	International Civil Aviation Organization
ISO	International Organization for Standardization
ITC	International Trade Centre
Mercosur	Regional trade association of Argentina, Brazil, Paraguay, Uruguay, and República Bolivariana de Venezuela
mg/kg	milligrams per kilogram
MOU	memorandum of understanding

NABL	National Accreditation Board for Testing and Calibration Laboratories (India)
NAFTA	North American Free Trade Agreement
NTM	nontariff measure
OSA	open skies agreement
PAL	ports and airports development levy (Sri Lanka)
PIC	Pharmaceutical Inspection Convention
PIC/S	Pharmaceutical Inspection Convention and Pharmaceutical Inspection Co-operation Scheme
PO	procedural obstacle
PRA	pest risk analysis
RTA	regional trade agreement
SAARC	South Asian Association for Regional Cooperation
SAFTA	South Asian Free Trade Area
SARSO	South Asian Regional Standards Organization
SITC	Standard International Trade Classification
SPS	sanitary and phytosanitary standard
TBT	technical barriers to trade
TR	technical requirement
UNCTAD	United Nations Conference on Trade and Development
VAT	value added tax
WHO	World Health Organization
WITS	World Integrated Trade Solution
WTO	World Trade Organization

Note: All dollar amounts are U.S. dollars ($) unless otherwise indicated.

Executive Summary

What if the trade between India and Pakistan were valued at $37 billion instead of $2 billion? What if trade between the countries of South Asia were valued at $67 billion instead of $23 billion?

These are not pipe dreams. They are the predictions of detailed econometric models. These models show that, given their proximity and the size of their economies, the countries of South Asia should be trading among themselves at three times the current levels.

Why Is There Such a Large Gap between the Reality and the Potential?

Many South Asian countries trade on better terms with distant economies than with their own neighbors. This can be shown through an index of trade restrictiveness. Based on global trade data, such an index generates an implicit tariff that measures a country's tariff and nontariff barriers on imports. In India, Nepal, Pakistan, and Sri Lanka, the indexes are two to nine times higher for imports from the South Asia region than for imports from the rest of the world.

The costs of trade are disproportionately high within South Asia compared with other regional trade blocks. For example, the average costs of trade within South Asia are 20 percent higher relative to country pairs in the Association of Southeast Asian Nations (ASEAN) and over three times higher than the corresponding costs among the countries of the North American Free Trade Agreement.

The agreement to implement the South Asian Free Trade Area (SAFTA) came into force in 2006, but SAFTA is still far from achieving the goal of tariff-free trade. Under SAFTA, South Asian countries have been lowering tariffs. However, several countries in the region have adopted opaque paratariffs, that is, duties imposed on imports, but not on domestic production. Paratariff elimination has been kept outside the ambit of SAFTA and other free trade agreements in the region. This has contributed to SAFTA's underperformance.

In addition, more than one-third of intraregional trade in South Asia falls under sensitive lists, comprising goods that are exempted from the tariff rationalization program under SAFTA. Intraregional trade in such goods is subject to normal tariffs, which can be quite high in many sectors, including consumer goods and agriculture.

Port restrictions on some bilateral trade in the region tend to diminish the advantages of shared land borders, including among the three biggest countries in the region. Pakistan allows only 138 items to be imported from India over the Attari–Wagah land route, the only land port between the two countries, despite the long, shared land border. This means that bilateral trade is dominated by trade along the sea route, which is not necessarily the most cost-effective avenue of trade for two contiguous countries with a long common border. Bangladesh and India also impose some restrictions on imports from each other at certain ports.

Access to each other's markets has also been eroded through the application of non-tariff measures (NTMs), that is, policy measures other than tariffs. While NTMs are applied in all countries to protect health and safety, they become nontariff barriers if they are unduly burdensome. Results of detailed surveys carried out for this report among traders involved in the Bangladesh–India and the India–Nepal trade demonstrate clearly that information asymmetries play a big role in creating misperceptions about the existence of nontariff barriers. Another common theme in the survey results is the delays stemming from inadequacies in border infrastructure and from cumbersome procedures.

Intraregional trade in services, such as tourism, education and medical services, and business services, is constrained by visa regimes, among other barriers. Visa regimes also limit intraregional foreign direct investment (FDI), which affects intraregional trade given the intricate links between investment and the growth of regional value chains.

Can We Begin to Imagine the Possibilities? Have There Been Any Actual Breakthroughs?

Two breakthroughs in the region have shed light on both the barriers and the opportunities. One relates to the hurdle created by the high costs of connectivity; the other centers on the lack of mutual trust between countries.

Even between capitals, regional air connectivity within South Asia is quite restricted. From this context emerged the India–Sri Lanka air services liberalization experience, which has involved the progressive liberalization of bilateral air connectivity. Today, Indians and Sri Lankans enjoy direct connections between Colombo and at least 12 Indian cities on around 147 flights per week. These multiple connections with India have allowed Sri Lanka to capitalize on the widespread growth of the Indian middle class.

By 2005, India had become the largest source of foreign tourists in Sri Lanka, and this also played a part in the post–civil war spurt in growth in the island country.

Trust promotes trade, and trade fosters trust, interdependency, and constituencies for peace. In South Asia, a complicated history and asymmetries in the size of economies, perpetuated by insufficient people-to-people interactions, have rendered trust a fragile commodity. An initiative by the governments of Bangladesh and India aimed at recapturing the once thriving economic and cultural relationships is now changing crossborder relations and reducing incentives for smuggling. This is occurring through haats, local border markets that enable small-volume trading among local communities on both sides of the border. The survey conducted for this report confirms significant increases in the income of vendors and in the creation of livelihood opportunities for women and marginalized workers, in India and Bangladesh. The haats have also led to a reduction in informal and illegal trading and generated a peace dividend. More than half the Indian respondents to the survey have a positive view of Bangladeshis, and an overwhelming proportion of Bangladeshi respondents have a positive view of Indians at the haats, views they attributed to their exposure to their Indian neighbors.

How Can South Asia Turn Its Proximity from a Burden to an Advantage?

A Glass Half Full: The Promise of Regional Trade in South Asia advocates an approach of open regionalism and views intraregional trade as complementary to and as a stepping-stone for deeper global integration. It unpacks four critical barriers to more effective intraregional trade integration and offers specific options for policy makers in the region to address these barriers. Given the context of South Asia, it focuses on incremental, yet concrete steps in four areas as the appropriate way to enhance intraregional trade in goods and services.

BORDER TAX DISTORTIONS

On the issue of border tax distortions, the report suggests targeting sensitive lists and paratariffs to enable real progress in SAFTA.

- Set the goal of adhering to an accelerated, time-bound schedule for the elimination of SAFTA sensitive lists within a period not to exceed 10 years, except for a few products of exceptional concern. A first step could be to lower the number of products in SAFTA sensitive lists to align them with sensitive lists in bilateral South Asian agreements.

- Form a panel of experts to establish a schedule for the elimination of paratariffs within a time frame that is credible, sufficiently ambitious, and acceptable to all parties. The exercise could begin with the reduction and accelerated removal of paratariffs on items not on sensitive lists.

NONTARIFF BARRIERS

With respect to nontariff barriers, the analysis points to a multipronged approach targeting information flows, procedures, and infrastructure. These can be seen as confidence-building measures that pave the way for eventual mutual recognition agreements. Many of the suggestions could be extended beyond India–Nepal and Bangladesh–India trade, which was the focus of the fieldwork.

Information Flows

• Explore a nontariff barrier resolution mechanism to enhance transparency and information flows and nudge the official system toward more rapid complaint settlement. This could be hosted by an institution that would provide traders with information to address problems, or direct their complaints to the relevant authorities while continuing to monitor progress until final resolution. A practical approach may involve establishing bilateral mechanisms and, based on demand, extending these to include other countries.

• Initiate information campaigns and workshops to reduce information asymmetry. For example, spread awareness about the need for and procedures relating to pest risk analysis (PRA) on agricultural products, including medicinal and aromatic plants, to enable imports of such products into India. Similarly, to reduce the historical dependence on the Central Food Laboratory in Kolkata for testing food products, inform stakeholders about the existence of the several notified and accredited laboratories in the private and public sectors.

Procedures and Infrastructure

• Establish a bilateral institutional mechanism between India and partner countries so that notification by the Food Safety and Standards Authority of India (FSSAI) of the partner country laboratories accredited by India's National Accreditation Board for Testing and Calibration Laboratories (NABL) is coordinated and expedited. This would help ensure that food imports to India are tested only on a random basis; it would also catalyze agricultural trade among countries in the region.

• Introduce electronic data interchange, risk management systems, and single windows at more locations along India's borders points to enable the realization of potential gains from coordination and efficiency. This is a prerequisite to enable FSSAI to execute risk-based profiling on-site for the efficient clearance of food imports.

• Streamline and enhance the transparency of procedures for importing pharmaceuticals and pharmaceutical raw materials into Bangladesh and Nepal. Currently, product registration and requisite authorization processes, which are mandatory for pharmaceutical imports, are cumbersome and time-consuming in both countries.

CONNECTIVITY COSTS

To improve air services and thereby reduce the costs of connectivity between countries, policy makers can draw several lessons from the liberalization of bilateral air services between India and Sri Lanka.

- Consider an approach that focuses on benefits to consumers and businesses and remains agnostic about the relative impact of liberalization on airline companies, irrespective of the country of origin.

- Deliberate on an incremental approach to free up air services as has been done by India and Sri Lanka. A gold standard such as an open skies agreement (OSA) is not necessary to begin liberalization.

- Support reforms that can reinforce the gains from air services liberalization. The Sri Lankan government's authorization of visa-on-arrival privileges for Indian tourists has complemented and may have even boosted the expansion in bilateral air services.

- Deliberate on the payoffs of policy persistence from the perspective of smaller countries. Thus, it was in the interest of the government of Sri Lanka to keep pushing for deeper liberalization in air services with India, given India's market size. Aviation authorities in other countries who do not have liberal air services agreements (ASAs) with India could envisage similar payoffs arising from policy persistence.

TRUST DEFICITS

South Asian policy makers could address the trust deficits among their countries by reinforcing the virtuous circle between trade and trust. The experience of Bangladesh–India border haats offers several useful, relevant insights.

- Reflect on ways to scale up the border haat initiative systematically in view of its strong positive impact on livelihoods and the building of relationships between people and officials on both sides of the border.

- Streamline procedures, improve facilities, and enhance the use of technology in haats to maximize welfare gains among the poor and largely poor people who participate in the haat program. All users of haats, including women and the poor, would benefit from efforts to minimize theft, expand opportunities for productive activities, and cut down on transport costs.

- Evaluate an approach that focuses on value limits rather than limitations on the number of products. Decision makers could consider the inclusion of products in high demand, which would boost the gains among both buyers and sellers. Overall purchase limits on buyers will ensure that trade volumes remain low and outside organized mainstream trade.

- Consider ways of capitalizing on the opportunities that haats offer to enhance women's participation. Unlike formal trade in South Asia, wherein women traders are not highly visible, the haats have enabled women to participate much more actively. This participation can be increased through modifications in haat design, location choices for new haats, operational guidelines to streamline the functioning of haats, and infrastructure upgrading.

- Deliberate on possible replication of the haat experience in the context of other land borders in South Asia, given the unambiguously positive impact that border haats have had in Bangladesh and India.

What Are the Considerations in the Careful Management of Trade Integration?

The South Asia trade integration strategy advocated in this report, similar to all trade reform, would create winners and losers. This calls for careful management of implementation. A sustainable process of trade integration, irrespective of who the trade partners are, will require the following ingredients: (1) precisely articulating the trade strategy, with timelines for reforms of all border taxes, communicated clearly and transparently to stakeholders; (2) Gradually phasing in trade liberalization in sectors where there are concerns about significant job displacement; (3) initiating a strategy to diversify sources of tax revenue that would reduce the often substantial dependence on trade taxes; (4) focusing on critical reforms that would help the economy and the private sector take advantage of trade liberalization, including improving trade facilitation, attracting high-quality FDI, and addressing key issues that constrain the ease of doing business; (5) negotiating enhanced market access within South Asia and in selected critical markets, especially in East Asia, which are underrepresented in the export basket of South Asian countries; (6) strengthening safety nets and training among those workers whose jobs are affected; (7) improving the links among education, training, and the job market to supply better skills to the sectors that gain from trade reform; and (8) defining a limited fiscal package with clear and transparent criteria for the firms or sectors that will be adversely affected by trade reforms.

Overview

SANJAY KATHURIA AND PRIYA MATHUR

The Issue

Trade has played a critical role in global poverty reduction. In harnessing the potential of trade, some of the most successful countries, such as economies in East Asia, Europe, and North America, have developed strong trade relationships with their neighbors. Intraregional trade accounts for 50 percent of total trade in East Asia and the Pacific and 22 percent in Sub-Saharan Africa, while it accounts for a little more than 5 percent of South Asia's total trade. Even in the case of the United States, a large continental economic power, its two largest trading partners are its immediate neighbors, Canada and Mexico. Using economic size as the denominator does not alter the result. Intraregional trade as a share of regional gross domestic product (GDP) hovers around only 1 percent in South Asia, versus 2.6 percent in Sub-Saharan Africa and about 11 percent in East Asia and the Pacific, reflecting low levels of trade within the South Asian region relative to the size of the economies (figure O.1).

In South Asia, both nature and man have contrived to fragment the region, denying countries and people the benefits of proximity. Gravity models show that total goods trade within South Asia could be worth $67 billion rather than the actual trade of only $23 billion. Formal trade between India and Pakistan could, for instance, be 15-fold more than current levels.

Despite these handicaps, trade among countries in South Asia continues to grow. Where the barriers are high, trade often flows along informal routes, through third

7

FIGURE O.1 Intraregional Trade as a Share of Regional GDP

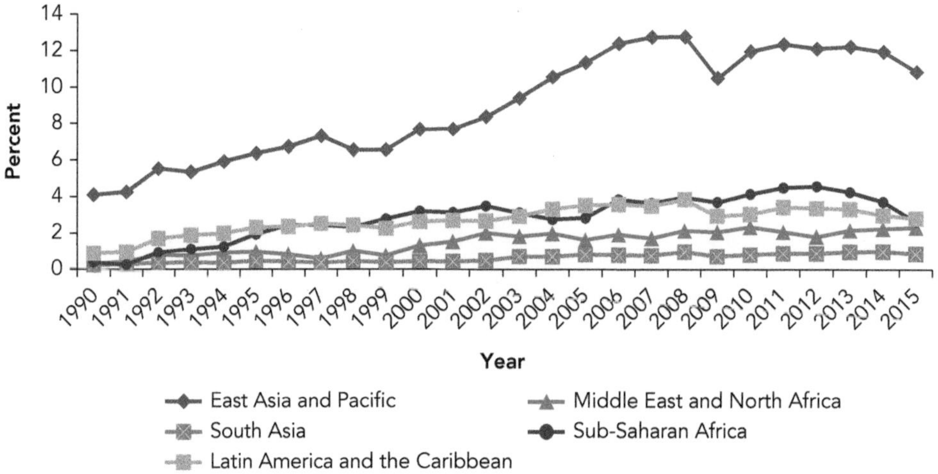

Sources: Data from UN Comtrade (United Nations Commodity Trade Statistics Database), Statistics Division, Department of Economic and Social Affairs, United Nations, New York, http://comtrade.un.org/db/; WITS (World Integrated Trade Solution) (database), World Bank, Washington, DC, http://wits.worldbank.org/WITS/.

countries or by avoiding customs checks. All countries in the region, irrespective of size, location, and endowments, gain from regional trade, although the impact is not symmetric. Consumers gain from access to a variety of food products, services, and consumer goods at lower prices. Producers and exporters gain from greater access to inputs, investment, and production networks. Firms, too, gain from regional trade through expanding market access in goods and services. Access to regional markets has also been important for services such as electricity and tourism. Gains from deeper cooperation are pronounced among landlocked countries and relatively isolated subregions.

And, yet, so much more is possible. India and Pakistan have merely scratched the surface of their bilateral trade potential. Only a fraction of the hydropower potential of the region has been tapped. Landlocked Afghanistan, Bhutan, and Nepal, as well as Northeast India and Khyber-Pakhtunkhwa and the Federally Administered Tribal Areas in Pakistan, could gain much more from better transit and connectivity. Regional tourism could grow much more quickly, as could trade in other services such as education, health care, and financial services. More foreign direct investment (FDI) within the region could help spawn regional and global value chains.

The report unpacks four of the critical barriers to effective integration and to resolving the unmet potential in trade in South Asia, as follows:

• Nontransparent and protective tariffs, especially paratariffs, which are taxes levied on imports, but not on domestic output. These paratariffs, along with the widespread exclusions from tariff preferences in the form of sensitive lists, have rendered the region's free trade agreement ineffective. They are analyzed in detail in the case of three countries that make extensive use of paratariffs.

• Real and perceived nontariff barriers, which exacerbate the trust deficit and affect the growth of trade. These are examined through the lens of specific products and trading relationships.

• Higher costs of connectivity, arising, for example, from restrictive bilateral air travel agreements. These are investigated using the India–Sri Lanka air travel agreement as a case study.

• The broader trust deficit, which has affected the overall South Asia integration effort. The analysis draws lessons from the Bangladesh–India border haats—local markets enabling small-volume trading among communities—that involve close people-to-people contacts and have helped reduce the trust deficit.

The report is not intended to be a complete treatment of country-specific trade issues, nor does it suggest that there be an exclusive focus on regional trade. The authors recognize that regional trade provides one among many development opportunities. First, intraregional trade is a subset of global trade, and global trading opportunities supply the greatest welfare gains. For example, most countries would benefit from greater trade with China; on the western side of the region, Afghanistan and Pakistan would benefit from expanded trade with the Islamic Republic of Iran and Turkey. Second, for a few small or landlocked countries in the region, a case may be made for diversification of trade sources within South Asia as well as beyond the region. The report focuses on the lost trading opportunities at the doorstep of South Asian countries—opportunities that, it shows, are significant and merit detailed examination. Moreover, the pursuit of intraregional trade need not occur at the expense of other trading opportunities; indeed, an open regionalism approach can help countries use regional integration as a stepping-stone to global integration. Finally, there are other regional cooperation possibilities in energy, transport connectivity, and water and ecological integrity, which are part of a broader World Bank Group program to support regional integration in South Asia.

The Symptoms

Actual intraregional trade in South Asia has not only been consistently below potential; the gap, based on the gravity model, has been widening, from only $7 billion in 2001 to $44 billion in 2015, partly because of the significant acceleration in GDP growth in South Asia relative to the world over that period (figure O.2).

Variations occur across countries in the gap between current and potential trade: India's trade with Pakistan, Bangladesh, and Afghanistan shows the highest levels of

FIGURE O.2 Intraregional Trade Potential in South Asia

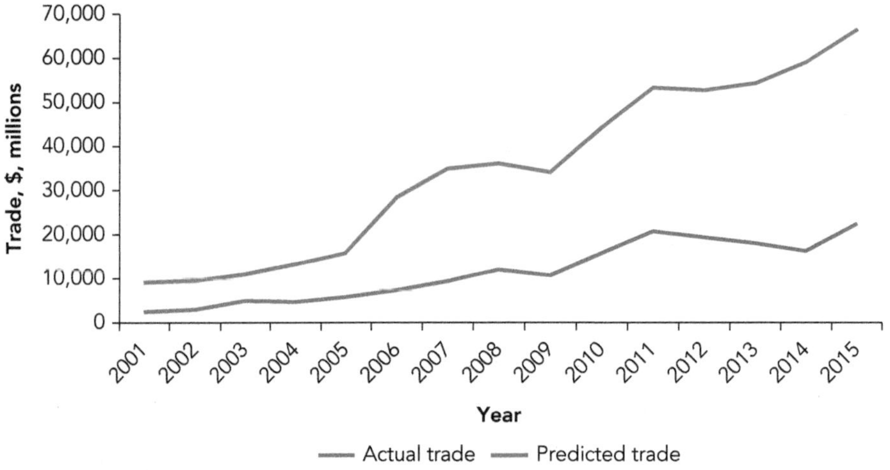

Source: Calculations based on data from CEPII Gravity Database, Centre d'Etudes Prospectives et d'Informations Internationales, Paris, http://www.cepii.fr/cepii/en/bdd_modele/presentation.asp?id=8; WITS (World Integrated Trade Solution) (database), World Bank, Washington, DC, http://wits.worldbank.org/WITS/.

undertrading (to the tune of $35 billion, $10 billion, and $700 million, respectively). In contrast, the trade between Afghanistan and Pakistan, India and Sri Lanka, and India and Nepal shows overtrading (of more than $1 billion in each case). However, further disaggregation between exports and imports reveals that Sri Lanka and Nepal underexport to India, even as they import more than predicted by the gravity model.

The force of gravity—the degree of trade attraction between countries—is also manifest in high levels of informal trade. Informal trade has been estimated at 50 percent of formal trade in South Asia, aggregating assessments of various studies for years between 1993 and 2005. India's informal trade with Nepal was as large as the formal trade; with Pakistan, it was 91 percent of formal trade; with Sri Lanka, it was about 30 percent; and, with Bhutan, it was almost three times the formal trade. More recent bilateral estimates of trade between India and Pakistan indicate that informal trade between the two countries in 2012–13 was almost double the value of formal trade, and most of this was routed through a third country.

The Barriers

The large gaps between actual and potential trade arise because countries in the region have erected barriers against each other. These barriers include high tariffs and paratariffs, despite a regional free trade agreement that came into force in 2006; disproportionately high costs of trading within the region that derive from poor transportation and logistics infrastructure and inefficient trade facilitation; complicated and nontransparent nontariff measures (NTMs), that is, policy measures other than tariffs that affect the free flow of goods and services across borders in the region; additional barriers to trade between the two largest economies in the region, India and Pakistan; constraints on trade in services, particularly in trade and visa regimes; and below-potential FDI, which also affects the deepening of regional value chains. Some of these barriers are highlighted below.

South Asian trade regimes discriminate against neighbors. In South Asia, protection is greater in the case of imports from within the South Asia region than from the rest of the world, as reflected in the overall trade restrictiveness index. This index measures the uniform tariff equivalent of a country's tariff and nontariff barriers that would generate the same level of import value for the country in a given year. As indicated in table O.1, the indexes are two to nine times higher for imports from the South Asia region than for imports from the rest of the world in all countries except Afghanistan. In the two largest economies in the region, India and Pakistan, the indexes are nine and six times higher, respectively, for imports from the South Asia region than for imports from the rest of the world. Moreover, although the average NTM burden may not appear high, it is high for specific product and market combinations in South Asia. It varies from over 75 percent to over 2000 percent; Sri Lanka's trade regime leads to that country's consistent appearance on the list of highest import ad valorem equivalents in the region.

Tariffs reappear in other forms. Even as South Asian countries have reduced tariffs, several countries in the region have simultaneously introduced protectionist paratariffs. Besides undermining tariff liberalization, these nontransparent paratariffs are not part of the phaseout program under the South Asian Free Trade Area (SAFTA) or other free trade agreements in the region, which reduces the preference margins for SAFTA partners. Bangladesh, Pakistan, and Sri Lanka maintain high paratariffs.

TABLE O.1 Overall Trade Restrictiveness Indexes, Selected Countries, South Asia, 2011

Importing country	Origin of imports	
	South Asia	Rest of world
Afghanistan	3.84	4.65
India	4.59	0.50
Sri Lanka	1.01	0.33
Nepal	10.59	6.87
Pakistan	3.00	0.51

Source: Chapter 1, box 1.2.
Note: The overall trade restrictiveness indexes are computed using applied tariffs that take into account bilateral preferences.

Shackled connectivity is reflected in the disproportionately high costs of trade. The costs of trading, which are a reflection of the transportation and logistics infrastructure and the efficiency of customs and border procedures, are considerably higher within South Asia than within other trade blocks of comparable size (figure O.3). For instance, the average level of trade costs is 20 percent higher between country pairs in South Asia than between country pairs in East Asia. It currently costs more to trade between some countries in South Asia than between these countries and, say, Brazil (shown for selected pairs in figure O.3).

Nontariff barriers erode market access. Complicated and nontransparent NTMs erode the market access granted by South Asian countries to each other and are sometimes held responsible for undermining the unrestricted market access granted to least developed countries by India. While all countries can legitimately impose NTMs to safeguard the interests of consumers and protect plant and animal life, NTMs become nontariff barriers if they are more burdensome than necessary to achieve a legitimate goal, for example, if border testing of imports takes inordinate amounts of time. An example of a nontariff barrier is the port restrictions imposed by several countries in the region. For instance, Pakistan allows only 138 items to be imported from India over the Attari–Wagah land route, the only land port between the two countries, despite the

FIGURE O.3 Average Intraregional and Interregional Trade Costs, 2010–15

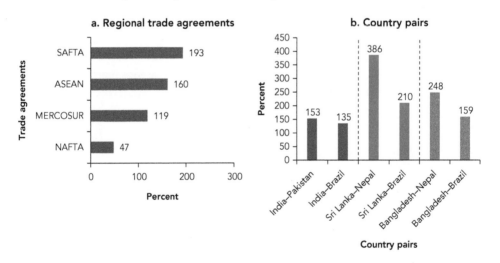

Source: Calculations based on data from the ESCAP–World Bank Trade Cost Database, United Nations Economic and Social Commission for Asia and the Pacific, Bangkok; World Bank, Washington, DC, http://www.unescap.org /resources/escap-world-bank-trade-cost-database.
Note: The unit of measurement is the ad valorem equivalent trade costs in percent. For the detailed methodology, see the source. The average intraregional trade costs are simple averages of the trade costs between country pairs in the respective trade blocs and across years; the average bilateral trade costs used in intraregional versus interregional comparisons are simple averages across years. ASEAN = Association of Southeast Asian Nations; MERCOSUR = Argentina, Brazil, Paraguay, Uruguay, and República Bolivariana de Venezuela; NAFTA = North American Free Trade Agreement; SAFTA = South Asian Free Trade Area.

long, shared land border. This means that bilateral trade is dominated by trade along the sea route, which is not necessarily the most cost-effective for two countries with a long shared land border. Bangladesh and India also impose some restrictions on imports from each other at certain ports.

Toward Realizing South Asia's Trade Potential

Given the context and situation in South Asia, incremental yet concrete steps to tap the potential of deeper integration are needed. This policy-focused report is advanced in this spirit, outlining specific actions to achieve concrete, measurable progress in different areas. It addresses four specific barriers that have constrained trade within South Asia: tariff and paratariff barriers; nontariff barriers, examined through the lens of selected products in Bangladesh–India and India–Nepal trade; the high costs of connectivity, focusing on air services and investigated using the India–Sri Lanka air travel agreement as a case study; and the trust deficit among South Asian countries, which underscores the importance of people-to-people interactions through initiatives such as the Bangladesh–India border haats program.

TARIFF AND PARATARIFF BARRIERS

Despite significant liberalization in tariff regimes by South Asian countries since the 1980s, average tariffs are still high. In 2016, average tariffs in South Asia were 13.6 percent, more than double the world average (6.3 percent) and the highest among major regions of the world. This high level of protection masks wide cross-sector variations in tariffs within many countries in South Asia, substantial protection on consumer goods, and a large wedge in protection between consumer goods and intermediate goods.

The study highlights two critical reasons that stand out in explaining the deficit in SAFTA's performance. First, each country maintains a long sensitive list of products that are exempted from the tariff liberalization program. Second, several countries in the region maintain high paratariffs, which have not been included in the tariff preference programs in free trade agreements.

Under SAFTA, the goal of duty-free trade is compromised by long sensitive lists that are maintained by all countries. Almost 35 percent of the value of intraregional trade in South Asia is subject to sensitive list tariffs; about 44 percent–45 percent of the imports from other SAFTA members fall under sensitive lists in Bangladesh and Sri Lanka; over 39 percent of India's exports to the region fall under the sensitive lists of various partners. SAFTA does not provide a clear guideline for phasing out the sensitive lists.

Maintained by several countries in the region, paratariffs are not part of the phaseout program under SAFTA or other free trade agreements in the region. By reducing the preference margins for SAFTA partners, paratariffs undermine the goals of SAFTA. Among the major economies in South Asia, Bangladesh, Pakistan, and Sri Lanka maintain high

TABLE O.2 Prevalence of Paratariffs in Bangladesh, Pakistan, and Sri Lanka

| Country, tariff | Tariff lines affected | | Rates, percent of affected tariff lines |
	Number	Share, %	
Bangladesh			
Regulatory duty	3,030	45.0	3 (99%), 15, 20
Supplementary duty	1,523	22.6	20 (61%), 45 (21%), 30 (5%), 10 (4%), 60 (4%), and six other rates between 100% and 500% (5%)
Value added tax	730	10.8	15 (100%)
Pakistan			
Regulatory duty	1,314	18.5	5 (30%), 10 (30%), 15 (26%), 30 (4%), and nine other rates between 2% and 60% (9.6%)
Additional duty, autos	146	2.1	15, 25, 30, 35
Additional duty, general	7,032	99.3	1 (100%)
Sri Lanka			
Ports and airports development levy	5,827	83.7	7.5 (89%), 2.5 (11%)
Cess	1,937	27.8	Ad valorem: 598 (1%–70%); specific: 522 (SL Rs 4/kg to SL Rs 6,000/kg); mixed: 817 (8% or SL Rs 25/kg to 35% or SL Rs 2,000/kg)

Source: In cooperation with the Policy Research Institute of Bangladesh, calculations based on data from the National Board of Revenue (Bangladesh), Sri Lanka Customs, and the Federal Bureau of Revenue (Pakistan). *Note:* Total number of tariff lines: Bangladesh = 6,739 (fiscal year 2016/17); Pakistan = 7,086 (fiscal year 2016/17); Sri Lanka = 6,965 (2016); kg = kilogram.

paratariffs (table O.2). They are not used in Nepal and are small in India. No data on paratariffs are available for Afghanistan, Bhutan, or Maldives.

Paratariffs can significantly increase the nominal protection rate. With the inclusion of paratariffs, the simple average tariff in Bangladesh in fiscal year 2016/17 almost doubles, from 13.3 percent to 25.6 percent; in Sri Lanka in 2016, the average tariff more than doubles, from 10.8 percent to 22.4 percent. For many individual products in these countries, the combination of paratariffs and customs duties results in high protection rates on the order of 40–80 percent.

The lack of effectiveness of SAFTA has created incentives for countries to pursue other free trade agreements both within and outside the region. For example, India has comprehensive economic partnerships, economic cooperation agreements, or free trade agreements with some 18 countries or country groups and is pursuing many others. Pakistan has 10 agreements in force, and more are being negotiated. Other countries, including Sri Lanka and Bangladesh, are also pursuing free trade agreements with multiple partners. Some of these other agreements could have led to the erosion of effective preferences within SAFTA and, in certain cases, may even have diverted some trade away from South Asian countries. Given that South Asian trade regimes discriminate against each other, an appropriate response is to eliminate such discrimination and make SAFTA (and other bilateral arrangements in South Asia) as effective as possible.

The report suggests three major areas of reform to make tariff liberalization under SAFTA more meaningful. They are also relevant to bilateral or subregional free trade agreements. These suggestions should be seen within the context of open regionalism, whereby regional trade integration is complementary to global integration.

First, to increase the volume of regional trade in South Asia and allow a genuine SAFTA to emerge, countries in the region should agree on an accelerated, time-bound schedule for the elimination of sensitive lists within a period not exceeding 10 years, except for a few products of exceptional concern. A first step could be to lower the number of products in SAFTA sensitive lists to align them with sensitive lists in bilateral South Asian agreements, such as the India–Sri Lanka and Pakistan–Sri Lanka free trade agreements.

Second, paratariffs need to be squarely addressed, with a panel of experts establishing a schedule for paratariff elimination within a time period that is credible, sufficiently ambitious, and acceptable to all parties. This will level the playing field between the countries that impose paratariffs and those that do not and enable tariff preferences to become more effective within SAFTA. An obvious starting point would be the reduction and accelerated elimination of paratariffs on items not on sensitive lists.

Third, SAFTA members should continue their efforts to eliminate tariffs on intraregional trade associated with their nonsensitive lists. Although the initial plan was to achieve full trade liberalization in SAFTA by 2016 (for nonsensitive items), some tariffs are still charged on imports from member countries. The goal should be to reduce all tariffs, inclusive of paratariffs, to zero for all products on nonsensitive lists (instead of the 0-to-5 percent range as originally planned). If the sensitive lists are reduced over 10 years, as suggested above, the zero-tariff formula for nonsensitive items would mean that protection would only occur (at least for SAFTA trade) through the sensitive list approach.

NONTARIFF BARRIERS

Traders across South Asia often complain about nontariff barriers. However, many complaints arise from lack of information on regulations and standards and inadequate infrastructure for measuring and certifying quality, rather than protection by the importing country.

It is necessary to address burdensome NTMs in South Asia by distinguishing between real and perceived complaints, thereby focusing the attention of policy makers on genuine issues; dealing with the misperceptions of traders; and, ultimately, bridging the gap between perceptions and objective evidence. This report examines NTMs in bilateral trade between Bangladesh and India and between India and Nepal in selected products of significance (exports of tea, cardamom, and medicinal and aromatic plants from Nepal to India; exports of processed foods, ready-made garments, and jute bags from Bangladesh to India; exports of pharmaceutical raw materials to Bangladesh from India; and exports of pharmaceuticals from India to Nepal). The study concentrates on measures relating to sanitary and phytosanitary standards (SPS) and technical barriers to trade (TBT), because these account for a majority of the nontariff barriers in South Asia. The study identifies procedural obstacles perceived by exporters in meeting SPS- and TBT-related NTM requirements, as captured through a survey. To distinguish between real and perceived issues, the information provided through the survey is triangulated with an assessment of the regulations and consultations with regulators in the three countries covered by the study.

The analysis underscores that information asymmetries are crucial in creating misperceptions, and a large part of the noise related to NTMs can be eliminated by dealing with information gaps. Another common theme is the delays stemming from inadequacies in border infrastructure and cumbersome procedures, such as those involved in product registration and renewal in the case of pharmaceutical products.

The report indicates several areas for policy consideration, targeting information flows, procedures, and infrastructure. Many of these can be seen as confidence-building measures that can pave the way for eventual mutual recognition agreements.

Information Flows

First, partners in South Asia could consider exploring a nontariff barrier resolution mechanism to enhance transparency and nudge the official system to settle NTM complaints more quickly. Drawing on the example of the mechanism set up by the African economic communities, such a system could include an online mechanism for reporting and monitoring complaints and hosted by an institution with some monitoring and evaluation capacity. This institution would provide traders with the necessary information to address their issues or to direct complaints to the relevant authorities within countries and continue monitoring each complaint until final resolution. Such an initiative would signal serious commitment to addressing nontariff barriers and could be an important step in reducing the trust deficit. A practical approach may involve establishing bilateral mechanisms and, based on demand, extend these to include other countries.

Second, partner countries could initiate information campaigns and workshops to reduce information asymmetry. For example, spreading awareness about the need for and procedures relating to pest risk analysis (PRA) on agricultural products, including medicinal and aromatic plants, would enable imports of such products into India. Requests for PRAs by importers in India and exporters in Bangladesh and Nepal could be fast-tracked under SAFTA/bilateral forums. This would also apply to other SAFTA countries.

Third, India as well as partner countries could spread awareness among exporters, importers, and regulators about all of the available public and private accredited laboratories in India. There has been historical dependence in India on only one public laboratory, namely, the Central Food Laboratory in Kolkata. This dependence continues to date because it is not widely known in Bangladesh, India, and Nepal that several laboratories in India now are accredited by the National Accreditation Board for Testing and Calibration Laboratories (NABL) and notified by the Food Safety and Standards Authority of India (FSSAI). Governments can develop marketing and communication strategies to familiarize traders with the various NABL-accredited and FSSAI-notified laboratories.

Procedures and Infrastructure

Fourth, establish a bilateral institutional mechanism to coordinate and expedite the FSSAI's notification of the partner country laboratories accredited by the NABL. It is not well known among traders and regulatory authorities in Bangladesh, India, and Nepal that test reports for food products issued by NABL-accredited laboratories in Bangladesh and Nepal are not accepted by Indian authorities unless these laboratories are also notified by the FSSAI.[1] Accordingly, it is suggested that an institutional mechanism be established bilaterally between the concerned countries so that notification by the FSSAI of NABL-accredited laboratories can be coordinated and expedited. This process would help ensure that food products imported into India are tested only on a random basis and help catalyze food trade, particularly agricultural trade, among countries in the region.

Fifth, introduce electronic data interchange, risk management systems, and single windows at more border points to enable realization of potential gains from coordination and efficiency. So far, electronic data interchange is operational between India and Nepal on one corridor along Kolkata to the Nepal border (Jogbani and Raxaul), while coordinated risk management has been introduced at the Bangladesh–India border (Petrapole/Benapole). Single-window systems at national levels have enabled greater coordination among agencies, thereby reducing transaction costs for traders. The FSSAI has been included in the single-window system and has introduced risk profiling to enable the system to identify high-risk consignments electronically. In general, electronic data interchanges can enhance risk profiling and are a prerequisite for single-window systems. Thus, if the goal is to achieve expedited clearance of food imports (with valid exporting-country test certificates recognized by India), electronic data interchange facilities need to be extended to other major land ports, such as Panitanki.

Sixth, streamline import procedures for pharmaceutical raw materials in Bangladesh and Nepal. Currently, product registration and requisite authorization processes, which are mandatory for pharmaceutical imports, are cumbersome and time-consuming in both countries. The Directorate General of Drug Administration (DGDA) in Bangladesh should streamline the process of product registration and reduce the time taken to register products and obtain requisite approvals. The pharmaceutical industry in Bangladesh would also benefit from this, given its heavy dependence on imports of pharmaceutical raw materials. Similarly, streamlining such processes in Nepal would benefit its local pharmaceutical industry.

THE HIGH COSTS OF CONNECTIVITY

A key obstacle to trade within South Asia is the disproportionately high costs of trading. The high costs arise from complex customs procedures, inadequate infrastructure at many border points, compliance costs associated with NTMs, and so forth. A key aspect of trade costs is connectivity, which depends on backbone transportation services between countries, such as air travel. The efficiency of air travel services can impact trade in goods because the transport of high-value, low-volume goods and trade in other services, such as tourism, health care, and education, often depend on air travel services. Moreover, the efficiency of air travel for business people can also affect FDI, and, ultimately, trade in goods and services.

Regional air connectivity within South Asia is restricted, and connectivity is poor even between capitals. Bilateral air connectivity is the best between India and Sri Lanka, which is a result of the progressive liberalization of air services between the two countries.

The report explores the issue of high connectivity costs in South Asia through the lens of air travel services by examining the liberalization of air services between India and Sri Lanka. The study tracks the evolution of the bilateral air services agreement (ASA) between India and Sri Lanka, focusing on the significant liberalization incorporated in the amendments of 2003 and 2011. The historical perspective is complemented by stakeholder interviews and econometric analysis to examine the impact of liberalization.

The first bilateral ASA between India and Sri Lanka, signed in 1948, has become progressively more liberal through decades of discussions, negotiations, and amendments. Although the agreement has not reached the status of a truly open skies arrangement, the major amendments of 2003 and 2011 have led to a freer bilateral air services market by allowing prices to be determined by the market, permitting private airlines to operate flights on bilateral routes, easing capacity limits and redefining them as flights per week rather than seats per week, and opening new destinations to bilateral air services.

The impact of the amendments of 2003 and 2011 on bilateral air services between India and Sri Lanka can be seen in the increase in the number of flights and seats between the two countries. During 2004–17, air services between India and Sri Lanka, in flights and seats, grew at a compound annual growth rate of about 6 percent. This bilateral air connectivity picked up pace after the end of the civil war in Sri Lanka in 2009: flights grew at 6.6 percent, and seats grew at 6.3 percent over 2010–17, more rapidly not only compared with the preceding years, but also relative to the air connectivity between India and Nepal (4.3 percent in flights and 5.1 percent in seats) and between Bangladesh and India (–1.3 percent in flights and 3.9 percent in seats) over the period. In 2017, air services between India and Sri Lanka continued to exceed, by a large margin, the services between the other two country pairs (figure O.4).

Econometric analysis applying a difference in differences approach reinforces the finding that the liberalization episode in 2011 had a positive effect on air connectivity

FIGURE O.4 Growth in Airline Seats Available between India and Selected Countries, 2004–17

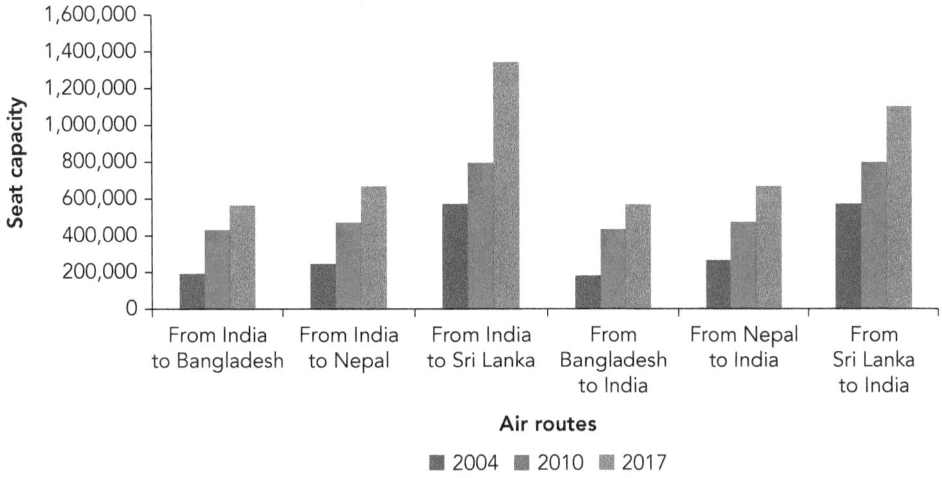

Source: Based on data from DIIO (Data In, Intelligence Out) (database), Diio, LLC, Reston, VA (accessed August 2017), https://www.diio.net/products/index.html.

between the two countries. The resulting estimates indicate increases of 16 flights and 2,442 seats a week attributable to the 2011 reforms.

Cargo volumes also received a stimulus from the 2003 and 2011 reforms, but growth in cargo volumes was less pronounced and less robust compared with passenger traffic growth. This finding can be partly explained by the dominance of low value-to-weight products, not typically transported by air freight, in the bilateral trade between India and Sri Lanka.

The reforms also had a positive impact on competition and pricing. Although historical pricing data are unavailable, stakeholder interviews confirm that prices fell, initially by as much as 20–40 percent on routes where there was competition, but the declines were rolled back partially as SriLankan Airlines came to dominate the bilateral air services market, accounting for 80 percent of the supply capacity. Another indication of the decline in airfares is the rising market share of low-cost carriers in seats and flights, which suggests that average fares should have declined over the period (table O.3). Similarly, fares on the New Delhi–to–Colombo route are typically much cheaper than those on another comparable major route, New Delhi to Dhaka, despite the fact that the flying time on the latter route is one-third less. Overall, while the impact on competition and prices has been positive, it could have been greater.

The demand for air services between India and Sri Lanka has been shaped not only by reforms, but also several other events, such as the end of the civil war in Sri Lanka in 2009, the authorization of visas upon arrival for Indian travelers by the Sri Lankan government

TABLE O.3 India–Sri Lanka: Growth in Seats and Flights, Low-Cost Carriers, and Other Alliances
Average number per month

Carrier type	Flights			Seats		
	2004–11	2011–16	Difference, %	2004–11	2011–16	Difference, %
Other alliances	401	475	19	69,273	79,084	14
Low-cost carriers	51	85	67	6,956	11,430	64

Source: Data of DIIO (Data In, Intelligence Out) (database), Diio, LLC, Reston, VA (accessed August 2017), https://www.diio.net/products/index.html.

in 2003, and the implementation of the India–Sri Lanka Free Trade Agreement in 2000. Together, these have meant that India–Sri Lanka air traffic continues to be the most robust and exceeds all other bilateral air traffic in the region.

The aviation industry, especially in Sri Lanka, has been a major beneficiary of the air services liberalization and the other factors that have shaped bilateral air services. For example, by 2007, SriLankan Airlines was the largest foreign airline operating in India in flights per week (94), although other carriers became more dominant in subsequent years. The economic impact has reached far beyond the aviation industry. For instance, the tourism industry has benefited in both countries, though more in Sri Lanka. India had become the largest source country of foreign tourists in Sri Lanka by 2005. There has also been steady growth since 2003 in the number of Sri Lankan tourists arriving in India.

Overall, the gains from air services liberalization between India and Sri Lanka have been substantial and can be increased by spurring more competition on the routes between the two countries. Other countries in South Asia can learn from this experience and strive for deeper air services liberalization with each other bilaterally or regionally.

First, the study suggests that policy makers remain agnostic about the relative impact of liberalization on specific airlines, irrespective of country of origin, because they should focus on bigger prizes, including the benefits to consumers of more choice in flights and airlines, better customer service, and lower prices, which could encourage deeper trade and investment.

Second, a key lesson for policy makers in South Asia is the understanding that a gold standard, such as an open skies agreement (OSA), is not necessary to begin liberalization. An alternative is to adopt an incremental approach, as has been done by India and Sri Lanka, toward the goal of freeing up air services.

Third, gains can be reinforced if air services liberalization is accompanied by supporting reforms. The Sri Lankan government's authorization of visa-on-arrival privileges for Indian tourists complemented and may even have boosted the expansion in bilateral air services.

Fourth, there are grounds to suggest that, although the liberalization of air services between India and Sri Lanka has had a significant beneficial impact, the gains could have been greater. The structural weaknesses faced by the airlines of the two countries, partly reflected in the losses of their respective national carriers, constrained the capacity of the airlines to serve on bilateral routes. In general, the biggest weaknesses usually involve capacity constraints arising from the lack of aircraft and poor service quality. These can be addressed through management contracts and strategic alliances as alternatives to or in conjunction with foreign equity participation. The Indian government's progressive liberalization of foreign investment in the airline sector may offer some lessons to other countries in South Asia.

Fifth, the study highlights that it was in the interests of the government of Sri Lanka to keep pushing for deeper air services liberalization with India, given the relative size of India's market and the potential benefits to Sri Lanka of greater access to that market. This policy persistence has paid off for Sri Lanka, as documented in this report. Aviation authorities in other countries that still do not have liberal ASAs with India could keep this in mind, especially now that India's National Civil Aviation Policy 2016 offers a reciprocal OSA with the countries of the South Asian Association for Regional Cooperation (SAARC).

THE TRUST DEFICIT

Trust promotes trade, and trade fosters trust, interdependency, and constituencies for peace. In South Asia, the virtuous circle between trust and trade has been broken by a history of mutual mistrust rooted in historical conflict and size asymmetries across economies, which prevent South Asian countries from reaping the full economic benefits of geographical proximity and complementary resource endowments. The trust deficit and the negative stereotypes are perpetuated by a lack of people-to-people interactions.

Historic ties in areas along the Bangladesh–India border have meant that goods, especially essential agricultural commodities, have always been traded in these areas. However, once the hard borders were established, fenced, and strictly policed, much of the legal trade was truncated and replaced by informal trading and smuggling, some of which involved skirmishes.

An initiative by the governments of Bangladesh and India aimed at recapturing the once thriving economic and cultural relationships is now changing crossborder relations and reducing incentives for smuggling. This is occurring through haats, that is, local border markets. Based on detailed fieldwork in the four operational haats, as well as focus group and stakeholder discussions, this report analyzes the impact of haats on people-to-people relationships and trust building, as well as on employment and income generation in the local communities.

The study finds that border haats have had a disproportionately large and positive impact on welfare in local communities on both sides of the border through three channels:

- First, a gain in real income and the creation of livelihood opportunities, including among women and some of the most marginalized workers, as well as benefits for buyers

- Second, improved crossborder relations through deeper people-to-people contacts

- Third, a reduction in informal and illegal trading and the resulting peace dividend.

The border haats offer a significant supplementary source of income. Among Indian vendors, 97.5 percent saw substantial increases in income ("okay," "quite a lot–a lot"), while the corresponding share was 67.5 percent among Bangladeshi vendors (figure O.5). The haats have created jobs for transporters, laborers, and providers of ancillary services and boosted their incomes. These opportunities are also open to women, and, although uptake is affected by sociocultural constraints, women's participation can be encouraged by affirmative action, capacity building, better haat infrastructure, and easier access to the markets.

Border haats help consumers in rural border regions by providing a wider variety of goods at cheaper prices, goods for which there is inherent local demand and supply complementarity. Many of these goods are basic food items—otherwise less available throughout the year—and simple household goods.

FIGURE O.5 Ratings of Income Increases from Haat Trade

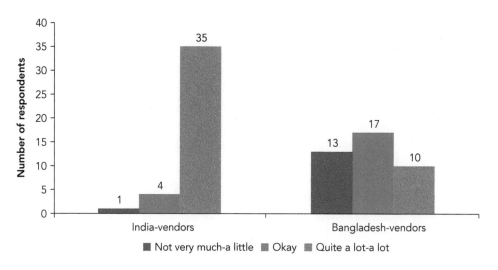

Source: Data from the India–Bangladesh border haats survey conducted by the Centre for International Trade, Economics, and Environment, Consumer Unity and Trust Society, Jaipur, India.

In supplying spaces for people to meet, reconnect, or establish fresh social and economic ties, the border haats have improved crossborder relations. Social mixing is a
large part of what a haat offers. Groups of people with a shared history have reconnected, including some families that had been separated for years. Over half the Indian
respondents have a positive view of Bangladeshis, and an overwhelming proportion
of Bangladeshi respondents express a positive view of Indians (figure O.6), views they
attribute to their exposure to their Indian neighbors at the haats.

Another positive impact of border haats has been a reduction in informal and illegal
trading and the resulting peace dividend. Bangladesh–India border trade has always
thrived, especially in essential agricultural commodities. According to Indian state government officials, informal trade was rampant before the border haats were created.
In formalizing informal trade and reducing smuggling, the haats have contributed to
the peace dividend and provided relief to agencies from the need for strict policing of
these regions.

A few key messages and policy implications derived from the analysis are as follows.
First, authorities could reflect on ways to scale up border haats systematically. The
study shows clearly that border haat trade comprises a very small proportion of formal
trade that would continue to be small even if the initiative is scaled up appreciably.
Haat trade does not detract from formal trade, given volume limitations, which make it
unattractive for more organized traders. It also has a disproportionately positive impact
on the livelihoods of people in nearby border regions. It similarly provides a bigger
peace- and relation-building dividend because of the face-to-face contacts involved

FIGURE O.6 The Views of Neighbors

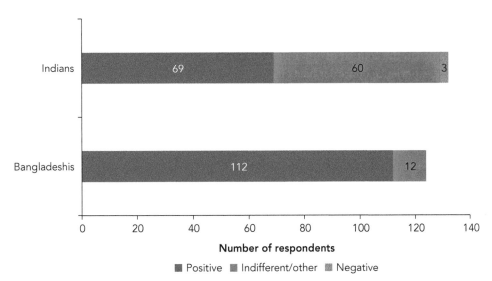

Number of respondents

■ Positive ■ Indifferent/other ■ Negative

Source: Data from the India–Bangladesh border haats survey conducted by the Centre for International Trade,
Economics, and Environment, Consumer Unity and Trust Society, Jaipur, India.

among vendors, laborers, buyers on both sides of the border, as well as among officials. This represents a strong case for aggressive expansion in the number of border haats.

Second, authorities could streamline procedures, improve facilities, and enhance the use of technology. Most people who participate in the haats are poor or very poor. Even small gains can be valuable to them. Currently, the haats are characterized by poor sanitary facilities, especially toilets; lack of running water, including drinking water; and substandard approach roads. These shortcomings exert a disproportionate impact on women and the poor. All users of haats, including women and the poor, would benefit from steps to minimize theft, expand opportunities for productive activities, cut down on transport costs, and so on, steps that are spelled out in some detail in the study.

Third, a focus on value limits rather than limitations on products would help increase welfare gains. Products currently traded include fresh fruits and vegetables and also manufactured products produced by reputable companies. The product list might be expanded to provide initially for more locally made or grown products, followed by other products in high demand, which would boost the gains among both buyers and sellers. The purchase limits on buyers will ensure that trade volumes remain low and outside the mainstream.

Fourth, local and national authorities could consider ways to capitalize on the opportunities that haats offer to enhance women's participation. Unlike formal trade in South Asia, wherein women traders are not highly visible, the haats have enabled women, particularly in Meghalaya, to participate actively as vendors and buyers. Much more is possible, even in societies that are not matrilineal. The study offers several suggestions to boost women's participation and ease their access to haats through modifications in haat design, the choice of location of new haats, operational guidelines to streamline the functioning of haats, capacity building for wider participation in haats, and infrastructure upgrading.

Fifth, countries in South Asia could deliberate on the possible replication of the haat experience in the context of other land borders in the region, given the unambiguously positive experience of border haats in Bangladesh and India.

A Synopsis

The objective of this report is to document systematically the gap between current and potential trade in South Asia and address important specific barriers that have held trade back. These barriers include tariffs and paratariffs, real and perceived non-tariff barriers, connectivity costs as manifest in the cost of air travel, and the broader trust deficit.

Much of the literature has addressed the obstacles to trade from a higher-level perspective and provided policy suggestions at a similar level of aggregation. However, such broad guidance does not seem to have catalyzed any significant momentum in South Asia toward removing critical policy obstacles.

This policy-focused report therefore pursues a different approach, undertaking in-depth studies on a curated list of barriers to trade and investment within South Asia that reflect the broader obstacles. The main focus is on four areas: tariff and paratariff barriers to trade; complicated and nontransparent NTMs; the disproportionately high costs of trade, especially because of poor transportation and logistics infrastructure, inefficient customs and border procedures, and poor intraregional connectivity; and the trust deficit in the region because of historical conflicts and size asymmetries. This approach is more pertinent to precise, actionable recommendations that are useful for policy makers.

The studies of four specific barriers described in this report are based on detailed knowledge gathering. Two are based on specific surveys and data collection, one of which includes focus group discussions; one is based on extensive stakeholder con-sultations; and the fourth has involved an analysis of tariffs, including new data on paratariffs. Two of the four studies (on air travel and border haats) highlight success stories and the related lessons.

Along the way, the report also documents experiences from around the world that clarify the motivations behind integration among various regional actors. Through an enumeration of the gains from existing trade, it illustrates current trade patterns and the potential benefits that deeper trade integration could help realize. It marshals new analysis that shows how trading regimes in South Asian countries discriminate against each other. It highlights the substantial problems in South Asia deriving from the lack of normal trade relations between the two largest economies in the region, India and Pakistan, and the special trading difficulties of transit and landlocked countries and subregions. It also illustrates the substantial advantages that could accrue to consumers, producers, exporters, and investors from more effective regional trade integration.

The South Asia trade integration strategy advocated in this report, like all trade reform, would create winners and losers. This calls for careful management of implementation. A sustainable process of trade integration, irrespective of the actors with whom a country is entering into a deeper partnership, will require the following ingredients:

- Precisely articulating the trade strategy, with timelines for reforms of all border taxes, communicated clearly and transparently to stakeholders

- Phasing in trade liberalization in sectors where there are concerns about large job displacement

- Implementing a strategy to diversify sources of tax revenue that would reduce the often substantial dependence on trade taxes

- Focusing on critical reforms that would help the economy and the private sector take advantage of trade liberalization, including improving trade facilitation, attracting high-quality FDI, and addressing key issues that constrain the ease of doing business

- Negotiating enhanced market access within South Asia and in selected critical markets, especially in East Asia, which are underrepresented in the export basket of South Asian countries

- Strengthening safety nets and training among those workers whose jobs are affected

- Improving the links among education, training, and the job market to supply better skills to the sectors that gain from trade reform

- Defining a limited fiscal package with clear and transparent criteria for the firms or sectors that will be adversely affected by trade reforms.

Note

1. In April 2017, the FSSAI authorized the Bangladesh Standards and Testing Institution (BSTI) to issue certificates of test analyses for 21 food products. See "Orders and Guidelines on Imports of Food Articles," Food Safety and Standards Authority of India, New Delhi, http:// fssai.gov.in/home/imports/order-guidelines.html.

CHAPTER 1

South Asia: A Work in Progress

SANJAY KATHURIA AND PRIYA MATHUR

Introduction

GENESIS

Trade has played a critical role in global poverty reduction. The number of the poor in the world declined from about 1.9 billion in 1990 to 0.8 billion in 2013, as measured by the poverty line of US$1.90 a day (2011 purchasing power parity); this decline was accompanied by an increase in the share of trade in the global economy, from about 39 percent in 1990 to over 60 percent in 2013.[1] In harnessing the potential of trade, some of the most successful countries, such as economies in East Asia, Europe, and North America, have developed strong trade relationships with their neighbors.

Yet, many countries in South Asia have trade regimes that discriminate against each other and thereby offset the positive impact of geography and proximity. Gravity models show that total goods trade within South Asia could be worth US$67 billion rather than the actual trade of only US$23 billion. Formal trade between India and Pakistan could, for example, be 15-fold more than current levels.

Nor has regional cooperation fulfilled expectations. A World Bank survey of informed regional stakeholders in Afghanistan, Bangladesh, Bhutan, India, Nepal, and Pakistan reveals that most people are dissatisfied with cooperation in the region; the share of dissatisfied respondents was 72 percent in Bangladesh and 85 percent–87 percent in India, Nepal, and Pakistan. Only Bhutan, at 42 percent, had a relatively higher share of satisfied respondents.[2]

Recognizing the lost development opportunity, the World Bank, based on consultations with external advisors on regional integration in South Asia, launched a program to build a more positive narrative on regional integration.[3] The program has three related pillars: knowledge generation, convening platforms and capacity building, and communications. The idea behind the program is to create a virtuous circle among the three pillars that could help gradually shape a more positive narrative. The present volume is one of the significant outputs of the program.

The objective of this report is to illustrate the gaps between current and potential trade in South Asia and address important specific barriers that have held trade back. These barriers include tariffs and paratariffs, real and perceived nontariff barriers, connectivity costs as manifested in the cost of air travel, and the broader trust deficit.[4] The report is not intended to be a complete treatment of country-specific trade issues.

The report's authors recognize that regional trade provides one among many development opportunities. First, intraregional trade is a subset of global trade, and global trading opportunities supply the greatest welfare gains. Thus, greater trade across regions is beneficial to all countries in the region; examples include China's trade with most countries, and the Islamic Republic of Iran and Turkey's trade with Afghanistan and Pakistan. Second, for a few small or landlocked countries in the region, a case may be made for the diversification of trade sources within South Asia, as well as beyond the region. Countries certainly have such choices, but the report focuses on the lost trading opportunities at the doorstep of South Asian countries—opportunities that, the report shows, are significant and merit detailed examination. Moreover, the pursuit of intraregional trade need not occur at the expense of other trading opportunities; indeed, an open regionalism approach can help countries use regional integration as a stepping-stone to global integration (see the following section).

Work on a crosscutting regional narrative is part of a broader program through which the World Bank is concentrating on interventions in critical sectors, including energy, transport connectivity, water, and ecological integrity; some of the initiatives are being developed through a coordinated approach across the countries of the region.

TRADE IN SOUTH ASIA

Intraregional trade accounts for a little more than 5 percent of South Asia's total trade, compared with 50 percent in East Asia and the Pacific and 22 percent in Sub-Saharan Africa. Even in the case of the United States, a large continental economy, the two largest trading partners are immediate neighbors, Canada and Mexico. Using economic size as the denominator does not alter the result. Intraregional trade as a share of regional gross domestic product (GDP) hovers around only 1.0 percent in South Asia, versus 2.6 percent in Sub-Saharan Africa and about 11.0 percent in East Asia and the Pacific, reflecting low levels of trade within the region relative to the size of the economies (figure 1.1). In South Asia, trade among the largest economies, particularly Bangladesh, India, and Pakistan, is well below potential. The latest gravity estimates, which have been carried out for this study, suggest that total potential merchandise trade in South Asia may be valued at around US$67 billion, almost three times the current trade value of US$23 billion. Moreover, because South Asia is the most rapidly growing region in the world, the gap between current and potential trade may continue to widen (figure 1.2).

FIGURE 1.1 Intraregional Trade as a Share of Regional GDP

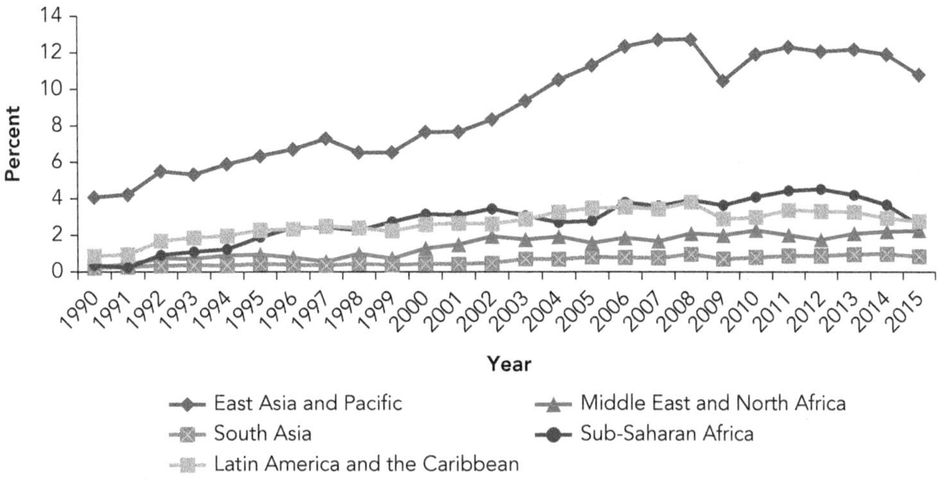

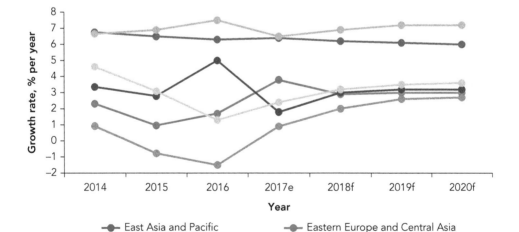

Source: Calculations based on data from UN Comtrade (United Nations Commodity Trade Statistics Database), Statistics Division, Department of Economic and Social Affairs, United Nations, New York, http://comtrade.un.org /db/; WDI (World Development Indicators) (database), World Bank, Washington, DC, http://data.worldbank.org /products/wdi; WITS (World Integrated Trade Solution) (database), World Bank, Washington, DC, http://wits .worldbank.org/WITS/.

FIGURE 1.2 South Asia Continues to be the Most Rapidly Growing Region in the World

Source: World Bank 2017, 2018.
Note: e = estimate; f = forecast.

Intraregional trade in South Asia falls short of its potential because of significant man-made barriers. In fact, as this chapter shows, the countries in the region erect discriminatory barriers against each other. These barriers include the following:

- High tariffs and paratariffs, despite a regional free trade agreement (FTA) that came into force in 2006

- Disproportionately high costs of trading within the region that arise because of poor transportation and logistics infrastructure and inefficient trade facilitation

- Complicated and nontransparent nontariff measures (NTMs) that especially affect the countries in the region

- Additional barriers to trade between the two largest economies in the region, India and Pakistan

- Constraints on trade in services, particularly in trade and visa regimes

- Below-potential foreign direct investment (FDI), which also affects the deepening of regional value chains (Kathuria and Shahid 2016).

An underlying theme in all these obstacles is the lack of mutual trust among South Asian countries, stemming from the complex history of these countries and reinforced by asymmetry in the size of economies. This dynamic also implies that confidence building through, for example, greater people-to-people interaction, will need to accompany traditional policy measures that address the barriers to trade.

Despite these handicaps, trade among countries in South Asia continues to grow and benefit consumers, exporters, and productive firms.[5] Where the barriers are high, trade often flows along informal routes, through third countries, or by avoiding customs checks. All countries in the region, irrespective of size, location, and endowments, gain from regional trade, although the impact is not symmetric. Consumers gain from access to a variety of food products, services, and consumer goods at lower prices. Producers and exporters gain from greater access to inputs, investment, and production networks. Firms, too, gain from regional trade through expanding market access in goods and services. Trade has been particularly useful for landlocked countries and subregions and for the smaller economies.

Even so, much more could be happening. India–Pakistan trade has merely scratched the surface. Only a fraction of the hydropower potential of the region has been tapped. Landlocked Afghanistan, Bhutan, Nepal, Northeast India, and Khyber-Pakhtunkhwa and the Federally Administered Tribal Areas in Pakistan could gain much more from better transit and connectivity. Regional tourism, such as in cultural circuits, could grow much more quickly, as could trade in other services, such as education, health care, and financial services. More FDI within the region could help spawn regional and global value chains.

More open trade in goods and services within South Asia represents the biggest prize for the individual. Other successful regions, such as East Asia, Europe, and

North America, demonstrate the possibilities of deeper integration translating into prosperity among the people. Deeper trade integration means consumers gain from access to a greater variety of food and other consumer products at lower prices. Job-seekers gain from employment related to exports and imports, which tend to be of higher quality than similar jobs in the domestic sector. A more liberal services trade regime would allow individuals to cross borders to study in schools or universities, use specialty hospitals, or explore job opportunities anywhere in the region with relative ease. It would also allow individuals to travel across borders for pleasure or to explore shared history or religion through the many opportunities for tourism offered in the region.

STRUCTURE OF THE REPORT

Much of the literature has addressed the obstacles to trade from a higher-level perspective and provided policy suggestions at a similar level of aggregation. However, such broad guidance does not seem to have catalyzed any significant momentum in South Asia to removing critical policy obstacles.

This policy-focused report addresses selected important and specific barriers that have held back trade and investment within South Asia. The World Bank has been pursuing a fresh approach to the subject by undertaking four specific, in-depth studies illustrating issues that are a subset of the broader obstacles that have been identified. This approach lends itself to more precise, actionable recommendations that are useful for policy makers. The four studies have produced detailed, on-the-ground knowledge. Two are based on surveys and data collection, one of which includes focus group discussions; the third is based on extensive stakeholder consultations; and the fourth has involved an analysis of tariffs that has put together new data on paratariffs. Two of the four studies (on air travel and border haats) highlight success stories and related lessons.[6] The barriers examined include the following:

- Nontransparent and protective tariffs, especially paratariffs, that, along with the widespread exclusions from tariff preferences in the form of sensitive lists, have rendered ineffective the region's FTA: These are analyzed in detail in three countries that make extensive use of paratariffs.

- Real and perceived nontariff barriers, which exacerbate the trust deficit and affect the growth of trade: These are examined through the lens of a handful of products and trading relationships.

- The higher costs of connectivity, arising, for example, from restrictive bilateral air travel agreements: These are investigated using the India–Sri Lanka air travel agreement as a case study.

- The broader trust deficit that has affected the overall South Asia integration effort: The analysis draws lessons from the Bangladesh–India border haats that involve close people-to-people contacts and have helped reduce the trust deficit.

Given the context and the current situation in South Asia, incremental, yet concrete, steps to tap the potential of deeper integration are appropriate. This report has been drafted in this spirit by outlining specific actions that could help achieve measurable progress in key areas.

Future reports will explore topics not covered in this volume. These will address, for example, the links between trade and border poverty, barriers to intraregional investment, the prospects of crossborder value chains in specific regions, and the promise of e-commerce as a possible means to surmount conventional barriers to trade.

The rest of this chapter is organized as follows. The next section documents experiences from around the world that clarify the motivations for integration among different regional groupings; it briefly discusses motivations beyond regional trade. The following section quantifies the untapped trade potential in South Asia. The subsequent section outlines the key barriers to deeper trade and investment relationships within South Asia. Through an enumeration of the gains from existing trade, the penultimate section analyzes current trade patterns and the potential benefits that deeper trade integration could help realize. The final section offers concluding thoughts.

The report often uses regional trade as shorthand for intraregional trade.

Establishing the Context for Intraregional Trade in South Asia

THE MOTIVATIONS FOR REGIONAL TRADE

In recent years, as multilateral trade liberalization has slowed, regional trade agreements (RTAs) have become the main instrument for reciprocal liberalization. As of April 26, 2018, 287 RTAs were in force worldwide, almost double the number in 2000; these agreements cover over half of all international trade.[7] Regionalism appears to be a useful tool to dismantle trade barriers if unilateral and multilateral efforts fail. Many factors have motivated regional integration, as amplified in the following paragraphs; some goals have been explicitly stated, while others are more implicit (Kritzinger-van Niekerk 2005; Schiff and Winters 2003).

Create Market Access for Enhanced Efficiency and Competition and Increased Trade
Regional integration enlarges the market for domestic firms, allowing them to exploit economies of scale and become more efficient. This is particularly important in small countries; market access through regional agreements can help them overcome the disadvantages of small domestic markets. Opening the economy also creates more competition, which induces firms to cut prices and improve efficiency, and enables them to compete more effectively in export markets. Notwithstanding the criticism of the North American Free Trade Agreement by the current U.S. administration, Mexico's experience after joining the agreement is a good example of sustained gains

in trade arising from an agreement between a smaller country, Mexico, and a much larger trading partner, the United States. U.S. imports from Mexico rose by about 500 percent from 1993, the year before the agreement, to 2012, more than twice as rapidly as imports from the rest of the world. U.S. exports to Mexico also rose more quickly than exports to the rest of the world (Kathuria and Shahid 2015). A 2006 study finds that Mexico has become an export platform for U.S. investors since 1994, a platform that has acted as a catalyst for Mexican export growth toward its agreement partners and the rest of the world (Tunea 2006).

Attract Enhanced Investment

Enlarged market access, along with improved policy credibility—through lock-in mechanisms in regional agreements—may also attract more FDI from within the region and from outside the region. FDI can supplement domestic investment and provide long-term balance of payments financing. It can help enhance the sophistication and competitiveness of exports through the introduction of new technologies and production processes. FDI can also enhance the access of producers to global production networks and facilitate the development of new activities within existing value chains. Since the establishment of the North American Free Trade Agreement, Mexico has seen a surge in FDI from the United States, a major expansion of its auto industry, improvement in labor skills, and a rise in manufacturing output (Scotiabank 2014).

Facilitate Deeper Integration

Regional agreements allow provisions to be adopted that are deeper than the more general standards applied by the World Trade Organization. The types of issues covered in such agreements are often more thoroughgoing than the traditional topics of tariffs and quantitative restrictions; they cover provisions related to NTMs, investment, labor migration, and more profound aspects of trade in services. Smaller groups with similar preferences make elements of deeper integration more likely. For example, in the Association of Southeast Asian Nations (ASEAN), regional cooperation has enabled enhanced trade facilitation (Kathuria, Shahid, and Ferrantino 2015). Most countries have established trade information portals, which allow traders to access electronically all the documents they need to obtain government approvals for export or import, or single windows, which allow the electronic submission of all documents. All national single windows are linked to the ASEAN Single Window, which supports a unified ASEAN customs declaration document and the exchange of intra-ASEAN certificates of origin.[8]

Enhance the Credibility of National Policy Reform through Lock-In Mechanisms

Regional agreements can help countries lock in difficult policy reforms and signal their commitment to such reforms. These commitment mechanisms apply not only to trade policy reform but also other economic reforms.[9]

Enhance Coordination on Regional Issues and Strengthen Bargaining Power in International Negotiations

Regional cooperation can allow countries to deal collectively and more effectively with common issues related to shared resources (for example, water), environmental issues such as flooding and glacier melt, or the spread of epidemics. Regional agreements may also enable countries to coordinate their positions in multilateral negotiations, such as at the World Trade Organization, and allow them to pool their limited financial resources and expert knowledge. The Caribbean Community, comprising small Caribbean nations, is an example of how a regional group can collectively improve visibility and bargaining power.[10]

Facilitate Trust Building and Enhance Security

Regional agreements can boost interdependency among countries by strengthening intraregional trade and investment links. This can foster deeper trust through people-to-people interaction and raise the opportunity costs of war, thereby reducing the risk of conflict between countries. Although regional arrangements may create tensions among member countries—for example, if one is seen to gain disproportionately more than others—developing a culture of and mechanisms for cooperation may improve intraregional security. It is widely believed that the creation of the European Economic Community in 1958 was motivated mostly by the desire to prevent future conflict among members (Freund and Ornelas 2010).[11]

Use Regional Integration as a Stepping-Stone to Global Integration

Regional integration need not detract from global integration. As discussed in a recent World Bank report, there are important complementarities between the two that make a region's international competitiveness and its ability to reach markets outside the region dependent on regional integration (Bown et al. 2017). Thus, in the context of the Latin America and Caribbean region, a combination of regional integration and global integration can boost the region's competitiveness for several reasons. First, the link between regional trade and global competitiveness can be best illustrated in the case of regionally traded goods, such as electricity and land transportation, which are typically traded only between neighbors because of the high costs associated with distance. Regional efforts to ensure efficient provision of these goods are important for the ability of the region to gain international competitiveness in sectors that use these goods intensively. The same argument can be extended to labor markets because the costs associated with migration are expected to increase with distance. The intraregional mobility of labor can enhance the regionwide efficiency of this migration. Second, knowledge diffusion and learning can be greater between nearby countries; however, the strength with which these channels affect a country's growth and competitiveness will be influenced by the stock of knowledge, the level of development, and the degree of global integration of partner nations. For example, the likelihood that a country will penetrate and survive in third markets is greater if the country's current trading partners are actively exporting to these markets. Thus, a country's ability to learn from the experience of its nearby partners depends on how open these partners are to global trade, which illustrates the complementarities between regional integration and global integration.

Despite the possible benefits, regional trading arrangements have faced serious challenges in all parts of the world. A key hurdle relevant to South Asia is the disproportionately large size of some countries within their respective regions, including Brazil, China, India, Nigeria, and South Africa, and the resulting perception that the large countries capture a disproportionate share of the benefits of regional trading arrangements (for example, see Sherov-Ignatiev and Sutyrin 2011). This is a frequent theme in this chapter.

BEYOND REGIONAL TRADE

In practice, most countries tend to pursue trading opportunities beyond their immediate region through preferential trading arrangements, as well as via the multilateral route. It is important for such countries to recognize the benefits of different agreements and to attempt to maximize their total benefits, given multiple trading agreements.

Among South Asian countries, trade beyond the region is a high priority. For example, China represents a trading opportunity that has not yet been fully tapped. This opportunity may even increase, as Chinese wages grow, imports continue to increase in China, and the Belt and Road Initiative of China becomes associated with a possible decline in the cost of exporting to and importing from China. Similarly, Afghanistan and Pakistan possess untapped trading opportunities in Central Asia, the Islamic Republic of Iran, Turkey, and beyond.

Landlocked countries in South Asia should consider an additional dimension. Their dilemma is the trade-off between more extensive trade with a large neighbor and the increasing dependency on that single neighbor and the costs this dependency might entail. Whatever the response to this problem, it is in the interests of landlocked countries to improve connectivity with the rest of the world and with other countries in South Asia.

Apart from the opportunities presented by the rest of the world, there are significant trading opportunities within South Asia that are underexploited. The task of this report is to quantify these opportunities and propose specific approaches to capitalize on them.

The Untapped Trade Potential

Several indicators highlight that South Asian trade may be below potential. First, gravity models as well as other approaches show that, in 2015, intraregional trade in goods in South Asia, valued at US$23 billion, was only about one-third of the trade potential of US$67 billion (box 1.1).[12] This is not surprising, given the many ways in which South Asian countries impose discriminatory barriers against each other, as documented in the next section. There are variations between country pairs in the gap between current and potential trade: India's trade with Pakistan, Bangladesh, and Afghanistan shows the highest levels of undertrading. In contrast, the trade between Afghanistan and

BOX 1.1 The Gravity Model Approach: Evidence of Untapped Trade Potential in
South Asia

Gravity models are based on the idea that geographically proximate countries tend
naturally to trade more with each other in the absence of barriers to trade. In the case of
South Asia, using the gravity model approach to determine potential trade flows (goods
only, throughout this discussion) among countries in the region suggests that intraregional
trade, valued at US$23 billion in 2015, represented only about one-third of the trade
potential of US$67 billion. Figure B1.1.1 shows that the actual intraregional trade in South
Asia has been consistently below potential and that the gap has risen, from only US$7
billion in 2001 to US$44 billion in 2015. The gap has been expanding partly because of the
significant acceleration in GDP growth in South Asia relative to the world over that period.

The big gap between trade potential and actual trade in 2015 may be largely attributed
to the gap in bilateral trade between Bangladesh and India and between India and
Pakistan, three of the largest economies in the region (table B1.1.1). The trade between
India and Pakistan, for example, was US$35 billion below potential. The model also
suggests that the trade between Afghanistan and Pakistan, India and Sri Lanka, and
India and Nepal exceeded potential by more than US$1 billion in 2015.

A more disaggregated analysis of the overtrading relationships reveals that the relatively
smaller countries, such as Afghanistan, Nepal, and Sri Lanka, generally import more
from their larger trading partners, such as India and Pakistan, than the model predicts.
However, exports from Nepal and Sri Lanka to India are significantly below potential. Only
Afghanistan's trade with Pakistan shows overtrading with respect to both imports and
exports (table B1.1.2).

FIGURE B1.1.1 Intraregional Trade in South Asia

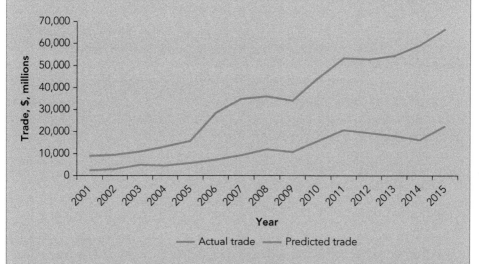

Source: Calculations based on data from CEPII Gravity Database, Centre d'Etudes Prospectives et
d'Informations Internationales, Paris, http://www.cepii.fr/cepii/en/bdd_modele/presentation.asp?id=8; WITS
(World Integrated Trade Solution) (database), World Bank, Washington, DC, http://wits.worldbank.org/WITS/.

box continues next page

BOX 1.1 The Gravity Model Approach: Evidence of Untapped Trade Potential in
South Asia *(continued)*

TABLE B1.1.1 Trade Relationships, South Asia
$, millions

Countries	Actual	Predicted	Actual–predicted
Undertrading			
India–Pakistan	2,117	36,915	−34,799
India–Bangladesh	6,522	16,441	−9,919
India–Afghanistan	448	1,124	−676
Bangladesh–Pakistan	837	1,376	−539
Bangladesh–Sri Lanka	150	573	−422
Overtrading			
Pakistan–Afghanistan	1,737	540	1,197
India–Sri Lanka	5,117	3,976	1,142
India–Nepal	4,498	3,362	1,136
Sri Lanka–Maldives	153	39	114
India–Maldives	232	229	3

Source: Calculations based on data from CEPII Gravity Database, Centre d'Etudes Prospectives et
d'Informations Internationales, Paris, http://www.cepii.fr/cepii/en/bdd_modele/presentation.asp?id=8; WITS
(World Integrated Trade Solution) (database), World Bank, Washington, DC, http://wits.worldbank.org/WITS/.

TABLE B1.1.2 Decomposition of Overtrading Relationships, South Asia
$, millions

Importer	Exporter	Actual import	Predicted import	Actual—predicted
India	Nepal	489.6	1,765.2	−1,275.7
India	Sri Lanka	848.8	2,113.0	−1,264.2
India	Maldives	5.1	125.6	−120.5
Sri Lanka	Maldives	20.0	20.2	−0.2
Pakistan	Afghanistan	390.4	276.4	114.0

Source: Calculations based on data from CEPII Gravity Database, Centre d'Etudes Prospectives et
d'Informations Internationales, Paris, http://www.cepii.fr/cepii/en/bdd_modele/presentation.asp?id=8; WITS
(World Integrated Trade Solution) (database), World Bank, Washington, DC, http://wits.worldbank.org/WITS/.

The gravity model results shown in tables B1.1.1 and B1.1.2 are based on the methodology
employed in Santos Silva and Tenreyro (2006). The traditional gravity equation framework
is used to predict trade flows between two countries based on selected key observable
variables, such as the economic mass of the two countries (measured by GDP), the
distance between the two countries, the remoteness of exporter and importer countries,
common borders, common language, common colonial legacy, common currency, and

box continues next page

BOX 1.1 The Gravity Model Approach: Evidence of Untapped Trade Potential in South Asia *(continued)*

participation in RTAs. The equation is estimated using the Pseudo–Poisson Maximum Likelihood method, which takes into account heteroskedasticity and zero trade flows. The estimating equation used is as follows:

$$T_{ijt} = \alpha_0 + \alpha_1 \log(dist_{ij}) + \alpha_2 \log(GDP_{it}) + \alpha_3 \log(GDP_{jt}) + \alpha_4 \log(Remoteness_{it})$$
$$+ \alpha_5 \log(Remoteness_{jt}) + \alpha_6\, CommonBorder_{ij} + \alpha_7\, CommonLang_{ij}$$
$$+ \alpha_8\, Colhist_{ij} + \alpha_9\, CommonCur_{ijt} + \alpha_{10}\, RTA_{ijt} + \gamma_t + \varepsilon_{ijt}$$

$$(B1.1.1)$$

where T_{ijt} are trade flows from country i to country j at time t; $dist_{ij}$ is the distance between country i and country j; GDP_{it} and GDP_{jt} are the GDP of country i and j, respectively, at time t; $Remoteness_{it}$ and $Remoteness_{jt}$ are indexes that measure the remoteness of country i and j, respectively, from all their trading partners at time t; and $CommonBorder_{ij}$, $CommonLang_{ij}$, $Colhist_{ij}$, $CommonCur_{ijt}$, RTA_{ijt} represent the common border dummy, common language dummy, colonial history dummy, common currency dummy, and RTA dummy, respectively. Time dummies γ_t are added to capture the business cycle effects. The gravity model was estimated for a sample of 196 countries and 38,220 country pairs from 1996 to 2015.

The data sources are as follows: imports between the country pairs were used to capture trade flows. Bilateral import data were collected from UN Comtrade via the World Integrated Trade Solution database.[a] Remoteness indexes were calculated following Wei (1996), also used by Santos Silva and Tenreyro (2006) as the arithmetically weighted average of the distance of exporter and importer countries from all their trading partners (GDP as weights).[b] Data on variables related to GDP, distance, common border, common language, common colonial history, and common currency were extracted from the CEPII gravity dataset originally generated by Head, Mayer, and Ries (2010).[c]

"Actual" trade is the existing trade between two countries; "predicted" or "potential" trade is the average level of trade between two countries predicted by the gravity model used; "trade gap" is the gap between the predicted and actual trade. "Overtrading" means that actual trade between two countries is greater than the predicted trade; "undertrading" means that the actual trade between two countries is lower than the predicted trade.

a. See UN Comtrade (United Nations Commodity Trade Statistics Database), Statistics Division, Department of Economic and Social Affairs, United Nations, New York, http://comtrade.un.org /db/; WITS (World Integrated Trade Solution) (database), World Bank, Washington, DC, http://wits .worldbank.org/WITS/.

b. The exporter and importer remoteness indexes control for multilateral trade resistance, that is, the barriers to trade that each country faces with all its trading partners, and have been used extensively in the gravity literature (Yotov et al. 2016). Another way of controlling for multilateral trade resistance is to use exporter and importer dummies. However, Fally (2015) explains that, with the Pseudo–Poisson Maximum Likelihood method, adding exporter and importer dummies implies that the fitted values of the estimated equation equal the observed values. Because the objective of this exercise is to estimate intraregional trade potential by calculating the difference between the actual level of trade and the level predicted by the model, the use of a remoteness index to control for the multilateral trade resistance term is deemed a better fit.

c. Details on the dataset can be found at CEPII Gravity Database, Centre d'Etudes Prospectives et d'InformationsInternationales,Paris,http://www.cepii.fr/cepii/en/bdd_modele/presentation.asp?id=8.

Pakistan, India and Sri Lanka, and India and Nepal shows overtrading. However, further disaggregation shows that Nepal and Sri Lanka still underexport to India.

Second, the high level of informal trade—trade that actually occurs but is not captured in official statistics—provides indirect evidence of trade potential that goes beyond what is captured in official statistics. For example, by aggregating the estimates of various studies for years between 1993 and 2005, Taneja (2014) finds that informal trade was 50 percent of formal trade in South Asia. India's informal trade with Nepal was as large as the formal trade. With Pakistan, it was 91 percent of formal trade. With Sri Lanka, it was about 30 percent, and, with Bhutan, it was almost three times the formal trade. More recent bilateral estimates of the trade between India and Pakistan indicate that informal trade between the two countries was as high as US$4.7 billion in 2012–13, almost double the value of formal trade, and most of this was routed through a third country (Taneja and Bimal 2016).

Third, the disproportionately high costs of intra–South Asia trade also penalize such trade and lead to significant substitution of South Asian exports by exports from the rest of Asia, Europe, and North America.

Barriers to Intraregional Trade and Investment

This section presents a curated list of barriers to trade and investment within South Asia, informed by research carried out for this report and drawing on the literature on the subject.

TARIFF AND PARATARIFF BARRIERS TO TRADE

Despite the significant liberalization of tariff regimes in South Asian countries since the 1980s, average tariffs in South Asia are still high compared with those in other regions of the world. In 2016, average tariffs in South Asia were 13.6 percent, compared with 7.3 percent in East Asia and the Pacific and the world average of 6.3 percent. This high level of protection masks wide variations in tariffs within many countries in South Asia, substantial protection for consumer goods, and a large wedge in protection between consumer goods and intermediate goods.

The South Asian Free Trade Area (SAFTA), which came into force in 2006, represents an attempt by the leaders of South Asia to trade on more favorable terms with each other than with the rest of the world. However, SAFTA has not been a success: in 2015, intraregional trade was only about 5 percent of South Asia's total trade, and accounted for less than 1 percent of the region's GDP.

Two major reasons stand out for the underperformance of SAFTA. First, each country maintains a long sensitive list, that is, goods that are exempted from the tariff liberalization program. Almost 35 percent of the value of the intraregional trade in the South Asian Association for Regional Cooperation (SAARC) is subject to sensitive list tariffs. In Bangladesh and Sri Lanka, as much as 44 percent–45 percent of the imports from other SAARC members fall under their sensitive lists, and over 39 percent of

India's exports to the region fall under the sensitive lists of various partners (chapter 2). This situation prevails because SAFTA does not provide a clear guideline for phasing out the sensitive lists. Although there is a working group to reduce the number of products on the sensitive lists and there is a provision for review of sensitive lists after every four years or earlier, progress has been incremental, at best.

Second, several countries in the region maintain high paratariffs, that is, taxes levied on imports but not on domestic output, in effect, import duties by another name. These paratariffs are not a part of the phaseout program under SAFTA or other FTAs in the region, which reduces the preference margins for SAFTA partners. Bangladesh, Pakistan, and Sri Lanka maintain high paratariffs. For example, if paratariffs are included, the simple average tariff in Bangladesh in fiscal year 2016/17 almost doubles to 25.6 percent, and, in Sri Lanka in 2016, it increases from 10.8 percent to 22.4 percent. In the case of many individual products in these countries, the combination of paratariffs and customs duties results in high protection rates on the order of 40–80 percent.

The ASEAN Free Trade Area offers a contrasting experience to SAFTA in reducing intraregional tariffs. It was established in 1992 with the signing of the Agreement on the Common Effective Preferential Tariff Scheme, under which successive rounds of intra-ASEAN tariff reductions began. The approach consisted of an accelerated elimination of tariffs for products on an inclusion list, the progressive shift of products from the sensitive list to the inclusion list, and the reduction of tariffs to the 0 percent–5 percent range for products on the sensitive list and the highly sensitive list (ASEAN and World Bank 2013). Thus, sensitive lists were to be progressively pruned. In 2009, ASEAN member states signed a new ASEAN Trade in Goods Agreement to accelerate the tariff elimination process. Through the agreement, the ASEAN-6, consisting of Brunei Darussalam, Indonesia, Malaysia, the Philippines, Singapore, and Thailand, eliminated intraregional import duties on nearly 99.7 percent of tariff lines, and Cambodia, the Lao People's Democratic Republic, Myanmar, and Vietnam reduced import duties to 0 percent–5 percent on almost 98.9 percent of tariff lines.[13] The tariffs that are not subject to elimination under the agreement are associated with only a few products in schedule D (sensitive agricultural goods on which tariffs can be maintained at 0 percent–5 percent) and schedule H (general exclusion list, not subject to liberalization, comprising 1.6 percent of all tariff lines) (ASEAN and World Bank 2013).

If SAFTA is to be effective, the issue of the sensitive lists and paratariffs must be addressed. Chapter 2, while examining the role of import duties in the underperformance of SAFTA, highlights the issue of paratariffs. It explores the complexity of the tariff structures in South Asia, including details on the structure of paratariffs in Bangladesh, Pakistan, and Sri Lanka and their negative impact on the level of overall protection as well as intersectoral tariff dispersion. It analyzes the constraints that tariffs and paratariffs impose on the effective functioning of SAFTA, including the widespread exclusions from tariff preferences in the form of sensitive lists, and the noninclusion of paratariffs in the tariff concessions given to partners in FTAs.

THE DISPROPORTIONATELY HIGH COSTS OF TRADE

High costs of trading, whether because of poor transportation and logistics infra-structure or inefficient customs and border procedures, adversely impact the competitiveness of products, discouraging trade. Although global tariffs have fallen, and, indeed, tariffs in many countries are now at historical lows, overall trade costs remain high (Arvis et al. 2013). Worldwide, reducing the trade costs associated with border administration, transport, and communication infrastructure even halfway to global best practice would lead to an additional $2.6 trillion in global GDP (4.7 percent) (WEF 2013).

A key obstacle to trade within South Asia is the disproportionately high cost of trading. The costs of trading are considerably higher within South Asia than within other trade blocks of comparable size (figure 1.3). For example, the average level of trade costs (including all direct and indirect costs of trading) is 20 percent higher between country pairs in South Asia than between country pairs in ASEAN.[14] It currently costs more to trade within some countries in South Asia than with, say, Brazil (shown for selected pairs in figure 1.3).[15]

FIGURE 1.3 Average Intraregional and Interregional Trade Costs, 2010–15

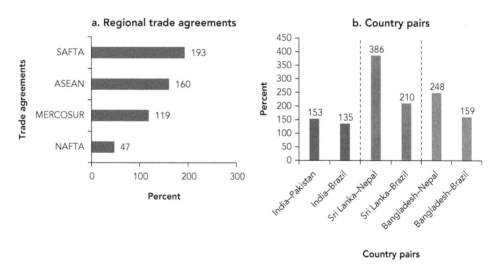

Source: Calculations based on data from ESCAP–World Bank Trade Cost Database, United Nations Economic and Social Commission for Asia and the Pacific, Bangkok; World Bank, Washington, DC, http://www.unescap.org /resources/escap-world-bank-trade-cost-database.
Note: The unit of measurement is the ad valorem equivalent trade costs in percent. The trade costs include transport costs, tariffs, costs at customs, and so on. For the detailed methodology, see the source. The average intraregional trade costs are simple averages of the trade costs between country pairs in the respective trade blocs and across years; the average bilateral trade costs used in intraregional versus interregional comparisons are simple averages across years. ASEAN = Association of Southeast Asian Nations; MERCOSUR = Argentina, Brazil, Paraguay, Uruguay, and República Bolivariana de Venezuela; NAFTA = North American Free Trade Agreement; SAFTA = South Asian Free Trade Area.

These high trade costs are reflected in simulations of the impact of trade facilitation. The high costs of trade in South Asia arise from complex customs procedures, poor infrastructure at many border points, the compliance costs associated with NTMs, and so forth. Recent studies find that the welfare impact of trade facilitation significantly exceeds the impact of a full-fledged FTA in goods in South Asia (Raihan 2012; UNESCAP 2017).

A key aspect of trade costs is connectivity, which depends on backbone transportation services between countries, such as air travel. The efficiency of air travel services can impact trade in goods because the transport of high-value, low-volume goods as well as trade in services, such as tourism, health care, and education, often depend on air travel services. Moreover, the efficiency of business travel can also affect trade in goods and services as well as FDI. This underscores the importance of services liberalization, especially backbone services, an important determinant of trade costs and the operating costs of firms, as a means to boost overall regional trade and investment.

Chapter 4 explores the issue of high connectivity costs in the context of air services by examining the liberalization of air services between India and Sri Lanka. The study tracks the evolution of the bilateral air services agreement (ASA) between India and Sri Lanka, focusing on the major liberalization entailed in the amendments of 2003 and 2011. It analyzes the impact of the resulting changes in air connectivity on the flow of passengers and cargo between the two countries, with the objective of drawing lessons for policy makers in other South Asian countries.

COMPLICATED AND NONTRANSPARENT NONTARIFF MEASURES

NTMs refer to all measures other than tariffs that affect the free flow of goods and services across borders. The United Nations Conference on Trade and Development (UNCTAD) classifies NTMs into three categories. The first two apply to imports, and the third to exports, as follows: (1) technical measures, which include measures related to product standards and quality specifications and largely comprise sanitary and phytosanitary standards (SPS) and technical barriers to trade (TBT); (2) nontechnical measures, which include measures such as import licensing, price control measures, import subsidies, and rules of origin; and (3) export-related measures, such as export subsidies, prohibitions, and quotas (ADB and UNCTAD 2008). (The annexes in chapter 3 provide the complete list.) All countries can legitimately impose NTMs to safeguard the interests of consumers and protect plant and animal life. However, NTMs become nontariff barriers if they are more burdensome than necessary to achieve a legitimate goal, for example, if customs officials behave arbitrarily and do not apply rules uniformly, or if border testing of imports takes inordinate amounts of time. In South Asia, much of the concern centers around SPS and TBT measures. According to one study, SPS and TBT measures account for 85 percent of all nontariff barriers in South Asia (ADB and UNCTAD 2008).

Traders across South Asia often complain about nontariff barriers, which create noise and exacerbate the trust deficit. However, many complaints arise from lack of information on regulations and standards and inadequate infrastructure for measuring and certifying quality, rather than protection by the importing country.

Port restrictions constitute a genuine nontariff barrier in South Asia. Many countries in the region permit only a restricted list of import products through certain custom stations or ports, citing inadequate testing facilities or other infrastructure deficits to hinder the free flow of all goods. Implicitly, the authorities are saying that, if imports were allowed through restricted ports, this could cause delays at the border. However, private sector traders routinely deal with such port delays in any case. Moreover, long delays lead to greater awareness of bottlenecks and pressure on the authorities to resolve the bottlenecks. Port restrictions mean that imports must be brought in over more circuitous routes, imposing additional costs on importers, exporters, and, eventually, consumers. They thus become more difficult to justify, seem to be imposed to protect domestic industry, and should be phased out.

Several examples illustrate the problem of port restrictions. Under the India–Sri Lanka Free Trade Agreement, which was signed in December 1998 and became operational in March 2000, India allowed a tariff rate quota (lower tariffs for quantities within the quota and higher rates for quantities outside the quota) on imports of tea and garments—two items that were otherwise on its negative list (items that were not granted tariff concessions)—but also specified the ports of entry where these imports would become eligible for the tariff rate quotas: Cochin and Kolkata in the case of tea and Chennai and Mumbai in the case of garments.[16] The port restrictions on tea and garments were subsequently removed, after repeated representations, in June 2007 and April 2008, respectively (CBEC 2007, 2008). In India–Pakistan trade, the land route is the most cost-effective and time-efficient way to move goods between the respective northern states or provinces of India and Pakistan, but Pakistan allows only 138 items to be imported from India through the Attari–Wagah Integrated Check Post, the only operational land port for road cargo between the two countries. In Bangladesh–India trade, as recently as June 2016, during the Tenth Meeting of the Joint Working Group on Trade, both sides petitioned each other for the lifting of port restrictions (Ministry of Commerce and Industry, India, and Ministry of Commerce, Bangladesh 2016). India cited port restrictions as one of the key reasons for the small amount of exports to Bangladesh through the Agartala–Akhaura Integrated Check Post; Bangladesh does not permit exports of items such as vulcanized rubber, yarn, milk powder, fish, sugar, and potatoes through this integrated check post. Bangladesh cited similar problems in exporting to India; for example, Bangladesh indicated that exports of ceramics and electronic goods are prohibited through the Dawki–Tamabil customs station.

Nontariff barriers add substantially to the cost of trading across borders and constitute a deterrent to intraregional trade. Similarly, calculations on overall protection that are based on combining data on tariffs and nontariff barriers show that imports are more restricted within South Asia than from the rest of the world (box 1.2). Such trade restrictions encourage traders to rely on informal channels, which deprives governments of revenue. By various accounts, the size of the informal trade within South Asia is substantial (see "The untapped trade potential" section).

NTMs also disproportionately impact small and medium enterprises. Given that compliance with importing-country NTMs involves information access, capacity, and financial resources, small and medium enterprises face more difficulty in complying with the regulatory burden of NTMs, and this affects their exporting capacity.

Although the average NTM burden may not appear high, it could be significant for specific product and market combinations in South Asia. Box 1.2, table B1.2.1 shows the average overall trade restrictiveness index for imports, which, at first sight, may not appear high for South Asian trade but may conceal significantly higher indexes for individual products. On closer inspection, this seems to be the case for product-specific ad valorem equivalents of NTMs in bilateral trade in South Asia. (The top 50 ad valorem equivalents in bilateral trade in South Asia are listed in annex 1A, table 1A.1.)[17]

BOX 1.2 South Asia: Overall Trade Restrictiveness Indexes Are Higher in Regional Trade

In South Asia, as reflected in the overall trade restrictiveness index, protection is greater in the case of imports from within the South Asia region than from the rest of the world. The index captures the trade policy distortions that each country imposes on the import bundle. It measures the uniform tariff equivalent of the country's tariff and nontariff barriers that would generate the same level of import value for the country in a given year.

As indicated in table B1.2.1, the indexes are two to nine times higher for imports from the South Asia region than for imports from the rest of the world in all countries except Afghanistan. In the two largest economies in the region, India and Pakistan, the indexes are nine and six times higher, respectively, for imports from the South Asia region than for imports from the rest of the world.

TABLE B1.2.1 Overall Trade Restrictiveness Indexes, Selected Countries, South Asia, 2011

Importing country	Origin of imports	
	South Asia	Rest of world
Afghanistan	3.84	4.65
India	4.59	0.50
Sri Lanka	1.01	0.33
Nepal	10.59	6.87
Pakistan	3.00	0.51

Source: Updated estimates by Kee and Nicita in 2017 based on methodology in Kee and Nicita (2017).
Note: The overall trade restrictiveness indexes are computed using applied tariffs that take into account bilateral preferences.

These equivalents are indeed high, varying from over 75 percent to over 2000 percent; Sri Lanka's trade regime leads to that country's consistent appearance on the list of highest import ad valorem equivalents in the region.

Evidence on missing markets is also relevant. Raihan, Khan, and Quoreshi (2014) examine bilateral trade between India and other South Asian countries and list the top 50 missing products in the case of India, as well as each of the seven countries, that is, products in which the level of exports to the South Asian partner is close to zero even as significant export capacity exists in the form of exports to the rest of the world. The reasons for this gap could include high trade costs and inability to comply with NTMs at a reasonable cost.

This missing market problem may partly arise from a lack of capacity to cope with legitimate NTMs. With the exception of India, most countries in the region depend on a handful of products for export earnings. The textile and clothing sector, for example, accounts for more than 80, 55, and 45 percent of merchandise exports in Bangladesh, Pakistan, and Sri Lanka, respectively. In this sector, exporting countries in South Asia have developed a globally acceptable standards and quality infrastructure. However, India, which is the largest market in South Asia and one of the largest in the world, is also a global player in textile and clothing products, and its imports in this sector are limited. In products that India imports, neighboring countries often do not have well-developed export capacity or the ability to cope with the quality standards set by India, which are imposed on domestic products as well as imports.

It is necessary to address burdensome NTMs in South Asia by distinguishing between real and perceived complaints to focus the attention of policy makers on genuine issues, dealing with the misperceptions of traders, and, ultimately, bridging the gap between perceptions and objective evidence. This is the goal of the study in chapter 3 that examines NTMs in bilateral trade between Bangladesh and India and between India and Nepal in selected products of significance. Although there are many types of NTMs, the study focuses on SPS and TBT measures because these account for a majority of the nontariff barriers in South Asia. The study identifies procedural obstacles perceived by exporters in meeting SPS- and TBT-related NTM requirements, as captured through a survey. To distinguish between real and perceived issues, the information provided through the survey is triangulated with an examination of the regulations and consultations with regulators in the three countries covered by the study. The study provides concrete actionable suggestions to policy makers to address the issues raised. Implementation of such measures could go a long way toward building trust among trading partners.

Box 1.3 offers an example of a nontariff barrier resolution mechanism in Africa and suggests consideration of some of these ideas in the South Asian context as another confidence-building measure.

BOX 1.3 Nontariff Barrier Resolution Mechanism: A Possibility in South Asia?

Complaints about nontariff barriers have been persistent in the recent discourse on regional integration in South Asia. Apart from hampering trade flows by creating unpredictability in a rules-based framework for crossborder trade, nontariff barriers exacerbate the trust deficit between countries. Thus, the resolution of nontariff barriers is critical to progress on the regional integration agenda.

Current Nontariff Barrier Resolution Mechanisms in South Asia

The multilateral SAFTA processes to address nontariff barriers have been slow moving. The Committee of Experts, which was formed to monitor and facilitate SAFTA implementation, in its first meeting in April 2006, set up a subgroup to address NTMs and paratariff measures in the region but without much progress. Even where bilateral trade agreements exist between countries (such as the India–Sri Lanka Free Trade Agreement), while nontariff barriers are addressed in a consultative manner through intergovernmental meetings (such as frequent or annual meetings of commerce secretaries), there is no transparent formal mechanism for recording and following up on complaints and no effective dispute resolution mechanism. How can South Asia deal more effectively with the nontariff barrier challenge?

Africa's Nontariff Barrier Resolution Mechanism

A useful starting point could be the online mechanism for reporting, monitoring, and eliminating nontariff barriers among African economic communities—the Common Market for Eastern and Southern Africa, the East African Community, and the Southern African Development Community—that was set up with the help of TradeMark Southern Africa, an initiative aimed at improving trade performance in Eastern and Southern Africa and funded by the U.K. Department for International Development.[a] The online system is supported by an institutional structure, consisting of national focal points and national monitoring committees in each country, to facilitate the resolution of reported barriers. The national monitoring committees include representatives of government ministries and departments, private sector organizations, trade associations, and major exporters and importers. A lodged complaint is sent to the system administrator, who forwards it to the national focal points, who then forward it to the relevant national monitoring committees for resolution and follow-up.[b] The mechanism allows for a structured consultative process, involving, if necessary, inspections and country missions.

The African nontariff barrier mechanism has several advantages:

- Because it is online and publicly available, it is more transparent than a system involving the offline filing of complaint forms.

- It offers the governments of member countries a systematic 24–7 mechanism for sharing nontariff barrier complaints with each other, as opposed to waiting for periodic intergovernmental meetings for resolution.

- It creates a repository of all reported nontariff barriers. Thus, the data can be used by policy makers to prioritize areas of action and by other stakeholders, such as researchers and traders, to put pressure on governments to take the required action.

- Inasmuch as it can sift through genuine and perceived nontariff barriers, the mechanism can help ameliorate the trust deficit among trading nations.

box continues next page

BOX 1.3 Nontariff Barrier Resolution Mechanism: A Possibility in South Asia?
(continued)

A transparency-enhancing initiative for South Asia

This study suggests that governments in South Asia consider a mechanism designed along the lines of the African mechanism, essentially to enhance transparency and nudge the official system to settle NTM complaints more quickly.[c] A practical approach would be to establish a mechanism at the bilateral level and, based on opportunity and demand, extend it to include other countries. The elements of this system could include an online mechanism for reporting and monitoring complaints, hosted by an institution with some monitoring and evaluation capacity to enable the institution to provide traders with the necessary information to address their issues or to direct the complaints to the relevant authorities in the relevant country and to continue to monitor each complaint until final resolution.

A study tour to Africa by interested South Asian commerce ministry officials could provide useful inputs for designing a mechanism that would need to be tailored to South Asian needs.

An initiative along the lines suggested here, if implemented successfully, would signal serious commitment to addressing nontariff barriers and could be an important step in reducing the persistent trust deficit.

a. The TradeMark Southern Africa Program was officially closed in March 2014 because the financial support of its sole financier, the U.K. Department for International Development, was terminated.

b. TradeMark Southern Africa was the administrator of the online system.

c. If this system works and is found to be useful, a more ambitious phase 2 could be designed that would facilitate consultations between the concerned governments and include voluntary arbitration through an independent body or expert panel.

LACK OF NORMAL TRADE RELATIONS BETWEEN THE TWO LARGEST ECONOMIES IN THE REGION

Complex relations between the two largest countries in South Asia, India and Pakistan, have adversely affected India–Pakistan bilateral trade as well as trade within the region. The two countries account for 88 percent of South Asia's GDP and 86 percent of its population.[18] The lack of normal bilateral trade relations between the two countries also affects the formation or deepening of regional value chains, such as in textiles and clothing, and automobiles and automobile parts.

A key factor leading to suboptimal trade between India and Pakistan is the long list of product restrictions in bilateral trade; this bilateral trade relationship is the most restrictive in South Asia. Under SAFTA, both countries have reduced tariffs to a maximum of 5 percent, and India has reduced them to zero on imports from the least developed countries. However, India and Pakistan continue to maintain long sensitive lists including items (at the 6-digit level) on which no tariff concessions are granted. Pakistan has a long list of 936 items (almost 17.9 percent of tariff lines) that applies to imports from all SAFTA countries. India has a sensitive list of 25 items (0.5 percent of tariff lines, which are only goods such as alcohol, firearms, and so forth) for least developed countries (Afghanistan, Bangladesh, Bhutan, Maldives, and Nepal). However, it has a much longer list of 614 items (almost 11.7 percent of tariff lines) for the non–least developed countries, Pakistan and Sri Lanka, but which effectively applies only to Pakistan because India applies a smaller sensitive list to Sri Lanka as part of a separate India–Sri Lanka Free Trade Agreement. Items on the Indian sensitive list can be imported at most-favored-nation tariffs from any SAFTA country, including Pakistan, because India accorded Pakistan most-favored-nation status in 1996, soon after the accession of the two countries to the World Trade Organization. However, Pakistan has not yet granted India most-favored-nation status or nondiscriminatory market access. In addition, the preferential access granted by Pakistan on 82.1 percent of tariff lines under SAFTA is partially blocked in the case of India because Pakistan maintains a negative list comprising 1,209 items that cannot be imported from India. In practice, many of these items are exported from India to Pakistan through third countries, usually the United Arab Emirates.

Another barrier to bilateral trade is the proliferation of NTMs, some of which take the form of nontariff barriers, such as port restrictions. Lahore (Pakistan) and Amritsar (India) are close to the India–Pakistan border and are only 54 kilometers apart via the Attari–Wagah border post (which is an integrated check post on the Indian side), the only trading point despite the long land border between India and Pakistan. Although geographical proximity should make for low transit costs and times between the states or provinces in northern India and Pakistan, port restrictions offset this advantage. Pakistan allows only 138 items to be imported from India over the Attari–Wagah land route. Furthermore, cargo trucks from either side cannot move beyond their border zones, which means that goods must be transloaded at the border, adding to the time and cost of trading. This route is also restricted for Afghanistan–India trade. Although Afghanistan can export to India through the Attari Integrated Check Post (the trucks use the land transit route via Pakistan), Indian goods cannot be exported to Afghanistan along this route.[19] The alternative land route between India and Pakistan, by rail, is in a state of deterioration: wagons are unavailable; warehousing is lacking; there is no fixed schedule for the operation of trains; and pilferage is common (Taneja, Dayal, and Bimal 2016). Thus, bilateral trade is dominated by trade along the sea route, which is not necessarily the most cost-effective for two countries with a long shared land border.

Imports into Pakistan from South Asian countries may also be handicapped by China's preferential access through the Pakistan–China Free Trade Agreement, although much of China's growing market share in Pakistan is in line with its global export performance (box 1.4).

Another factor impeding bilateral trade in goods and services, as well as FDI, is the encumbered visa regime that India and Pakistan have created for each other, which restricts the mobility of people between the two countries. In South Asia, although visas are generally available for tourists from most other South Asian countries with minimal conditions, visas for business travel, employment, and purposes such as

BOX 1.4 A Tale of Two Free Trade Agreements

China and Pakistan signed an agreement on trade in goods and investment in 2006 and an agreement on trade in services in 2009. Since the entry into force of the Pakistan–China Free Trade Agreement, Chinese imports into Pakistan have grown, from 9.8 percent of total imports in 2006 to 25.0 percent in 2015 (table B1.4.1). The share of Chinese imports grew much more quickly in the post–free trade agreement period, 2009–15, than in the pre–free trade agreement period, 2000–06, while the share of Indian imports and total imports from South Asia grew more slowly than in the earlier period.[a] In contrast, in Bangladesh, a comparable large country in South Asia, the share of Chinese imports increased by 5 percentage points in both periods; though the increase in the shares of Indian and South Asian imports occurred at a slower pace in the second period, the increase was still significantly greater in Bangladesh than the corresponding increase in Pakistan.

India and Sri Lanka implemented the India–Sri Lanka Free Trade Agreement in 2000. India obtained progressive market access until full implementation in 2008. India increased its market share in Sri Lanka from 9.5 percent to 22.5 percent in 2000–15; China, without the benefit of a free trade agreement, increased its share from 4.0 percent to 19.7 percent over the same period.

Overall, China has performed strongly in South Asia, in line with the country's global export performance, irrespective of its trading status in various South Asian countries.

TABLE B1.4.1 Bangladesh, Pakistan, and Sri Lanka: Origin of Imports Pre- and Post-Free Trade Agreements

Percent

Year	Pakistan China	Pakistan India	Pakistan South Asia	Sri Lanka China	Sri Lanka India	Sri Lanka South Asia	Bangladesh China	Bangladesh India	Bangladesh South Asia
2000	5.0	1.7	2.7	4.0	9.5	11.2	11.3	8.1	9.6
2006	9.8	3.7	4.4	8.0	18.5	20.3	16.4	12.0	13.1
2008	11.2	4.0	4.6	8.1	20.8	22.4	18.8	13.0	14.8
2009	12.0	3.4	4.2	9.3	18.0	20.4	16.5	10.1	11.9
2015	25.1	3.8	5.0	19.7	22.5	24.4	21.5	12.2	14.2
Change in share									
2000–06 (pre-FTA)	4.8	2.1	1.7	n.a.	n.a.	n.a.	5.1	3.9	3.5
2000–08 (pre-FTA)	n.a.	n.a.	n.a.	4.1	11.3	11.2	7.5	4.9	5.1
2009–15 (post-FTA)	13.1	0.4	0.8	10.3	4.5	3.9	5.0	2.1	2.3

Source: Calculations based on data from UN Comtrade (United Nations Commodity Trade Statistics Database), Statistics Division, Department of Economic and Social Affairs, United Nations, New York, http://comtrade.un.org/db/; WITS (World Integrated Trade Solution) (database), World Bank, Washington, DC, http://wits.worldbank.org/WITS/.
Note: FTA = free trade agreement. The FTA is the Pakistan–China Free Trade Agreement in the case of Pakistan and the India–Sri Lanka Free Trade Agreement in the case of Sri Lanka. The Pakistan–China Free Trade Agreement was fully implemented in 2007, while the agreement between India and Sri Lanka was fully implemented in 2008. n.a. = not applicable.

box continues next page

BOX 1.4 A Tale of Two Free Trade Agreements *(continued)*

Thus, over 2000–15, Pakistan's imports from China (a free trade agreement country) grew by 22.1 percent; Sri Lanka's grew by 19.9 percent; and Bangladesh's imports from China grew by 18.1 percent. (All growth rates are compound annual growth rates.)

The implication is that, while there is the possibility of some trade diversion in Pakistan's imports toward China, the aggregate magnitude of this diversion is mitigated by China's strong global export record, including in South Asian countries where China does not have a special trading status.

a. According to the Pakistan Business Council (PBC 2013), a possible cause of the rapid increase in imports from China is trade diversion; more than 170 tariff lines were found to indicate diversion in trade toward China after the free trade agreement came into effect.

medical travel and education are more cumbersome to obtain. Visas are typically given on a single-entry basis for short durations (15–30 days); multiple entry visas are not the norm (Chanda 2014). The visa regime between India and Pakistan is particularly cumbersome, despite the liberalized bilateral visa agreement the two countries signed in 2012 to boost trade and people-to-people contacts.[20] Because of security concerns, the documentation requirements are onerous, and the processing time is often lengthy, given the obligation to possess security agency clearances—an average 35 days for a visa for India or Pakistan. Visa rejection rates can be high and spike following any security incident or diplomatic impasse between the two countries (Bhalla 2016; Laskar 2015; Press Trust of India 2017).[21] Visas are issued for specific ports of entry and exit, as well as for specific cities to be visited; furthermore, there are requirements to report at the local police station or registration authority for Indians and Pakistanis when arriving in the other country or when moving to another city (within 24 hours of arrival), unless exempted from police reporting.[22] The availability of Pakistani consular services only in New Delhi compounds the difficulty in obtaining visas for those residing in other cities. Indian visa application facilities are available in several Pakistani cities.[23] However, the Indian e-visa facility, introduced in November 2014 for 43 countries and currently available to more than 160 countries under the three separate subcategories of e-tourist visa, e-medical visa, and e-business visa, excludes Afghanistan, Bangladesh, and Pakistan from the list of eligible countries.[24] India introduced visa-on-arrival for Pakistani citizens in 2013, but this is restricted to citizens older than age 65 entering on foot at the Attari Integrated Check Post.[25]

The restrictions are reflected in the current level of trade and in estimates of the significant gap between current and potential trade. In 2015, bilateral trade between the two countries accounted for about 10 percent of South Asia's intraregional trade, but it was small relative to the trade of these two countries with the rest of the world. Bilateral India–Pakistan trade accounted for less than 0.5 percent of India's global trade and 3.0 percent of Pakistan's global trade.[26] According to the estimates in this study, potential formal trade between the two countries could be 15 times greater than its current value.[27] A telling indicator of the bilateral trade potential is the size of the informal trade between the two countries, pointing to the significant demand on either side of the border. Taneja et al. (2013) estimate the value of the informal trade between India and Pakistan at between US$250 million and US$4 billion. More recent bilateral estimates in Taneja and Bimal (2016) indicate that the informal trade between the two countries was as high as US$4.7 billion in 2012–13, almost double the formal trade; most of this trade is routed through third countries.

THE TRUST DEFICIT

Mutual trust is the underlying foundation of any trading relationship. Trust promotes trade, and trade fosters trust, interdependency, and constituencies for peace. Trade can improve trust and security in various ways. It creates economic interdependence between the countries involved, which increases the stake that each country has in the welfare of its neighbor, thus making war and conflict costlier. Polachek (1992, 1997) finds that trade has a significant negative impact on conflict: a 6 percent increase in trade lowers his measure of conflict by about 1 percent.[28] The greater people-to-people interaction fostered by trade creates a better understanding among neighbors, dispelling myths and thereby engendering greater trust. Greater trust may also lead to a peace dividend with a fall in military expenditures over time, creating fiscal space for more productive expenditures, such as in education and health care. Through all of these channels, trade can build trust, and more trust leads to more trade, creating a virtuous cycle. In South Asia, the virtuous cycle between trust and trade has been broken by a long history of mutual mistrust rooted in conflict and size asymmetry across the economies, which prevents South Asian countries from reaping the full economic benefits of geographical proximity and complementary resource endowments.

Trust is a fragile commodity in South Asia and is persistently in short supply. South Asian nations have a long history of political tensions and mutual suspicion, often stemming from their colonial history and the circumstances under which the countries were born. The 1947 division of the subcontinent resulted in preoccupation with national identity and internal consolidation and in a tendency to view neighboring countries with mistrust. Regional relationships and mindsets have tended to be dominated by security concerns, leaving less space for consideration of economic integration issues. Continued political tensions and lack of normal trade relations between India and Pakistan have cast a shadow over cooperation efforts within South Asia, contributing to the lack of progress in the regional cooperation agenda of SAARC and SAFTA. Tensions between Afghanistan and Pakistan and between Bangladesh and Pakistan have also grown in recent years. There is still uneasiness in relations between Bhutan and Nepal. The growing presence of China in South Asian countries has complicated relationships in the region, given the rivalry between China and India.

The trust deficit in South Asia is also generated by the asymmetry in the size of countries in the region. India's large size and economic clout generates concerns among smaller neighbors that crossborder openness could result in economic domination by

India. Trade deficits in favor of India add to this perception of economic domination.[29] Adding to this mix, many countries still have protective trade regimes, including complicated and nontransparent NTMs (sometimes real, sometimes only perceived), as well as paratariffs, which add to the noise and reinforce the lack of trust among countries.

An inadequate dispute resolution mechanism under SAFTA perpetuates the trust deficit between the countries. SAFTA's Article 10 on institutional arrangements establishes the Committee of Experts as the primary dispute settlement body and the SAFTA Ministerial Council as the highest decision-making body mandated with the administration and implementation of the agreement. Article 20 lays down the dispute settlement mechanism, including provisions for consultations, review by the Committee of Experts, appellate review of a decision by the SAFTA Ministerial Council, and the timelines to be followed. However, the framework falls short in several areas. The SAFTA agreement does not clearly specify the scope and jurisdiction of the dispute settlement mechanism (Nath 2007). It does not lay down rules of procedure for the committee or the council; the two bodies draw up their own working procedures for dispute settlement on a case-by-case basis (Khan et al. 2009). Since the Committee of Experts comprises state nominees, and the SAFTA Ministerial Council consists of ministers of commerce or trade, review at both levels could be vulnerable to bias.[30]

Meanwhile, the SAARC Arbitration Council was set up as a specialized body under SAARC. The agreement to establish the council entered into force on July 2, 2007. The council is an intergovernmental body mandated to resolve commercial, industrial, trade, banking, investment, and other such disputes, but its effectiveness and credibility are yet to be established.

The fragility of the trust deficit means that trust-building efforts are often easily eroded by an adverse episode in bilateral relations; the memory of such episodes can endure.[31]

One manifestation of the trust deficit in South Asia is the low level of intraregional FDI. In South Asia, on average, overall FDI is well below potential, and intraregional FDI is even more so. Intraregional FDI stocks account for only 1.1 percent of total outward FDI in South Asia. India is a significant global investor, with total outward investment stock at around US$85 billion in 2015. It is also the biggest investor in South Asia, with sizable investments in countries such as Bangladesh, Nepal, and Sri Lanka (see annex 1A, table 1A.2). Yet, India's total South Asian investments represent less than 1 percent of its total outward investment. This also affects regional trade. FDI and trade are inextricably connected, each reinforcing the other through increasingly intricate links.[32] Value chains tend to become established regionally before they become global, and they are often likely to be galvanized by regional FDI. Low intraregional FDI means that South Asia has not been able to use its proximity advantage to create regional value chains or regionally based export platforms, as has been done, for example, by ASEAN countries.

Intraregional FDI in South Asia has been constrained by various factors. These include overall investment climate issues in South Asia, as well as political undertones that constrain intraregional FDI.[33] Kelegama (2014), for instance, points to the unfriendly attitude toward Indian FDI in the region. A key constraining factor is the restrictive visa policy, especially the visa regimes of India and Pakistan as applicable to each other, another reflection of the trust deficit.

The trust deficit and the negative stereotypes that cast a shadow over cooperation efforts are perpetuated by lack of people-to-people interaction. Hence, efforts to promote direct interaction among the populations of South Asian countries can help rebuild trust and create a lasting foundation for peace and greater regional cooperation. Border haats, local border markets set up between India and its neighbors, represent an example of a successful effort to promote people-to-people interactions. The haats were initially established as a confidence-building measure between neighbors. They have had a positive impact, even beyond that original objective.

Chapter 5 examines the operations of the four operational border haats on the Bangladesh–India border to analyze their impact on rural livelihoods and local communities and on building positive relationships. The study finds that border haats have had a significant welfare-enhancing impact on the local communities on both sides of the border, and the welfare impact has been disproportionately large compared with the small volume of trade that takes place at the haats. The positive impact on welfare occurs through three channels: first, a gain in real income and the creation of livelihood opportunities, including among women and some of the most marginalized workers, such as laborers and rickshaw pullers, as well as benefits for buyers; second, improved crossborder relations through deeper people-to-people contacts; and third, a reduction in informal and illegal trading and the resulting peace dividend.

The Benefits of Current Trade Patterns

All countries in the region, irrespective of size, location, and endowments, gain from regional trade, although the impact is not symmetric. Consumers gain from access to food products, services, and consumer goods. Producers and exporters gain from greater access to inputs, investment, and production networks. Firms gain from expanding market access in goods and services. Gains from deeper energy cooperation are pronounced, as are the gains among landlocked countries and subregions. The expansion of trade reduces the incentives for conflict, although trade would need to grow additionally to ramp up the opportunity costs of conflict. This section spells out the trade patterns and benefits that are already accruing along these lines and that demonstrate why regional trade is important in South Asia. Nonetheless, so much more is possible.

BENEFITS TO CONSUMERS

Most countries in South Asia import vegetables, fruits, and other food products from each other. Taking the example of vegetables and fruits, intraregional imports account for 12 percent of the total imports of such products by South Asian countries (table 1.1). Furthermore, the share of imports from within South Asia in total regional imports is

TABLE 1.1 Shares of Intraregional Trade, South Asia, 2015
Percent

Indicator	All products	Consumer goods	Vegetables and fruits	Small cars	Motorcycles	Pharmaceuticals	Intermediate goods	Capital goods
Exports	6.9	4.3	24.8	32.5	25.0	4.0	8.6	9.8
Imports	4.4	9.2	11.6	44.3	64.9	22.4	4.4	3.6

Source: Calculations based on data from UN Comtrade (United Nations Commodity Trade Statistics Database), Statistics Division, Department of Economic and Social Affairs, United Nations, New York, http://comtrade.un.org/db/; WITS (World Integrated Trade Solution) (database), World Bank, Washington, DC, http://wits.worldbank.org/WITS/.
Note: All products are classified according to the 2002 version of the Harmonized Commodity Description and Coding Systems (HS) (database), Statistics Division, Department of Economic and Social Affairs, United Nations, New York, https://unstats.un.org/unsd/tradekb/Knowledgebase/50018/Harmonized-Commodity-Description-and-Coding-Systems-HS. Consumer, intermediate, and capital goods refer to UNCTAD SOP3, SOP2, and SOP4 of the United Nations Conference on Trade and Development, respectively, under HS2002; see Reference Data (database), World Integrated Trade Solution, World Bank, Washington, DC, http://wits.worldbank.org/referencedata.html. Vegetables and fruits are defined as SITC 05: Vegetables and fruits under SITC revision 3. See SITC (Standard International Trade Classification) (database), Statistics Division, United Nations, New York, https://unstats.un.org/unsd/cr/registry/regcst.asp?Cl=14. Other products refer to the following codes under HS2002: (a) small cars refer to the product code 870321: motor cars and other motor vehicles principally designed for the transport of persons of a cylinder capacity not exceeding 1,000 cubic centimeters; (b) motorcycles refer to the product code 8711: motorcycles (including mopeds) and cycles fitted with an auxiliary motor, with or without sidecars; and (c) pharmaceuticals refers to the following product codes: 3003: medicaments (excluding goods of heading 30.02, 30.05, or 30.06) and 3004: medicaments (excluding goods of heading 30.02, 30.05, or 30.06).

highest among small landlocked economies such as Afghanistan (97 percent), Bhutan (75 percent), and Nepal (33 percent). It is lower, but still high, among small island nations such as Maldives (25 percent) and Sri Lanka (33 percent), and it is even lower, yet still significant among large countries such as Bangladesh (13 percent) and Pakistan (20 percent) (see annex 1A, table 1A.3). These products have a direct bearing on food prices and, hence, welfare, especially among the poor, who spend a large proportion of their incomes on food. India imports a small share of vegetables and fruits from within the region (5 percent); it is often one of the major sources of South Asia's imports.

In addition to food products, South Asian countries procure a significant share of other consumer goods from within the region. The share of intraregional imports in total imports of all consumer goods is 9 percent in South Asia (see table 1.1). As in the case of vegetables and fruits, the intraregional share is highest among small landlocked economies such as Afghanistan (99 percent), Bhutan (85 percent), and Nepal (63 percent), and, although it is much lower among large countries such as Bangladesh (8 percent), it is still significant (see annex 1A, table 1A.4). Although India imports only a small share from within the region (2 percent), it is a major source country for imports from within the region. This is evident, for instance, in the case of key consumer goods, such as small cars, motorcycles, medicines, and refined petroleum.

In the case of small cars (cylinder capacity not exceeding 1,000 cubic centimeters) and motorcycles, India is the largest source of imports in several South Asian countries, including Bangladesh, Bhutan, Nepal, and Sri Lanka. South Asian countries together account for about 33 percent of India's total small car exports and 25 percent of its total motorcycle exports (see annex 1A, tables 1A.5 and 1A.6). India has become a global hub for the production of small and subcompact cars, which is relevant for the existing and aspiring middle class in rapidly growing South Asia.

Similarly, in the case of pharmaceutical products (including packaged medicines for retail sale and medicines not in measured doses or in packaging for retail sales), India is the largest source country for Bhutan, Maldives, Nepal, and Sri Lanka and the second largest for Afghanistan. India also exports pharmaceutical products to Bangladesh and Pakistan, but accounts for a much smaller share of their total imports (9 percent and 4 percent, respectively). Pakistan accounts for 55 percent of Afghanistan's pharmaceutical imports. South Asian countries together account for about 3 percent of India's total exports of pharmaceutical products. The corresponding figures for the other two significant exporters, Pakistan and Bangladesh, are about 49 percent and 23 percent, respectively (see annex 1A, table 1A.7).

Refined petroleum is an important essential commodity that enjoys consumer as well as industrial demand and of which India is a major source for all South Asian countries. Refined petroleum exports represent India's strength in refining as well as the transport cost advantage of exporting a bulky product to a proximate location. Because of its rapid growth in crude oil refining capacity over the past decade, India now ranks fourth globally in total refining capacity. Thus, it has emerged as one of the world's largest exporters of refined petroleum products.

It is worth recalling that, in a few cases, especially among small or landlocked countries, there may be overtrading in the region. The gravity model shows that Nepal and Sri Lanka import more than the model predicts from India and that Afghanistan exports more to and imports more from Pakistan than predicted. This suggests there may be a case for greater diversification in trade sources. Among landlocked countries, diversification can be encouraged by improving connectivity to the rest of the world, which might involve, somewhat ironically, better access through the countries with which they overtrade. For example, Rocha (2017) suggests that updating and removing bottlenecks in the Afghanistan–Pakistan Transit Trade Agreement can reduce uncertainties related to merchandise transportation and ensure gains from trade for Afghanistan.[34] Strengthening the Bangladesh, Bhutan, India, Nepal transit agreement can reduce transport costs, improve Nepal's connectivity with the rest of the region, and enhance Nepal's access to markets in East Asia with greater potential (Narain and Varela 2017). Apart from diversification beyond South Asia, Nepal and Sri Lanka can increase their exports to India and realize untapped export potential by plugging into India's local and regional value chains.

BENEFITS TO PRODUCERS AND EXPORTERS

Producers can benefit from greater integration via the enhanced competitiveness that arises from better access to imported inputs, foreign investment, and production networks. They also benefit from greater integration by gaining access to quality inputs, including intermediate goods and capital goods, at competitive prices, which enables them to compete more effectively in export and domestic markets. Trade and FDI are highly complementary; so opening trade leads to more FDI, and vice versa (Kathuria and Yatawara 2016). Greater FDI inflows from within and outside the region can enhance the sophistication and competitiveness of exports, as well as facilitate the access of producers to regional and global production networks.

Producers in South Asia are already accessing imported intermediate and capital goods from within the region (see table 1.1 and annex 1A, tables 1A.8 and 1A.9). The share in imports of intermediate goods procured from within South Asia is highest among the small landlocked economies, Afghanistan, Bhutan, and Nepal; lower, but it is still significant among the island nations, Maldives and Sri Lanka; it is even lower, but still not insignificant, among large countries such as Bangladesh and Pakistan. In capital goods, small countries, such as Bhutan, Nepal, and Sri Lanka, procure more than 40 percent of their imports from within South Asia; even in Bangladesh, as much as 12 percent of imports come from South Asia. India and Pakistan rely largely on the rest of the world for imports of intermediate products and capital goods. Clearly, there is room to import more from neighbors within the region, even for a large country such as India, which currently does not import many intermediate and capital goods from within South Asia. Raihan, Khan, and Quoreshi (2014) examine bilateral trade between India and the other South Asian countries and list the top 50 products—largely intermediate goods—in India, as well as each of the other seven countries, in the context of bilateral trade among them, where actual exports to the partner are close to zero, although significant export capacity exists.

In the case of FDI, some intraregional FDI flows are already taking place (see annex 1A, table 1A.2). Reasonable levels of foreign investments from South Asia, primarily from India, are seen in Bangladesh, Nepal, and Sri Lanka. Although India accounted for 15 percent of the total foreign investment stock in Nepal as of 2015, it only accounted for 1 percent and 4 percent in Bangladesh and Sri Lanka, respectively. Furthermore, investment to South Asia represented a small share of the total outward investment of India (less than 1 percent). South Asia's share in foreign investment is also significant in the case of Afghanistan (28 percent), Maldives (13 percent), and Bhutan (12 percent), among which the primary source countries within the region are, respectively, Pakistan, Sri Lanka, and India. However, overall, the flow of intraregional FDI is small in South Asia, which indicates the substantial scope for gains from greater regional integration that also embraces easing the constraints on FDI.

Nascent regional value chains exist in some sectors, such as textiles and clothing. The textile and clothing sector accounts for 89, 59, 48, and 14 percent of merchandise export earnings in Bangladesh, Pakistan, Sri Lanka, and India, respectively.[35] The textile and clothing sectors in all four countries import from each other. The share of imports from the other three countries in total imports from the world is about 26 percent in Sri Lanka, 22 percent in Bangladesh, 18 percent in Pakistan, and 9 percent in India.[36] About 13 percent of the South Asian FDI stock in Bangladesh as of the end of June 2017 was in the textile and clothing sector.[37] This was partly because of the preferential access to world markets granted to Bangladesh as a least developed country.[38] Clearly, in South Asia, a regional value chain is emerging in apparel. A recent World Bank report documents that the value of the intraregional apparel trade in South Asia rose sharply, from US$400 million in 2003 to US$2.5 billion in 2013, and the share of imported intermediate apparel inputs from within the region increased from 18 percent to 24 percent over the same period (Lopez-Acevedo, Medvedev, and Palmade 2017). With export shares of final apparel goods at 86 percent and 44 percent of total exports, respectively, Bangladesh and Sri Lanka source many apparel inputs from India and Pakistan, which focus relatively less on final apparel (6 percent and 18 percent of total exports, respectively). In 2013, two-thirds of India's exports of knit and crochet fabric were directed to Bangladesh and Sri Lanka, and nearly half of Pakistan's exports of woven cotton denim went to Bangladesh and Sri Lanka. Nonetheless, even in the textile and clothing sector, more regional value chain activity can be catalyzed, especially through greater intraregional FDI.

MARKET ACCESS

Access to regional markets has been important for small countries in South Asia (table 1.2, table 1A.10). For some small economies in the region, such as Afghanistan, Bhutan, and Nepal, regional markets dominate merchandise exports, accounting for

TABLE 1.2 Regional Market Shares, Merchandise Trade, South Asian Countries, 2015
Percent

Indicator	Afghanistan	Bangladesh	Bhutan	India	Maldives	Nepal	Pakistan	Sri Lanka
Exports	72.8	1.9	88.8	6.5	14.2	66.2	13.7	8.7
Imports	29.4	13.2	74.3	0.6	13.6	48.5	5.3	30.6

Source: Calculations based on data from UN Comtrade (United Nations Commodity Trade Statistics Database), Statistics Division, Department of Economic and Social Affairs, United Nations, New York, http://comtrade .un.org/db/; WITS (World Integrated Trade Solution) (database), World Bank, Washington, DC, http://wits .worldbank.org/WITS/.
Note: All shares are calculated according to the 2002 version of the Harmonized Commodity Description and Coding Systems (HS) (database), Statistics Division, Department of Economic and Social Affairs, United Nations, New York, https://unstats.un.org/unsd/tradekb/Knowledgebase/50018/Harmonized-Commodity-Description -and-Coding-Systems-HS. Export share refers to total exports to the region, divided by total exports to the world by the respective countries except for Bhutan; for Bhutan, mirror data are used. Import share refers to total imports from the region, divided by total imports from the world. Total imports from the region are calculated from mirror data of the respective countries; total imports from the world are reported by the respective countries. See annex 1A, table 1A.10 for details.

close to 73 percent, 89 percent, and 66 percent, respectively, of total exports. For Bhutan and Nepal, India is the top export market; for Afghanistan, Pakistan is the largest export market, followed by India. In the case of the other small South Asian economies, such as Maldives and Sri Lanka, regional markets may not dominate their exports, but still play a significant role, especially proximate markets, Sri Lanka in the case of Maldives and India in the case of Sri Lanka.

Even for the larger South Asian economies, market access within the region has been vital. For Pakistan, regional markets account for about 14 percent of overall merchandise exports. For India, regional exports represent 6.5 percent of merchandise exports. Bangladesh is still among India's top 10 markets in the world and the largest in South Asia. Moreover, markets within the region account for a significant share of important exports from South Asian countries, as the examples in table 1.3 illustrate. Thus, in India, passenger cars, nonretail cotton yarn, and raw cotton account for 2.0 percent, 1.4 percent, and 0.7 percent, respectively, of total exports. Similarly, in Bangladesh, jute yarn accounts for 1.6 percent of exports. In all these cases, regional markets play an important role.

Although regional markets have played a significant role among the economies in South Asia, there is wide scope for enhancing this role. The untapped trade potential in the region documented in this report looms even larger given that South Asia is the most rapidly growing region in the world. Growth has exceeded 7 percent a year in the past three years, while growth in the rest of the world, including South Asia's major markets in Europe and North America, has been slowing (see figure 1.2).

Access to regional markets has been noteworthy in the case of some services, but here, too, there is scope for deeper market access. The first example relates to energy. In many countries in South Asia, inadequate, poor-quality energy supply is a binding constraint to growth. Regional trade in electricity can help create more reliable, cost-effective, and cleaner electricity supply systems. In the Doing Business database,

TABLE 1.3 Regional Market Share, Selected Products, Bangladesh and India, 2015
Percent

Exporting country	Product	Share in total exports	Regional export of product (percent of total product exports)				
			Bangladesh	India	Nepal	Pakistan	Sri Lanka
India	Passenger cars	2.0	1.1	—	1.1	0.0	6.2
	Nonretail cotton yarn	1.4	14.2	—	0.2	2.9	1.9
	Raw cotton	0.7	36.4	—	0.0	27.2	0.0
Bangladesh	Jute yarn	1.6	—	11.3		0.4	0.2

Source: Calculations based on data from UN Comtrade (United Nations Commodity Trade Statistics Database), Statistics Division, Department of Economic and Social Affairs, United Nations, New York, http://comtrade .un.org/db/; WITS (World Integrated Trade Solution) (database), World Bank, Washington, DC, http://wits .worldbank.org/WITS/.
Note: The data refer to product codes according to the 2002 version of the Harmonized Commodity Description and Coding Systems (HS) (database), Statistics Division, Department of Economic and Social Affairs, United Nations, New York, https://unstats.un.org/unsd/tradekb/Knowledgebase/50018/Harmonized-Commodity -Description-and-Coding-Systems-HS. The 4-digit codes for the various products are 8703: passenger cars; 5205: nonretail cotton yarn; 5201: raw cotton; and 5307: jute yarn. — = not applicable.

the average ranking on the getting electricity indicator is 121 for South Asia in 2018, the second lowest of all the regions, only slightly above Sub-Saharan Africa.[39] Regional cooperation in energy can provide more optimal matching of the demand for and supply of energy using differences in capacity, demand, and seasonal patterns of supply and demand across countries and the right mix of the diverse energy resources available in the region. This is especially true of run-of-river plants that produce a larger output in summer than in winter.[40] In addition, regional cooperation in the electricity sector can facilitate economies of scale in investment, enhance competition and joint undertakings, improve efficiency, and strengthen the capability to finance investments in the sector, especially in small countries. For example, Bhutan and Nepal have immense hydro potential; the development of this potential could transform the countries, while benefiting the region at large. This requires leveraging foreign investment and expertise from within and outside South Asia and, most importantly, exports to bigger markets, including Bangladesh, India, and Pakistan.

Developments are promising (see annex 1A, table 1A.11 for an overview of existing and proposed crossborder electricity trading arrangements.) In Bhutan, electricity is the principal export commodity and the largest revenue earner, and India is the principal export market. In recent years, Bangladesh–India energy trade has also commenced and is rapidly deepening. Currently, India is supplying 660 megawatts of power to Bangladesh by linking power generation in the states of West Bengal and Tripura to Bangladesh. Much more is in the offing. Bangladesh–India–Nepal trade also holds much promise. Similar progress is also seen on the western side of South Asia, where the CASA-1000 Project will enable 1,300 megawatts of electricity to be sold from the Kyrgyz Republic and Tajikistan to Afghanistan and Pakistan and also lay the foundation for a possible Central Asia–South Asia regional electricity market.

The second example in services relates to tourism. Tourism is another major service export of Bhutan, Nepal, and Sri Lanka, and India is the largest source of tourists to these countries. In the case of Bhutan, India accounted for 65 percent of all foreign tourist arrivals for leisure (which comprised 84 percent of all foreign tourist arrivals) in 2016 (TCB 2016). In Nepal, in 2012/13, tourism accounted for about 5 percent of foreign exchange earnings, and India accounted for 23 percent of all foreign tourist arrivals in 2013 (Ministry of Culture, Tourism, and Civil Aviation 2014). In the case of Sri Lanka, where tourism accounts for 14 percent of total foreign exchange earnings, India is the largest source of tourists, accounting for 17 percent of all foreign tourist arrivals in 2016 (Sri Lanka Tourism Development Authority 2016).

Even India relies on South Asia for a high and growing share of tourist arrivals; Bangladesh is India's largest market. South Asian tourists (2.2 million tourists) accounted for 25 percent of all foreign tourist arrivals in India; Bangladesh, with a 16 percent share in global tourist arrivals into India in 2016 (and even higher in 2017), was the number one source of tourists.[41] In the case of medical tourism, where India has emerged as a major destination, medical tourists from South Asia dominate. Bangladesh alone accounts for the largest number of medical tourists to India (165,000 patients or 35 percent of estimated total medical tourist arrivals) and the largest share of medical tourism revenues (US$343 million, more than 50 percent of the estimated medical tourism revenues) (DGCI&S 2017).

Overall, intra-SAARC travel accounted for 20 percent of all foreign tourist arrivals in SAARC countries (Chanda 2014). Recognizing the potential of tourism to create jobs and deepen people-to-people contacts, SAARC has identified tourism as a priority sector that would benefit from intergovernmental cooperation.

TRANSIT AND LANDLOCKED COUNTRIES AND SUBREGIONS

Trade integration and connectivity can play an important role in enhancing the welfare of landlocked countries in South Asia, such as Afghanistan, Bhutan, and Nepal, and relatively isolated subregions, such as Northeast India and Khyber-Pakhtunkhwa and the Federally-Administered Tribal Areas in Pakistan. Lack of efficient transit through neighboring countries can increase the costs of transportation and logistics, pushing up the prices of imported, essential, and nonessential consumer goods, as well as the prices of inputs. Similarly, higher transportation and logistics costs can often render products from landlocked areas uncompetitive beyond local markets, thus confining these areas to production in volumes that are insufficient to reap economies of scale and limited primarily to sale in nearby markets. Better connectivity and trade integration with neighboring countries can allow consumers to access a wider variety of cheaper, better-quality goods and permit firms to access world-class inputs at competitive prices, thereby enabling access to wider markets and economies of scale. Through transport corridors that offer connectivity and transit, better integration also has the potential to affect poverty, which tends to be higher in landlocked and border subregions (Ahmed and Ghani 2010).[42] Transport corridors can grow into economic corridors with improved transportation, logistics, and energy infrastructure.[43] Thus, they can bring greater economic opportunities to border and landlocked areas and help reduce poverty by improving poor people's access to jobs, lowering the costs of the goods and services they consume, and providing better access to essential infrastructure services such as electricity. Bridging selected Central Asian countries with South Asia through energy transit, Afghanistan can reduce its energy shortage, add 3.1 percent to its export growth annually, and gain US$530 million in terms of revenue by 2030 (Rocha 2017).

Landlocked countries, such as Bhutan and Nepal, rely on transit trade facilities from India and, to a lesser extent, Bangladesh to reach the ports that enable imports from and exports to the rest of the world. Similarly, Afghanistan relies on trade and transit through Pakistan and the Islamic Republic of Iran.

The importance of transit for landlocked regions is underscored by the fact that landlocked countries and border subareas have tended to do better when they have been better connected to neighboring countries. As Ahmed and Ghani (2010) note, Afghanistan and Nepal prospered in the 18th and 19th centuries on the basis of free trade and commerce with neighbors, but conflict and border restrictions placed a constraint on this source of growth. Similarly, Northeast India flourished before the division of the subcontinent in the 20th century; thereafter, it gradually fell behind the rest of India in growth and development (box 1.5).

MANAGING CHANGE

The South Asia trade integration strategy advocated in this report will, like all trade reform, create winners and losers. This calls for careful management of implementation. A sustainable process of trade integration, irrespective of the countries with whom the country is entering into a deeper partnership, will require the following ingredients:

- Precisely articulating the trade strategy, with timelines for reforms of all border taxes, communicated clearly and transparently to stakeholders

- Gradually phasing in trade liberalization in sectors where there are concerns about large job displacement

- Implementing a strategy to diversify sources of tax revenue that reduces the often substantial dependence on trade taxes

- Focusing on critical reforms that would help the economy and the private sector take advantage of trade liberalization, including improving trade facilitation, attracting high-quality FDI, and addressing key issues that constrain the ease of doing business

- Negotiating enhanced market access within South Asia and in selected critical markets, especially in East Asia, which are underrepresented in the export basket of South Asian countries

BOX 1.5 Trade and Lagging Regions: The Case of Northeast India

Northeast India is endowed with abundant natural resources, such as oil and gas, coal, limestone, hydroelectricity potential, tropical forests with rich biodiversity, pristine natural beauty, and clean environs.[a] Northeast India was at the forefront of development in India almost 150 years ago, as noted in *North Eastern Region Vision 2020* (MDONER and NEC 2008). The rapid spread of tea gardens and the export of tea followed the establishment of the first tea garden in 1835. The discovery of oil and establishment of the first refinery in Digboi in 1890 laid the foundation for the economic development of an undivided Assam. Missionaries laid an early foundation for widespread literacy. Global trade was conducted through the seaports of Chittagong (now in Bangladesh) and Kolkata, well-connected to the region through a network of inland waterways and road and railway networks through present-day Bangladesh. The railway network between Dibrugarh (in Assam, India) and Chittagong was one of the earliest projects in India.

The trajectory of Northeast India's growth and development changed with the division of the subcontinent, first in 1947, with the split of colonial India into India and Pakistan (West and East) and then, in 1971, with the separation of East Pakistan from West Pakistan and the creation of Bangladesh. This division caused the interruption of inland water, road, and railway communications through Bangladesh and the loss of access to the port of Chittagong, the gateway to East and Southeast Asia. Furthermore, the incorporation of Tibet into China, replacing the earlier soft territorial frontier, and the virtual closure of the border with Myanmar added to the isolation of Northeast India by cutting its traditional economic links with surrounding areas. Northeast India became a peninsula, connected to the rest of India only through the 27-kilometer-wide Chicken's Neck or Siliguri corridor. To access a port, traders need to travel 1,600 kilometers from Agartala in Tripura to Kolkata in West Bengal, via Siliguri, instead of 200 kilometers to access the nearby port of Chittagong in Bangladesh; this is true for all states in the region. People and goods travel through the Chicken's Neck to reach Northeast India from the rest of India and vice-versa, resulting in greater transit times and higher costs. Poor transport and logistics within Northeast India worsen the situation. Accessing mainland India can add between 8 percent and 15 percent to the costs of products, making consumer goods coming into Northeast India more expensive for consumers in the region. The situation makes the products of Northeast India more expensive in the rest of India, often rendering them uncompetitive outside local markets. Northeast India's geographical isolation has prevented this landlocked region, comprising an area of 263,000 square kilometers and a population of 46 million, from benefiting from the trickle-down effect of the booming economies of South Asia and Southeast Asia. Today, the region accounts for 8 percent of India's land area and 4 percent of its population, but only about 3 percent of its GDP.

Some recent developments that would provide better connectivity to the region offer hope for Northeast India's economic development. First, the Government of India, with its Act East Policy, aims to provide an action-oriented thrust to its goal of unlocking Northeast India's development potential by connecting the region with neighboring countries in Southeast Asia. The government is backing the fast-tracking of a host of connectivity projects within Northeast India (deeper penetration of the railway network, expansion of the network of national highways and state roads, new airports, and so forth), as well as projects linking the region to Southeast Asia.

Second, the BBIN Motor Vehicles Agreement, which was signed between Bangladesh, Bhutan, India, and Nepal in June 2015, aims to allow vehicles registered in these countries to travel through each other's sovereign territories.[b] A pilot project carried out by the logistics company DHL in November 2015 showed that the movement of cargo from

box continues next page

> **BOX 1.5 Trade and Lagging Regions: The Case of Northeast India** *(continued)*
>
> Kolkata to Agartala in Northeast India would become extremely time- and-cost-effective if routed through Bangladesh, instead of the circuitous route through the Chicken's Neck, because it would cut the travel distance by more than 1,000 kilometers.
>
> Third, the deepening relationship between Bangladesh and India, cemented by several bilateral agreements in June 2015, will add further impetus to Northeast India's development, given the shared border of 1,880 kilometers between Northeast India and Bangladesh. For example, investments are being made to improve road and rail connectivity between the two countries, including through planned rail links between the Indian states of Tripura and Assam, and Bangladesh. The memorandum of understanding that grants India access to the ports of Chittagong and Mongla to ship goods to Northeast India, the Coastal Shipping Agreement that provides for direct connectivity between the seaports of East India and Bangladesh, and the Protocol on Inland Water Transit and Trade (Renewal) that allows for goods transportation using the river network will, together, provide multimodal connectivity, while lowering transportation costs and time for the flow of goods to and from Northeast India. Under the Inland Water Transit and Trade Protocol, transshipment of cargo through the Ashuganj port and Akhaura checkpoint of Bangladesh to the Northeast Indian state of Tripura has already begun.
>
> Coordinated infrastructure upgrades of land custom stations and integrated check posts, stressed by both governments as an urgent need, will smooth the flow of goods through border areas. The Bilateral Cooperation Agreement between the Bureau of Indian Standards and the Bangladesh Standards and Testing Institution (BSTI), which will facilitate compliance with and recognition of each other's standards, will further ease the flow of goods. Better connectivity within Northeast India and from Northeast India to the rest of India, as well as to neighboring Bangladesh, Bhutan, Myanmar, and Nepal will be key to unlocking the economic potential of the region.
>
> a. Northeast India consists of the eight Indian states of Arunachal Pradesh, Assam, Manipur, Meghalaya, Mizoram, Nagaland, Sikkim, and Tripura.
>
> b. Bhutan has since decided to defer its entry into the agreement, but has asked the other countries to proceed.

- Strengthening safety nets and training for those workers whose jobs are affected

- Improving the links among education, training, and the job market to supply better skills to the sectors that gain from trade reform

- Defining a limited fiscal package with clear and transparent criteria for the firms or sectors that will be adversely affected by trade reforms (Kathuria and Shahid 2015, 2016; Lederman, Lopez-Acevedo, and Savchenko 2014).

The government of Sri Lanka is preparing for a fresh round of trade liberalization based on these principles. It has articulated a new trade vision and begun autonomous trade liberalization through the November 2017 budget.[44] It signed a FTA with Singapore in January 2018, is negotiating a deeper FTA with India (one is ongoing), and is discussing new FTAs with Bangladesh and China.

Conclusions

The people of South Asia have not enjoyed many of the fruits of geographical and cultural proximity. In several ways, the countries of the region provide less than most-favored-nation treatment to their neighbors, and this is not only about India and Pakistan. Trade volumes are well below potential. Artificial barriers have thwarted the goals of free trade in the region. Inadequate infrastructure and inefficient trade procedures have led to disproportionately high intraregional trade costs, compounded by complex NTMs. Trade in services is held back by visa regimes, among other factors. The vibrant private sector in the region usually makes outward investment decisions beyond the immediate neighborhood, which limits trade and regional value chains. All of this reinforces a trust deficit that has persisted because of complex history and size asymmetry across economies.

Despite these obstacles, trade and investment links have grown, although haltingly. Where barriers are too high, trade takes an informal route. Trade has benefited consumers, exporters, and producers and has especially helped the inhabitants of landlocked countries and subregions and the smaller economies.

Yet, so much more is possible. All of the countries, including the large countries, such as Bangladesh, India, and Pakistan, have much more to gain from deeper integration within the region. One example is the large gaps between current and potential trade. For landlocked countries, such as Afghanistan, Bhutan, and Nepal, and subregions, such as Northeast India and Khyber-Pakhtunkhwa and the Federally-Administered Tribal Areas in Pakistan, better regional connectivity, increased regional exports, and access to regional value chains are key to unlocking economic potential.

Deeper integration in goods and services trade in South Asia holds the biggest prize for the individual. Benefits can be wide-ranging, including access to a greater variety of goods at lower prices, and ease of crossing borders to study in universities, use hospitals, or explore shared history. In turn, the greater people-to-people contacts implied by such access could help reduce the trust deficit.

Deeper trade relations in South Asia do not hamper advances in interregional or multilateral trade. Each country will have other underexploited markets, including ASEAN countries, Central Asian countries, China, the Islamic Republic of Iran, and Turkey. This report does not analyze these trading relationships. Its objective is to show that there are significant and unrealized benefits associated with deeper trade integration within South Asia and to indicate ways to realize some of these benefits.

The rest of this report is about unpacking the reasons for the unmet potential in four specific areas. Chapter 2 deals with tariffs and nontransparent paratariffs and how they inhibit the goals of free trade. Chapter 3 takes a deep dive into specific NTMs, focusing on SPS and TBT measures only, in the context of bilateral trade between Bangladesh and India and between India and Nepal in selected products; the chapter suggests ways to reduce the burden of NTMs. Chapter 4 explores the issue of the high costs of connectivity in the context of air services liberalization between India and Sri Lanka and illustrates lessons for other countries in the region. Chapter 5 analyzes the operation of border haats along the Bangladesh–India border to document their impact on people-to-people relationships and trust building, as well as on employment and income generation.

Annex 1A: Tables

TABLE 1A.1 Top 50 ad Valorem Equivalents of Nontariff Measures, Bilateral Trade, South Asia

Importer	Exporter	Cods (HS 2007)	AVE SPS/TBT (%)	Imports (Thousand US$)	Product description (HS 2007)
LKA	IND	291812	2,036	0.6	Tartaric acid
LKA	IND	854411	2,029	90.9	Winding wire, of copper
PAK	BGD	200899	1,293	4.7	Edible parts of plants, prepared/preserved, whether/not containing added sugar/other sweetening matter/spirit, n.e.s.
LKA	PAK	391530	1,091	172.5	Waste, parings and scrap, of polymers of vinyl chloride
LKA	IND	390791	541	214.8	Polyesters (excl. of 3907.10-3907.60. unsaturated, in primary forms
IND	BGD	853190	497	15.2	Parts of the apparatus of 85.31
LKA	IND	940510	446	80.3	Chandeliers and other electric ceiling/wall lighting fittings (excl. those of a Kind used for lighting public open spaces/thoroughfa res)
LKA	IND	110814	441	27.7	Manioc (cassava) starch
LKA	IND	290715	420	31.0	Naphthols and their salts
LKA	IND	200559	318	22.2	Beans (excl. Vigna spp., Phaseolus spp.), shelled, prepared/preserved othw. than by vinegar/acetic acid, not frozen, other than products of 20.06
LKA	IND	950670	296	0.0	Ice skates and roller skates, incl. skating boots with skates attached
IND	LKA	200899	286	1.0	Edible parts of plants, prepared/preserved, whether/not containing added sugar/other sweetening matter/spirit, n.e.s.
LKA	PAK	950699	243	38.2	Articles and equip. for sports, n.e.s. in Ch.95 (excl. gloves, strings for rackets, bags, clothing, footwear and nets); swimming pools & paddling pools
LKA	IND	761610	237	35.4	Nails, tacks, staples (excl. of 83.05), screws, bolts, nuts, screw hooks, rivets, cotters, cotter-pins, washers and similar articles, of aluminium
IND	PAK	220720	212	85.9	Ethyl alcohol and other spirits, denatured, of any strength
LKA	PAK	220720	196	18.8	Ethyl alcohol and other spirits, denatured, of any strength
LKA	IND	220720	192	10.2	Ethyl alcohol and other spirits, denatured, of any strength
LKA	IND	220830	190	63.5	Whiskies

table continues next page

TABLE 1A.1 Top 50 ad Valorem Equivalents of Nontariff Measures, Bilateral Trade, South Asia (continued)

Importer	Exporter	Cods (HS 2007)	AVE SPS/TBT (%)	Imports (Thousand US$)	Product description (HS 2007)
LKA	IND	841919	185	134.4	Instantaneous/storage water heaters, non-electric (excl. of 8419.11)
LKA	PAK	731816	181	1.9	Nuts of iron/steel
LKA	IND	380991	173	1,383.3	Finishing agents, dye carriers to accelerate the dyeing/fixing of dyestuffs and other products and preparations (e.g., dressings and mordants), of a kind used in the textile industries (excl. of 3809.10)
AFG	PAK	020629	167	0.0	Edible offal of bovine animals (excl. tongues and livers), frozen
IND	BGD	620331	161	6.3	Men's/boys' jackets and blazers (excl. knitted/crocheted), of wool/fine animal hair
NPL	IND	040221	160	262.0	Milk in powder/granules/other solid form, unsweetened, fat content by weight >1.5%
NPL	IND	020629	158	0.3	Edible offal of bovine animals (excl. tongues and livers), frozen
LKA	PAK	950890	147	0.2	Roundabouts, swings, shooting galleries and other fairground amusements; travelling theatres
LKA	PAK	390690	143	3.5	Acrylic polymers other than poly(methyl methacrylate), in primary forms
LKA	IND	841460	138	10.4	Ventilating/recycling hoods incorporating a fan, whether/not fitted with filters, having a maximum horizontal side not > 120cm
LKA	PAK	871499	127	3.4	Parts and accessories of the vehicles of 87.11–87.13, n.e.s. In 87.14
LKA	IND	390720	126	289.4	Polyethers other than polyacetals, in primary forms
LKA	IND	840999	123	1,403.3	Parts suit. for use solely/principally with the engines of 84.07/84.08 (excl. of 8409.10 and 8409.91)
LKA	IND	848220	123	512.9	Tapered roller bearings, incl. cone and tapered roller assemblies
LKA	PAK	950631	121	0.5	Golf clubs, complete
LKA	IND	732393	121	2,638.4	Table/kitchen/other h-hold. articles and parts thereof (ex cl. of 7323.10), of stainlesssteel
LKA	IND	830210	116	160.3	Hinges of basemetal
IND	LKA	220429	114	0.8	Wine other than sparkling wine of fresh grapes, incl. fortified; grape must with fermentation prevented/arrested by the addition of alcohol, in containters of >2|

table continues next page

TABLE 1A.1 **Top 50 ad Valorem Equivalents of Nontariff Measures, Bilateral Trade, South Asia** (continued)

Importer	Exporter	Cods (HS 2007)	AVE SPS/TBT (%)	Imports (Thousand US$)	Product description (HS 2007)
LKA	IND	950890	112	0.0	Roundabouts, swings, shooting galleries and other fairground amusements; travelling theatres
LKA	IND	220429	108	15.8	Wine other than sparkling wine of fresh grapes, incl. fortified; grape must with fermentation prevented/arnested by the addition of alcohol, in containters of >2|
LKA	IND	841533	107	14.4	Air-conditioning machines (excl. of 8415.10–8415.31), not incorporating a refrigerating unit
LKA	IND	701952	97	4.4	Woven fabrics of glass fibres (excl. of 7019.40), of a width >30cm, plain weave, weighing <250g/m2, of filaments measuring per single yarn >136tex
LKA	PAK	481930	93	0.4	Sacks and bags, havinga base of a width of 40cm/more
PAK	IND	090830	92	2,132.0	Cardamoms
IND	PAK	520842	89	66.8	Woven fabrics of cotton, containing 85%/ more by weight of cotton, of yarns of different colours, plain weave, weighing>100g/m2
LKA	IND	621143	87	109.4	Track suits (excl. knitted/crocheted), women's/girls'; other garments, n.e.s. (excl. knitted/crocheted), women 's/girls', of man-made fibres
LKA	IND	950691	82	133.0	Articles and equip, for general physical exercise/gymnastics/athletics
IND	PAK	620610	78	4.0	Women's/girls' blouses, shirts and shirt-blouses (excl. knitted/crocheted), of silk/ silk waste
LKA	IND	481420	78	0.2	Wallpaper and similar wall coverings, consisting of paper coated/covered, on the face side, with a grained/embossed/ coloured/design-printed/othw. decorated layer of plastics
LKA	IND	950590	77	21.C	Festive/carnival/other entertainment articles (excl. articles for Christmas festivities), incl. conjuring tricks and novelty jokes
LKA	IND	920810	76	0.5	Musical boxes
LKA	IND	560490	75	2.3	Other type of rubber thread and cord, textile covered

Source: Kee and Nicita 2017.
Note: Only SPS- and TBT-related NTMs are used in the computation of ad valorem equivalents. AFG = Afghanistan; BGD = Bangladesh; IND = India; LKA = Sri Lanka; NPL = Nepal; PAK = Pakistan; SPS = sanitary and phytosanitary standards; TBT = technical barriers to trade.

TABLE 1A.2 Intraregional Outward FDI Stock, South Asia, 2015
$, millions

Investment from/ Investment to	AFG	BGD	BTN	IND	MDV	NPL	PAK	LKA	Total inv to South Asia	Total inv to World	Inv to South Asia/Inv to World (%)
AFG	—	0.0	—	0.1	—	—	0.0	—	0.2	418.1	0.0
BGD	—	—	—	34.9	1.1	19.9	1.2	6.4	63.5	187.5	33.8
BTN	—	—	—	—	—	0.0	0.0	—	0.0	4.5	0.5
IND	—	140.6	19.6	—	20.9	131.5	—	431.4	744.0	84,826.4	0.9
MDV	—	—	—	—	—	—	—	17.3	17.3	140.4	12.3
NPL	—	0.2	—	0.7	—	—	—	—	0.9	72.2	1.2
PAK	9.6	22.6	—	—	5.3	3.4	—	15.6	56.5	307.7	18.4
LKA	—	10.2	—	30.5	53.7	0.9	—	—	95.2	659.8	14.4
Total Inv from South Asia	9.6	173.5	19.6	66.1	81.0	155.6	1.2	470.7	977.5	86,616.6	1.1
Total Inv from World	34.8	12352.27	167.4	312,152.0	617.4	904.9	1,230.9	9,971.9	337,431.4		
Inv from South Asia/Inv from World (%)	27.5	1.4	11.7	0.0	13.1	17.2	0.1	4.7	0.3		

Source: Calculations based on data from CDIS (Coordinated Direct Investment Survey) (database), International Monetary Fund, Washington, DC, http://data.imf .org/?sk=40313609-F037-48C1-84B1-E1F1CE54D6D5.

Note: The reporting countries in the rows and the investment flows reported refer to outward investment. These data may differ from data reported as inward investment by destination countries. Total Investment to the world is outward investment reported by the respective countries. Total investment from the world is reported by the respective countries, except Afghanistan and Maldives. In these two cases, mirror data are used. Inv = investment; — = not available. AFG = Afghanistan; BGD =Bangladesh; BTN = Bhutan; IND =India; LKA = Sri Lanka; MDV = Maldives; NPL = Nepal; PAK=Pakistan

TABLE 1A.3 Intraregional Trade in Vegetables and Fruits, South Asia, 2015
$, millions

Exporting country/ Importing country	AFG	BGD	BTN	IND	MDV	NPL	PAK	LKA	Total export to South Asia	Total export to World	Export to South Asia/Export to World (%)
AFG	—	—	—	89.4	—	—	43.3	—	132.6	183.6	72.2
BGD	0.1	—	0.2	25.5	0.2	—	0.0	1.4	27.4	168.7	16.2
BTN	—	13.1	—	1.3	—	—	—	—	14.4	14.6	98.7
IND	2.0	105.5	1.2	—	15.0	88.2	146.5	129.3	487.9	3,175.6	15.4
MDV	—	—	—	—	—	—	—	—	—	0.0	
NPL	—	6.6	—	56.9	—	—	—	—	63.5	64.6	98.3
PAK	221.6	7.1	—	69.6	0.9	—	—	23.8	323.0	702.0	46.0
LKA	—	—	—	79.4	11.0	0.1	10.1	—	100.6	329.3	30.6
Total import from South Asia	223.8	132.3	1.4	322.1	27.0	88.4	199.9	154.6	1,149.4	4,638.5	24.8
Total import from World	231.3	991.9	1.9	6,798.7	107.3	268.7	1,003.9	482.6	9,886.3		
Import from South Asia/ Import from World (%)	96.7	13.3	75.4	4.7	25.2	32.9	19.9	32.0	11.6		

Source: Calculations based on data from UN Comtrade (United Nations Commodity Trade Statistics Database), Statistics Division, Department of Economic and Social Affairs, United Nations, New York, http://comtrade.un.org/db/; WITS (World Integrated Trade Solution) (database), World Bank, Washington, DC, http://wits.worldbank.org/WITS/.

Note: The reporting countries in the rows and the trade flows reported refer to exports, except for Bhutan. Mirror data of the other reporting countries are used for Bhutan. Total imports from and total exports to the world refer to the data reported by the respective reporting countries except for Afghanistan and Bhutan imports. Mirror data from the world are used in both these cases. Vegetables and fruits are defined as STIC 05: vegetables and fruit under SITC revision 3 (see the text). — = not available. AFG = Afghanistan; BGD = Bangladesh; BTN = Bhutan; IND = India; LKA = Sri Lanka; MDV = Maldives; NPL = Nepal; PAK = Pakistan.

TABLE 1A.4 Intraregional Trade in Consumer Goods, South Asia, 2015
$, millions

Exporting country/ Importing country	AFG	BGD	BTN	IND	MDV	NPL	PAK	LKA	Total Export to South Asia	Total Export to World	Export to South Asia/Export to World (%)
AFG	—	0.6	—	14.2	—	—	89.0	—	103.8	132.3	78.4
BGD	4.2	—	2.2	291.5	1.7	2.1	6.9	17.2	325.8	29,637.9	1.1
BTN	—	12.3	—	7.7	—	0.0	—	—	20.0	22.0	90.6
IND	303.5	859.3	166.6	—	64.0	1,397.1	280.6	2,234.7	5,305.9	117,805.7	4.5
MDV	—	—	—	0.1	—	—	—	0.8	0.9	15.2	5.8
NPL	9.1	0.1	0.3	184.9	0.0	—	0.1	0.0	194.6	361.2	53.9
PAK	726.6	17.7	—	15.4	5.4	1.7	—	54.0	820.8	12,703.2	6.5
LKA	0.5	31.4	0.0	364.0	45.0	1.5	31.7	—	474.1	8,153.8	5.8
Total import from South Asia	1,043.9	921.4	169.2	877.7	116.1	1,402.3	408.3	2,306.7	7,245.8	168,831.5	
Total import from World	1,055.2	11,162.1	199.4	43,593.2	949.4	2,224.8	13,628.7	6,166.6	78,979.3		
Import from South Asia/ Import from World (%)	98.9	8.3	84.9	2.0	12.2	63.0	3.0	37.4	9.2		

Source: Calculations based on data from UN Comtrade (United Nations Commodity Trade Statistics Database), Statistics Division, Department of Economic and Social Affairs, United Nations, New York, http://comtrade.un.org/db/; WITS (World Integrated Trade Solution) (database), World Bank, Washington, DC, http://wits.worldbank.org/WITS/.
Note: The reporting countries in the rows and the trade flows reported refer to exports, except for Bhutan. Mirror data of the other reporting countries are used for Bhutan. Total imports from and total exports to the world refer to the data reported by the respective reporting countries except for Bhutan. Mirror data from the world are used for Bhutan. Consumer goods refer to UNCTAD SOP3 under HS2002 provided in WITS (see the text). — = not available. AFG = Afghanistan; BGD = Bangladesh; BTN = Bhutan; IND = India; LKA = Sri Lanka; MDV = Maldives; NPL = Nepal; PAK = Pakistan.

TABLE 1A.5 Intraregional Trade in Small Cars, South Asia, 2015
$, millions

Exporting country/Importing country	AFG	BGD	BTN	IND	MDV	NPL	PAK	LKA	Total export to South Asia	Total export to World	Export to South Asia/Export to World
AFG	—	—	—	—	—	—	—	—	—	—	—
BGD	—	—	—	0.0	—	—	—	—	0.0	0.0	100.0
BTN	—	—	—	—	—	—	—	—	—	—	—
IND	2.3	57.1	16.2	—	—	4.1	—	319.0	398.7	1,225.8	32.5
MDV	—	—	—	—	—	—	—	—	—	—	—
NPL	—	—	—	—	—	—	—	—	—	—	—
PAK	0.1	0.3	—	0.0	—	—	—	—	0.4	0.6	62.4
LKA	—	—	—	—	—	—	—	—	—	0.0	—
Total import from South Asia	2.4	57.3	16.2	0.0	0.0	4.1	0.0	319.0	399.1	1,226.5	32.5
Total import from World	2.7	59.0	16.2	0.3	2.4	8.6	345.9	466.6	901.8		
Import from South Asia/Import from World (%)	88.9	97.2	100.0	3.1	0.0	47.3	0.0	68.4	44.3		

Source: Calculations based on data from UN Comtrade (United Nations Commodity Trade Statistics Database), Statistics Division, Department of Economic and Social Affairs, United Nations, New York, http://comtrade.un.org/db/; WITS (World Integrated Trade Solution) (database), World Bank, Washington, DC, http://wits.worldbank.org/WITS/.

Note: The reporting countries in the rows and the trade flows reported refer to exports, except for Bhutan. Mirror data of the other reporting countries are used for Bhutan. Total imports from and total exports to the world refer to the data reported by the respective reporting countries except for Bhutan, Afghanistan imports, and Bangladesh imports. Mirror data from the world are used in these cases. Small cars refer to the product code 870321: motor cars and other motor vehicles principally designed for the transport of persons of a cylinder capacity not exceeding 1,000 cubic centimeters, under HS2002 (see the text). — = not available. AFG = Afghanistan; BGD = Bangladesh; BTN = Bhutan; IND = India; LKA = Sri Lanka; MDV = Maldives; NPL = Nepal; PAK = Pakistan.

TABLE 1A.6 Intraregional Trade in Motorcycles, South Asia, 2015
$, millions

Exporting country/Importing country	AFG	BGD	BTN	IND	MDV	NPL	PAK	LKA	Total export to South Asia	Total export to World	Export to South Asia/Export to World (%)
AFG	—	—	—	—	—	—	—	—	—	—	—
BGD	—	—	—	—	—	—	—	—	—	0.0	—
BTN	—	—	—	—	—	—	—	—	—	—	—
IND	0.3	130.1	0.5	—	0.1	87.0	—	223.3	441.4	1,783.6	24.7
MDV	—	—	—	—	—	—	—	—	—	—	—
NPL	—	—	—	—	—	—	—	—	—	—	—
PAK	4.5	0.8	—	—	—	—	—	0.0	5.3	5.4	97.5
LKA	—	—	—	0.0	0.0	—	0.0	—	0.0	0.3	14.4
Total Import from South Asia	4.9	130.9	0.5	0.0	0.1	87.0	0.0	223.3	446.7	1,789.3	25.0
Total Import from World	51.4	141.5	0.6	47.0	9.4	94.9	104.8	238.8	688.4		
Import from South Asia/Import from World (%)	9.4	92.5	81.8	0.1	1.1	91.6	0.0	93.5	64.9		

Source: Calculations based on data from UN Comtrade (United Nations Commodity Trade Statistics Database), Statistics Division, Department of Economic and Social Affairs, United Nations, New York, http://comtrade.un.org/db/; WITS (World Integrated Trade Solution) (database), World Bank, Washington, DC, http://wits.worldbank.org/WITS/.
Note: The reporting countries in the rows and the trade flows reported refer to exports, except for Bhutan. Mirror data of the other reporting countries are used for Bhutan. Total imports from and total exports to the world refer to the data reported by the respective reporting countries except for Bhutan and Afghanistan imports. Mirror data from the world are used in these cases. Motorcycles refer to the product code 8711: Motorcycles (including mopeds) and cycles fitted with an auxiliary motor, with or without sidecars; sidecars, under HS2002 (see the text). — = not available; AFG = Afghanistan; BGD = Bangladesh; BTN = Bhutan; IND = India; LKA = Sri Lanka; MDV = Maldives; NPL = Nepal; PAK = Pakistan.

TABLE 1A.7 Intraregional Trade in Pharmaceutical Products, South Asia, 2015
$, millions

Exporting country/ Importing country	AFG	BGD	BTN	IND	MDV	NPL	PAK	LKA	Total export to South Asia	Total export to World	Export to South Asia/Export to World (%)
AFG	—	—	—	—	—	—	—	—	—	—	—
BGD	3.5	—	0.1	0.0	0.1	1.0	0.5	10.3	15.5	68.7	22.6
BTN	—	—	—	—	—	0.0	—	—	0.0	0.9	0.0
IND	31.7	7.8	1.9	—	9.9	115.6	14.2	167.7	348.8	11,564.2	3.0
MDV	—	—	—	—	—	—	—	—	—	—	—
NPL	—	—	—	6.0	—	—	0.0	—	6.0	6.2	97.8
PAK	73.7	0.7	—	0.3	1.2	0.0	—	21.9	97.8	200.6	48.7
LKA	—	0.0	—	0.4	1.0	—	—	—	1.3	2.3	59.5
Total Import from South Asia	108.9	8.4	2.0	6.7	12.2	116.6	14.7	199.9	469.5	11,842.9	4.0
Total Import from World	133.4	82.7	3.3	880.2	19.0	247.0	368.5	359.5	2,093.7		
Import from South Asia/ Import from World (%)	81.6	10.2	61.7	0.8	64.2	47.2	4.0	55.6	22.4		

Source: Calculations based on data from UN Comtrade (United Nations Commodity Trade Statistics Database), Statistics Division, Department of Economic and Social Affairs, United Nations, New York, http://comtrade.un.org/db/; WITS (World Integrated Trade Solution) (database), World Bank, Washington, DC, http://wits.worldbank.org/WITS/.
Note: The reporting countries in the rows and the trade flows reported refer to exports, except for Bhutan. Mirror data of the other reporting countries are used for Bhutan. Total imports from and total exports to the world refer to the data reported by the respective reporting countries except for Bhutan and Afghanistan imports. Mirror data from the world are used in these cases. Pharmaceuticals refers to the following product codes under HS2002: (a) 3003: medicaments (excluding goods of heading 30.02, 30.05 or 30.06) consisting of two or more constituents which have been mixed together for therapeutic or prophylactic uses, not put up in measured doses or in forms or packings for retail sale. (b) 3004: medicaments (excluding goods of heading 30.02, 30.05 or 30.06) consisting of mixed or unmixed products for therapeutic or prophylactic uses, put up in measured doses (including those in the form of transdermal administration systems) or in forms or packing for retail sale (see the text). — = not available.

TABLE 1A.8 Intraregional Trade in Intermediate Goods, South Asia, 2015
$, millions

Exporting country/ Importing country	AFG	BGD	BTN	IND	MDV	NPL	PAK	LKA	Total export to South Asia	Total export to World	Export to South Asia/Export to World (%)
AFG	—	—	—	0.0	—	—	0.1	—	0.1	1.9	7.6
BGD	—	—	0.2	90.2	0.1	0.0	3.8	4.3	98.7	926.6	10.7
BTN	—	1.1	—	186.5	—	0.0	0.1	—	187.6	212.2	88.4
IND	198.6	2,512.0	62.8	—	35.3	898.0	945.1	1,145.3	5,797.1	85,251.5	6.8
MDV	—	0.1	—	—	—	—	—	8.3	8.5	10.8	78.3
NPL	—	6.6	0.1	196.7	—	—	0.0	0.0	203.4	240.8	84.5
PAK	670.0	613.2	0.0	128.5	1.3	0.1	—	161.9	1,574.9	6,275.0	25.1
LKA	—	46.8	0.0	75.4	12.4	0.1	14.4	—	149.2	809.8	18.4
Total Import from South Asia	868.6	3,179.7	63.1	677.4	49.2	898.2	963.5	1,319.8	8,019.5	93,728.5	8.6
Total Import from World	1,431.1	22,148.1	70.2	133,903.4	301.9	2,333.8	14,071.8	6,458.3	180,718.4		
Import from South Asia/ Import from World (%)	60.7	14.4	89.9	0.5	16.3	38.5	6.8	20.4	4.4		

Source: Calculations based on data from UN Comtrade (United Nations Commodity Trade Statistics Database), Statistics Division, Department of Economic and Social Affairs, United Nations, New York, http://comtrade.un.org/db/; WITS (World Integrated Trade Solution) (database), World Bank, Washington, DC, http://wits.worldbank.org/WITS/.
Note: The reporting countries in the rows and the trade flows reported refer to exports, except for Bhutan. Mirror data of the other reporting countries are used for Bhutan. Total imports from and total exports to the world refer to the data reported by the respective reporting countries except for Bhutan. Intermediate goods refer to UNCTAD SOP2 under HS2002 provided in WITS (see the text). — = not available; AFG = Afghanistan; BGD = Bangladesh; BTN = Bhutan; IND = India; LKA = Sri Lanka; MDV = Maldives; NPL = Nepal; PAK = Pakistan.

TABLE 1A.9 Intraregional Trade in Capital Goods, South Asia, 2015
$, millions

Exporting Country/ Importing Country	AFG	BGD	BTN	IND	MDV	NPL	PAK	LKA	Total export to South Asia	Total export to World	Export to South Asia/Export to World (%)
AFG	—	—	—	—	—	—	—	—	—	—	—
BGD	0.4	—	—	15.2	4.1	0.5	0.6	2.4	23.3	292.7	8.0
BTN	—	0.0	—	0.0	—	—	0.0	—	0.0	1.2	0.7
IND	24.7	961.0	83.2	—	16.2	584.9	68.3	1,693.2	3,431.4	35,860.9	9.6
MDV	—	—	—	—	—	—	—	—	—	0.3	—
NPL	0.0	—	1.0	1.8	—	—	—	0.4	3.2	11.7	27.0
PAK	42.3	20.1	—	14.5	0.0	0.4	—	1.8	79.2	514.5	15.4
LKA	—	2.9	—	75.1	6.5	1.2	0.7	—	86.4	482.8	17.9
Total Import from South Asia	67.5	984.0	84.3	106.5	26.9	587.1	69.6	1,697.7	3,623.5	37,164.0	9.8
Total Import from World	509.2	8,242.9	173.9	77,634.5	417.9	1,342.1	9,013.8	3,736.0	101,070.3		
Import from South Asia/ Import from World (%)	13.2	11.9	48.5	0.1	6.4	43.7	0.8	45.4	3.6		

Source: Calculations based on data from UN Comtrade (United Nations Commodity Trade Statistics Database), Statistics Division, Department of Economic and Social Affairs, United Nations, New York, http://comtrade.un.org/db/; WITS (World Integrated Trade Solution) (database), World Bank, Washington, DC, http://wits.worldbank.org/WITS/.
Note: The reporting countries in the rows and the trade flows reported refer to exports, except for Bhutan. Mirror data of the other reporting countries are used for Bhutan. Total imports from and total exports to the world refer to the data reported by the respective reporting countries except for Bhutan. Mirror data from the world are used for Bhutan. Capital goods refer to UNCTAD SOP4 under HS2002 provided in WITS (see the text). — = not available; AFG = Afghanistan; BGD = Bangladesh; BTN = Bhutan; IND = India; LKA = Sri Lanka; MDV = Maldives; NPL = Nepal; PAK = Pakistan.

TABLE 1A.10 Intraregional Merchandise Trade, South Asia, 2015
$, billions

Exporting country/ Importing country	AFG	BGD	BTN	IND	MDV	NPL	PAK	LKA	Total export to South Asia	Total export to World	Export to South Asia/Export to World (%)
AFG	—	0.00	—	0.19	—	—	0.23	0.00	0.42	0.57	72.8
BGD	0.00	—	0.00	0.52	0.01	0.00	0.05	0.03	0.61	31.73	1.9
BTN	—	0.04	—	0.20	—	0.00	0.00	—	0.24	0.27	88.8
IND	0.53	5.52	0.38	—	0.17	3.20	1.96	5.50	17.26	264.38	6.5
MDV	—	0.00	—	0.00	—	—	—	0.02	0.02	0.14	14.2
NPL	0.01	0.01	0.00	0.42	0.00	—	0.00	0.00	0.44	0.66	66.2
PAK	1.72	0.70	—	0.31	0.01	0.00	—	0.26	3.00	21.89	13.7
LKA	0.00	0.09	0.00	0.64	0.08	0.00	0.07	—	0.89	10.20	8.7
Total Import from South Asia	2.27	6.36	0.38	2.28	0.26	3.21	2.31	5.80	22.87	329.85	
Total Import from World	7.72	48.06	0.51	390.74	1.90	6.61	43.79	18.97	518.31		
Import from South Asia/ Import from World (%)	29.4	13.2	74.3	0.6	13.6	48.5	5.3	30.6	4.4		

Source: Calculations based on data from UN Comtrade (United Nations Commodity Trade Statistics Database), Statistics Division, Department of Economic and Social Affairs, United Nations, New York, http://comtrade.un.org/db/; WITS (World Integrated Trade Solution) (database), World Bank, Washington, DC, http://wits.worldbank.org/WITS/.
Note: The reporting countries in the rows and the trade flows reported refer to exports, except for Bhutan. Mirror data of the other reporting countries are used for Bhutan. Total imports from and total exports to the world refer to the data reported by the respective reporting countries except for Bhutan. Mirror data from the world are used for Bhutan. — = not available; AFG = Afghanistan; BGD = Bangladesh; BTN = Bhutan; IND = India; LKA = Sri Lanka; MDV = Maldives; NPL = Nepal; PAK = Pakistan.

TABLE 1A.11 Existing and Proposed Crossborder Electricity Trade Arrangements, South Asia

Participants	Crossborder electricity trade
India–Nepal	In fiscal year 2016/17, imports from India through various transmission lines, including Dhalkebar–Mujaffarpur, reached an average of 250 megawatts.
Bhutan–India	India has existing arrangements with Bhutan for importing 1,416 megawatts from the hydroelectric power plants at Tala (1,020 megawatts), Chukha (336 megawatts), and Kurichu (60 megawatts). For future imports from upcoming hydropower plants in Bhutan, such as Punatsangchu-I (1,200 megawatts), Punatsangchu-II (990 megawatts), and Mangdechu (720 megawatts), two crossborder interconnection lines are under implementation: Punatsangschu-I (Bhutan)–Alipurduar (India) and Jigmeling (Bhutan)–Alipurduar (India).
Bangladesh–India	Total imports from India are 660 megawatts through interconnections at Bheramara–Bahrampur (500 megawatts) and Tripura–South Comilla (160 megawatts). In April 2017, it was agreed that Bangladesh would draw an additional 500 megawatts from India through the existing Bheramara–Bahrampur interconnection after a capacity expansion program and that a power transmission line would be constructed from Assam to Bihar across Bangladesh, which will also allow the latter to import 1,000 megawatts of electricity.
India–Sri Lanka	A feasibility study was carried out for two 500-megawatt high-voltage direct current bipole lines between Madurai (India) and New Anuradhapura (Sri Lanka), including submarine cable for the sea portion.
India–Pakistan	Following discussions between the two countries, Pakistan submitted a draft memorandum of understanding to India on importing 1,200 megawatts of electricity with a transmission link from Amritsar to Lahore.
Iran, Islamic Rep.–Pakistan	Pakistan imported 419 gigawatt hours of electricity in 2014 (375 gigawatt hours in the previous year) from the Islamic Republic of Iran.
Afghanistan–Central Asia	Afghanistan imported 77 percent of its total generation from Uzbekistan (1,567 gigawatt hours), Tajikistan (1,359 gigawatt hours), the Islamic Republic of Iran (932 gigawatt hours), and Turkmenistan (599 gigawatt hours) in fiscal year 2015/16.

Sources: Ghalib 2017; MOF 2017; MOP 2017; NEA 2017; Singh et al. 2015.

Notes

1. The links among trade, jobs, and poverty reduction are complex. However, trade openness is key to successful poverty reduction, although it alone is insufficient. Trade contributes positively by opening new opportunities for jobs and lowering the prices for the goods the poor consume. Yet, trade is also associated with greater exposure to external shocks. Harnessing the full potential of trade requires growth-promoting policies, including trade openness, along with policies that allow the poor to participate fully in the new opportunities and institutions that adequately protect people who experience temporary or permanent job losses as a result of trade-related changes in production structures (World Bank and WTO 2015).

2. The survey of 384 stakeholders across the six countries was conducted via face-to-face interviews in 2014.

3. For more detail, see "One South Asia," World Bank, Washington, DC, http://www.worldbank.org/en/programs/south-asia-regional-integration.

4. Paratariffs are extra fees or taxes imposed on imports over and above customs duties.

5. Intra–South Asia exports and imports grew at a compound annual growth rate of, respectively, about 13.7 percent and 11.0 percent per year from 1990 to 2015, doubling their share in total exports (from 3.4 percent to 6.9 percent) and total imports (from 2.0 percent to 4.3 percent) in the region during this period. Furthermore, the intraregional export share grew across all countries in the region, except Bangladesh and Maldives, during the period; it grew in the larger countries, such as India and Pakistan, but even more significantly across small landlocked economies, such as Bhutan and Nepal.

6. In South Asia, a haat is a market, typically one that opens periodically.

7. See RTA-IS (Regional Trade Agreements Information System) (database), World Trade Organization, Geneva (accessed April 26, 2018), http://rtais.wto.org/UI/Public MaintainRTAHome.aspx.

8. Another example is provided by the Mercosur Residence Agreement, which allows foreign workers from the region to reside and work for up to two years in the host state; the residence permit can be extended to a permanent one if the worker can prove that he or she can support themselves and their family through work. This represents a major step in facilitating trade in services that require personal presence for the most effective delivery (Kathuria, Shahid, and Ferrantino 2015).

9. Regional agreements may function as a commitment to uphold democracy and human rights, as in the case of Mercosur, in which democracy is a prerequisite for membership. See Schiff and Winters (2003) for details.

10. The community was established in 1973 to formulate common policy stances and pool the negotiation resources of constituent countries. It has been particularly active in negotiating preferential access to European and North American markets, negotiating for consistent and remunerative commodity prices, obtaining larger flows of concessionary finance, and raising the region's profile in multilateral institutions. See Schiff and Winters (2003) for more detail.

11. Similar motives were behind the creation of ASEAN, that is, to reduce tensions between Indonesia and Malaysia (DeRosa 1995).

12. A recent report of the United Nations Economic and Social Commission for Asia and the Pacific (UNESCAP 2017) uses the gravity model approach and finds that intraregional trade in South Asia was less than one-third of the potential in 2014, that is, 67 percent of the trade potential remains unexploited. Bangladesh exhibits the highest unexploited proportion (93 percent), followed by Maldives (88 percent), Pakistan (86 percent), Afghanistan (83 percent), and Nepal (76 percent). Although there are differences between the study and this report in terms of the structure of the gravity model and the estimation methodology, the results are similar.

13. See "ASEAN Trade in Goods Agreement," Association of Southeast Asian Nations, Jakarta, http://investasean.asean.org/index.php/page/view/asean-free-trade-area-agreements /view/757/newsid/872/asean-trade-in-goods-agreement.html.

14. Trade costs are directly inferred from observable bilateral and intranational (domestic) trade data and can vary depending on the underlying assumptions. This report follows the database guidelines that advise using the database to compare across country pairs or across time and avoid standalone interpretations of the data on single pairs. For the detailed methodology, see ESCAP–World Bank Trade Cost Database, United Nations Economic and Social Commission for Asia and the Pacific, Bangkok; World Bank, Washington, DC, http://www .unescap.org/resources/escap-world-bank-trade-cost-database.

15. The transport cost component can be particularly high for landlocked countries such as Nepal. Despite the physical proximity between Bangladesh and Nepal, transporting a 20-foot or 40-foot container from Chittagong port in Bangladesh to Nepal costs about $500 and $900 more, respectively, compared with transporting it from Chittagong to Santos, Brazil. This is partly because there is limited direct (land) traffic between Bangladesh and Nepal, and cargo has to be transported through Kolkata port in India to Nepal, which increases the cost significantly.

16. At the time of the signing of the India–Sri Lanka Free Trade Agreement, the tariff rate quota arrangements allowed a margin of preference of 50 percent on the applied most-favored-nation tariff rate on imports of tea up to 15 million kilograms per year and on imports of garments up to 8 million pieces per year, 6 million pieces of which had to contain Indian fabric. See CBEC (2000).

17. The ad valorem equivalents of NTMs are estimated in product-specific, quantity-based gravity regressions involving pooling across the bilateral trade in the products between importing and exporting countries. Tariffs and NTMs are included in the regressions; the quantity of imports is the dependent variable. Bilateral variations in ad valorem equivalents are obtained by interacting tariffs and NTMs with variables that are specific to the importing and exporting countries. The endogeneity of tariffs and NTMs is corrected with instruments; the large presence of zeros in the bilateral trade data is addressed with zero-inflated count regressions.

18. 2016 data from WDI (World Development Indicators) (database), World Bank, Washington, DC, http://data.worldbank.org/products/wdi.

19. See Rocha (2017); "ICP Attari," Land Ports Authority of India, New Delhi, http://www.lpai.gov.in/content/innerpage/icp-attari.php.

20. "Q. 81 New Visa Regime with Pakistan," Media Centre, Ministry of External Affairs, New Delhi, November 29, 2012, http://www.mea.gov.in/bilateral-documents.htm?dtl/20856/Q81+New+visa+regime+with+Pakistan.

21. See also "India to Expedite Visa Process for Pakistani Citizens," *Hindu*, May 27, 2016, http://www.thehindu.com/news/national/india-to-expedite-visa-process-for-pakistani-citizens/article8651991.ece; "Pakistani Passport Holders," High Commission of India, Islamabad (accessed October 10, 2017), https://www.india.org.pk/pages.php?id=114.

22. See "Pakistani Passport Holders," High Commission of India, Islamabad (accessed October 10, 2017), https://www.india.org.pk/pages.php?id=114; "Visa Policy (for Indian Nationals)," Directorate General of Immigration and Passports, Ministry of Interior, Islamabad (accessed October 10, 2017), http://www.dgip.gov.pk/Files/VisaforIndian.aspx.

23. The cities are Faisalabad, Gujranwala, Hyderabad, Islamabad, Karachi, Lahore, Mirpur Khas, Multan, Peshawar, Quetta, Sialkot, and Sukkur. For details, see "TCS Visatronics/Gerry's International," High Commission of India, Islamabad (accessed October 10, 2017), https://www.india.org.pk/pages.php?id=134.

24. The e-visa facility allows visa applications to be submitted online. Visa collection occurs upon arrival at 24 designated airports and three designated seaports in India. See "e-Visa," National Informatics Center and Ministry of Home Affairs, New Delhi (accessed October 10, 2017), https://indianvisaonline.gov.in/evisa/tvoa.html.

25. See "Visa on Arrival for Pak Nationals," Bureau of Immigration, Ministry of Home Affairs, New Delhi (accessed October 10, 2017), http://boi.gov.in/content/visa-arrival-pak-nationals.

26. UN Comtrade (United Nations Commodity Trade Statistics Database), Statistics Division, Department of Economic and Social Affairs, United Nations, New York, http://comtrade .un.org/db/; WITS (World Integrated Trade Solution) (database), World Bank, Washington, DC, http://wits.worldbank.org/WITS/.

27. Kathuria and Shahid (2016) summarize several other estimates, showing the gap at 10–27 times the current trade.

28. The measure used is the relative frequency of conflict, that is, the frequency of conflictual events, minus the frequency of cooperative events.

29. Although the bilateral trade deficit is not a useful economic concept, such deficits have become a politically sensitive issue in South Asia as in the rest of the world.

30. The nominees are senior economic officials with expertise in trade matters.

31. Examples of trust-building efforts include India's acceptance of asymmetrical market access, as witnessed in the opening of its market to all least developed countries in the region as part of SAFTA (chapter 2) and to Sri Lanka as part of the India–Sri Lanka Free Trade Agreement. Pakistan has also provided greater concessions to Sri Lanka than vice versa, as part of the Pakistan–Sri Lanka Free Trade Agreement (de Mel 2008). India also provides medical treatment for citizens of South Asian countries; Afghans are significant users of Pakistani medical facilities.

32. See Kathuria and Yatawara (2016) for a discussion of trade and investment links.

33. See Kathuria and Malouche (2016) for a discussion in the context of Bangladesh.

34. According to Rocha (2017), although the Afghanistan–Pakistan Transit Trade Agreement allows the use of various ports for transit trade along specific routes, it faces some barriers to full implementation, such as expensive bank guarantees and border delays. The agreement also permits Afghan trucks to transport exports up to the Indian border at Wagah–Attari, but does not allow them to return through Pakistan carrying Indian goods. Moreover, it does not cover road transport vehicles from third countries.

35. 2015 data, WITS (World Integrated Trade Solution) (database), World Bank, Washington, DC, http://wits.worldbank.org/WITS/.

36. 2015 data, WITS (World Integrated Trade Solution) (database), World Bank, Washington, DC, http://wits.worldbank.org/WITS/.

37. Data are taken from Bangladesh Bank Open Data Initiative (database), Bangladesh Bank, Dhaka, Bangladesh, https://www.bb.org.bd/econdata/index.php. Among South Asian countries, the data relate to only India, Pakistan, and Sri Lanka, which account for 99.9 percent of South Asian FDI stock in Bangladesh (see annex 1A, table 1A.2).

38. Bangladesh obtains liberal market access under the Everything But Arms Initiative from the European Union. Pakistan has access to the European Union Generalized Scheme of Preferences (GSP Plus), and Sri Lanka gained access to GSP Plus in May 2017.

39. Doing Business (database), International Finance Corporation and World Bank, Washington, DC, http://www.doingbusiness.org/data.

40. The published tariff for storage projects in Nepal is NPR 12 per kilowatt hour, while the winter tariff for run-of-river is at NPR 8.4 per kilowatt hour. The summer tariff is NPR 4.8 per kilowatt hour.

41. "Nationality-Wise Foreign Tourist Arrivals in India, 2014–2016," Bureau of Immigration, Ministry of Home Affairs, New Delhi, http://tourism.gov.in/sites/default/files/Other /Countrywise%20Fig%202014-16.xlsx.

42. This may occur through the establishment of routes that connect economic centers within and across countries, providing fast-track connectivity services. A forthcoming report will also discuss the issue of trade and border poverty in South Asia.

43. See ADB et al. (2018) for an in-depth discussion on transport and economic corridors.

44. "Vision 2025: A Country Enriched," press material, Prime Minister's Office, Colombo, Sri Lanka, http://www.pmoffice.gov.lk/download/press/D00000000061_EN.pdf.

References

ADB (Asian Development Bank), DFID (U.K. Department for International Development), JICA (Japan International Cooperation Agency), and World Bank. 2018. *The WEB of Transport Corridors in South Asia*. Washington, DC: World Bank.

ADB (Asian Development Bank) and UNCTAD (United Nations Conference on Trade and Development). 2008. *Quantification of Benefits from Economic Cooperation in South Asia*. New Delhi: Macmillan India.

Ahmed, Sadiq, and Ejaz Ghani. 2010. "Making Regional Cooperation Work for South Asia's Poor." In *Promoting Economic Cooperation in South Asia: Beyond SAFTA*, edited by Sadiq Ahmed, Saman Kelegama, and Ejaz Ghani, 30–68. Washington, DC: World Bank; New Delhi: Sage Publications India.

Arvis, Jean-François, Yann Duval, Ben Shepherd, and Chorthip Utoktham. 2013. "Trade Costs in the Developing World: 1995–2010." Policy Research Working Paper 6309, World Bank, Washington, DC.

ASEAN (Association of Southeast Asian Nations) and World Bank. 2013. *ASEAN Integration Monitoring Report*. Report 83914. Washington, DC: World Bank; Jakarta: ASEAN.

Bhalla, Abhishek. 2016. "Why India Rejected over 17,000 Visa Applications from Pakistan." *Mail Today*, June 17. http://indiatoday.intoday.in/story/india-pakistan-visa-applocations-rejected/1/694047.html.

Bown, Chad P., Daniel Lederman, Samuel Pienknagura, and Raymond Robertson. 2017. *Better Neighbors: Toward a Renewal of Economic Integration in Latin America*. World Bank Latin American and Caribbean Studies Series. Washington, DC: World Bank.

CBEC (India, Central Board of Excise and Customs). 2000. "Notification No. 26/2000: Customs." (March 1), CBEC, Department of Revenue, Ministry of Finance, New Delhi. http://www.cbec.gov.in/htdocs-cbec/customs/cs-act/notifications/notfns-2000/cs-tarr2000/cs26-2k.

———. 2007. "Notification No. 75/2007: Customs." CBEC, Department of Revenue, Ministry of Finance, New Delhi. http://www.cbec.gov.in/htdocs-cbec/customs/cs-act/notifications/notfns-2007/cs-tarr2007/cs75-2k7.

———. 2008. "Notification 52/2008: Customs." CBEC, Department of Revenue, Ministry of Finance, New Delhi. http://www.cbec.gov.in/htdocs-cbec/customs/cs-act/notifications/notfns-2008/cs-tarr2008/cs52-2k8.

Chanda, Rupa. 2014. 'Services Trade Liberalization in South Asia." Background paper, Asian Development Bank and South Asian Association for Regional Cooperation Secretariat, Manila.

de Mel, Deshal. 2008. "India–Sri Lanka, Pakistan–Sri Lanka Bilateral Free Trade Agreements." Institute of Policy Studies of Sri Lanka, Colombo, Sri Lanka.

DeRosa, Dean A. 1995. "Regional Trading Arrangements among Developing Countries: The ASEAN Example." Research Report 103, International Food Policy Research Institute, Washington, DC.

DGCI&S (Directorate General of Commercial Intelligence and Statistics). 2017. "Export of Health Services: A Primary Survey in India." Ministry of Commerce and Industry, New Delhi.

Fally, Thibault. 2015. "Structural Gravity and Fixed Effects." *Journal of International Economics* 97 (1): 76–85.

Freund, Caroline, and Emanuel Ornelas. 2010. "Regional Trade Agreements." *Annual Review of Economics: Annual Reviews* 2 (1): 139–66.

Ghalib, Amanullah. 2017. "Afghanistan Energy Sector Development Plans." Presentation at the Ministry of Economy, Ankara, Turkey, January 2. https://www.ekonomi.gov.tr/portal/content /conn/UCM/uuid/dDocName:EK-236901;jsessionid=K-M8GZmdX0-bSKpv0O7NR8 _CD-VSxKcz_UZZqpyDWSK6Oq9YaU-M!3487174.

Head, Keith, Thierry Mayer, and John Ries. 2010. "The Erosion of Colonial Trade Linkages after Independence." *Journal of International Economics* 81 (1): 1–14.

Kathuria, Sanjay, and Mariem Mezghenni Malouche. 2016. *Toward New Sources of Competitiveness in Bangladesh: Key Insights of the Diagnostic Trade Integration Study.* Directions in Development: Trade Series. Washington, DC: World Bank.

Kathuria, Sanjay, and Sohaib Shahid. 2015. "Opening Up Markets to Neighbors: Gains for Smaller Countries in South Asia." SARConnect 1 (January), World Bank, Washington, DC.

———. 2016. "Boosting Trade and Prosperity in South Asia." In *Regional Integration in South Asia: Essays in Honour of Dr. M. Rahmattulah,* edited by Prabir De and Mustafizur Rahman, 7–34. New Delhi: KW Publishers Pvt. Ltd.

Kathuria, Sanjay, Sohaib Shahid, and Michael Joseph Ferrantino. 2015. "How Has Regional Integration Taken Place in Other Regions: Lessons for South Asia." SARConnect 2 (April), World Bank, Washington, DC.

Kathuria, Sanjay, and Ravindra Yatawara. 2016. "Trade-Investment Links Get Increasingly Intricate." *Trade Insight* 12 (2): 10–20, South Asia Watch on Trade, Economics, and Environment, Kathmandu, Nepal.

Kee, Hiau Looi, and Alessandro Nicita. 2017. "Trade Fraud, Trade Elasticities and Non-Tariff Measures." Paper presented at the First Mid-Atlantic International Trade Workshop, University of Virginia, Charlottesville, VA, December 8–9.

———. 2017. "Short-Term Impact of Brexit on the United Kingdom's Export of Goods." Policy Research Working Paper 8195, World Bank, Washington, DC.

Kelegama, Saman. 2014. "Why Is Indian FDI Shying away from South Asia?" East Asia Forum, Crawford School of Public Policy, Australian National University, Canberra. http://www.east asiaforum.org/2014/09/12/why-is-indian-fdi-shying-away-from-south-asia.

Khan, Shaheen Rafi, Moeed Yusuf, Faisal Haq Shaheen, and Azka Tanveer. 2009. "Regional Trade Agreements in South Asia: Trade and Conflict Linkages." In *Integration and Conflict Resolution,* edited by Shaheen Rafi Khan, 69–101. Ottawa, Canada: International Development Research Center.

Kritzinger-van Niekerk, Lolette. 2005. "Regional Integration: Concepts, Advantages, Disadvantages and Lessons of Experience." World Bank, Washington, DC. http://sitere -sources.worldbank.org/EXTAFRREGINICOO/Resources/Kritzinger.pdf.

Laskar, Rezaul H. 2015. "The Mad Mad World of Indian and Pakistani Visa Rules." *Hindustan Times*, May 11. http://www.hindustantimes.com/india/the-mad-mad-world-of-indian-and-pakistani-visa-rules/story-YtkZGlA7Nk191gFmf8jHTJ.html.

Lederman, Daniel, Gladys Lopez-Acevedo, and Yevgeniya Savchenko. 2014. "Trade Adjustment Assistance Programs." World Bank, Washington, DC.

Lopez-Acevedo, Gladys, Denis Medvedev, and Vincent Palmade, eds. 2017. *South Asia's Turn: Policies to Boost Competitiveness and Create the Next Export Powerhouse.* South Asia Development Matters Series. Washington, DC: World Bank. https://openknowledge.world bank.org/bitstream/handle/10986/25094/9781464809736.pdf.

MDONER (Ministry of Development of North Eastern Region) and NEC (North Eastern Council). 2008. *North Eastern Region Vision 2020*, vol. 1. New Delhi: MDONER.

Ministry of Commerce and Industry, India, and Ministry of Commerce, Bangladesh. 2016. "10th Meeting of India-Bangladesh Joint Working Group on Trade: Agreed Minutes." Department of Commerce, New Delhi, June 8–9. http://commerce.gov.in/writereaddata/UploadedFile /MOC_636014410789638795_10th_meeting_JWG_between_India_Bangladesh_8th_9th _June_2016.pdf.

Ministry of Culture, Tourism, and Civil Aviation. 2014. *Nepal Tourism Statistics 2013.* Statistical Section, Planning and Evaluation Division, Ministry of Culture, Tourism, and Civil Aviation, Kathmandu. http://www.tourismdepartment.gov.np/tourism-statistics.

MOF (Ministry of Finance, Bangladesh). 2017. *Bangladesh Economic Review 2017.* Dhaka, Bangladesh: Ministry of Finance.

MOP (Ministry of Power, India). 2017. *Annual Report 2016–17.* New Delhi: Ministry of Power. http://powermin.nic.in/sites/default/files/uploads/MOP_Annual_Report_2016-17.pdf.

Narain, Ashish, and Gonzalo Varela. 2017. "Trade Policy Reforms for the Twenty First Century: The Case of Nepal." World Bank, Washington, DC.

Nath, Amala. 2007. "The SAFTA Dispute Settlement Mechanism: An Attempt to Resolve or Merely Perpetuate Conflict in the South Asian Region." *American University International Law Review* 22 (2): 333–59.

NEA (Nepal Electricity Authority). 2017. *A Year in Review 2017.* Kathmandu, Nepal: Nepal Electricity Authority. http://www.nea.org.np/admin/assets/uploads/supportive_docs/87757284.pdf.

PBC (Pakistan Business Council). 2013. *Preliminary Study on Pakistan and China Trade Partnership Post FTA.* Trade Study Series. Karachi: PBC. http://www.pbc.org.pk/wp-content /uploads/21-Oct_Pakistan_China_Trade_Study_2013.pdf.

Polachek, Solomon William. 1992. "Conflict and Trade: An Economics Approach to Political Interactions." In *Economics of Arms Reduction and the Peace Process: Contributions from Peace Economics and Peace Science*, edited by Walter Isard and Charles H. Anderton, 89–120. Amsterdam: North-Holland.

———. 1997. "Why Democracies Cooperate More and Fight Less: The Relationship between International Trade and Cooperation." *Review of International Economics* 5 (3): 295–309. http://harvey.binghamton.edu/~polachek/reprints/polachek%20Review%20of%20interna tional%20economics.pdf.

Press Trust of India. 2017. "No Medical Visas for Pakistanis, Islamabad Summons Indian Envoy: Media Reports." *Hindustan Times*, May 6. http://www.hindustantimes.com/india-news /no-medical-visa-for-pakistanis-islamabad-summons-indian-envoy-media-reports/story -nLuwky40Q4X8nnF6yaK3eO.html.

Raihan, Selim. 2012. "SAFTA and the South Asian Countries: Quantitative Assessments of Potential Implications." South Asian Network on Economic Modeling, University of Dhaka, Dhaka, Bangladesh.

Raihan, Selim, Mostafa Abid Khan, and Shaquib Quoreshi. 2014. "NTMs in South Asia: Assessment and Analysis." South Asian Association for Regional Cooperation–Trade Promotion Network, Kathmandu, Nepal.

Rocha, Nadia. 2017. "Trade as a Vehicle for Growth in Afghanistan: Challenges and Opportunities." World Bank, Washington, DC.

Santos Silva, João M. C., and Silvana Tenreyro. 2006. "The Log of Gravity." *Review of Economics and Statistics* 88 (4): 641–58.

Schiff, M., and L. Alan Winters. 2003. *Regional Integration and Development*. Washington, DC: World Bank; New York: Oxford University Press.

Scotiabank. 2014. "NAFTA: What's Next?" Special Report, Scotiabank, Toronto.

Sherov-Ignatiev, Vladimir G., and Sergei F. Sutyrin. 2011. "Peculiarities and Rationale of Asymmetric Regional Trade Agreements." Discussion forum: World Trade Report 2011 (August 2), World Trade Organization, Geneva. https://www.wto.org/english/res_e /publications_e/wtr11_forum_e.htm.

Singh, Anoop, Tooraj Jamasb, Rabindra Nepal, and Michael Toman. 2015. "Cross-Border Electricity Cooperation in South Asia." Policy Research Working Paper 7328, World Bank, Washington, DC.

Sri Lanka Tourism Development Authority. 2016. "Annual Statistical Report 2016." Research and International Relations Division, Sri Lanka Tourism Development Authority, Colombo, Sri Lanka. http://www.sltda.lk/sites/default/files/annual-statical-report-2016.pdf.

Taneja, Nisha. 2014. "Informal Trade in South Asia." Background paper, Asian Development Bank, Manila.

Taneja, Nisha, and Samridhi Bimal. 2016. "India's Informal Trade with Pakistan." ICRIER Working Paper 327 (July), Indian Council for Research on International Economic Relations, New Delhi. http://www.icrier.org/pdf/Working_Paper_327.pdf.

Taneja, Nisha, Isha Dayal, and Samridhi Bimal. 2016. "Facilitating India-Pakistan Trade through the Land Route." ICRIER Working Paper 318 (May), Indian Council for Research on International Economic Relations, New Delhi. http://icrier.org/pdf/Working_Paper_318.pdf.

Taneja, Nisha, Mishita Mehra, Prithvijit Mukherjee, Samridhi Bimal, and Isha Dayal. 2013. "Normalizing India Pakistan Trade." ICRIER Working Paper 267 (September), Indian Council for Research on International Economic Relations, New Delhi.

TCB (Tourism Council of Bhutan). 2016. "Annual Report: Bhutan Tourism Monitor 2016." Tourism Council of Bhutan, Thimphu, Bhutan. http://tcb.img.ebizity.bt/attachments /tcb_041217_bhutan-tourism-monitor-2016.pdf.

Tunea, Claudiu. 2006. "Patterns of FDI in Mexico after NAFTA: The Role of Export Markets and Geographical Determinants." Paper presented at the Canadian Economic Association Annual Conference 2006, Concordia University, Montreal, May 26–28.

UNESCAP (United Nations Economic and Social Commission for Asia and the Pacific). 2017. "Unlocking the Potential of Regional Economic Cooperation and Integration in South Asia: Potential, Challenges, and the Way Forward." UNESCAP, Bangkok.

WEF (World Economic Forum). 2013. "Enabling Trade: Valuing Growth Opportunities." WEF, Geneva.

Wei, Shang-Jin. 1996. "Intra-National versus International Trade: How Stubborn Are Nations in Globalization?" NBER Working Paper 5531, National Bureau of Economic Research, Cambridge, MA.

World Bank. 2017. *Global Economic Prospects, June 2017: A Fragile Recovery.* Washington, DC: World Bank.

———. 2018. *Global Economic Prospects, January 2018: Broad-Based Upturn, but for How Long?* Washington, DC: World Bank.

World Bank and WTO (World Trade Organization). 2015. "The Role of Trade in Ending Poverty." WTO, Geneva.

Yotov, Yoto V., Roberta Piermartini, José-Antonio Monteiro, and Mario Larch. 2016. *An Advanced Guide to Trade Policy Analysis: The Structural Gravity Model.* Geneva: World Trade Organization. https://www.wto.org/english/res_e/booksp_e/advancedwtounctad2016_e.pdf.

CHAPTER 2

Border Tax Distortions in South Asia: The Impact on Regional Integration

SANJAY KATHURIA AND GUILLERMO ARENAS

Introduction

Regional trade agreements (RTAs) have proliferated over the past decades and now account for most of the world's trade. According to the World Trade Organization, as of April 26, 2018, some 287 RTAs were in force.[1] The largest RTAs are the European Union, the North American Free Trade Agreement, and the Association of Southeast Asian Nations (ASEAN). Together, these three RTAs represented 56 percent of world exports (US$8.7 trillion) and 60 percent of world imports (US$9.5 trillion) in 2016 (WTO 2017).

The most well-known RTAs have been associated with significant trade among their members. For example, intraregional trade in the European Union, the North American Free Trade Agreement, and ASEAN stood at 63 percent, 50 percent, and 24 percent, respectively, of their total trade in 2015 (WTO 2017). However, intraregional trade remains low in regions covered by other RTAs, such as Mercosur (14 percent) and the agreement that led to the South Asian Free Trade Area (SAFTA) (about 5 percent) in 2015.[2]

This chapter starts from the premise that South Asian countries undertrade with each other. Not only is intraregional trade in South Asia low compared with more successful RTAs, but it is well below its potential. There are many reasons for this (explored in chapter 1), including the high costs of trading, the greater trade restrictiveness in intraregional trade, additional barriers to trade between India and Pakistan, and constraints on trade in services and intraregional foreign direct investment (FDI).

SAFTA represents an attempt by the leadership of South Asia to capitalize on the advantages of RTAs. However, it is largely perceived as unsuccessful a decade after it came into force in 2006. The nomenclature "free trade agreement" reflects an aspiration among member countries to conduct duty-free, quota-free trade among themselves. The reality in South Asia is far from this aspiration. Thus, for example, 34.7 percent of intraregional trade was restricted under sensitive lists in 2015.[3]

Accordingly, this chapter discusses a key reason for SAFTA's underperformance: the role of border taxes (import duties), especially the little-explored paratariffs, which are additional taxes or fees imposed on goods over and above customs tariffs. The next section explores the complexity of tariff structures in South Asian countries, including details on the structure of paratariffs—tariffs in all but name—in Bangladesh, Pakistan, and Sri Lanka, as well as their negative impacts on the levels of overall protection and intersectoral tariff dispersion. The subsequent section analyzes the constraints that tariffs and paratariffs impose on the effective functioning of SAFTA, including the widespread exclusions from tariff preferences in the form of sensitive lists and the noninclusion of paratariffs in the tariff concessions given to partners in free trade agreements. The final section follows up the analysis and suggests possible directions of reform.

Trade Protection in South Asia

After a long period of experimentation with import-substituting industrialization, most countries in South Asia started to dismantle their highly protective tariffs in the 1980s; Sri Lanka began in 1977. Figure 2.1 shows the sharp decline in tariffs that took place in the region between 1987 and 2016; most of the tariff liberalization took place around 2007. Tariffs in the largest economies in the region averaged 98.8 percent (India), 81.8 percent (Bangladesh), and 68.9 percent (Pakistan) in 1987 (Sri Lanka was an exception), but had been reduced to close to 10 percent by 2016. However, trade liberalization in South Asia has not been smooth. Several countries have experienced reform reversals in the past two decades: Bangladesh in the late 1990s, and Pakistan and Sri Lanka after the global financial crisis in the late 2000s. Tariff reform in India was not derailed even during the global financial crisis; the country has managed to preserve most of its low tariffs (Pursell 2011). However, India's 2018 budget has increased tariffs on a range of products, such as auto parts, footwear, mobile phones, and so on.[4]

Despite the reforms, tariffs in South Asia are still high compared with those in other regions. The simple average tariff in South Asia is 13.6 percent, which is more than double the world average (6.3 percent) and the highest among major regions in the world, as follows: North America, 2.7 percent; Europe and Central Asia, 4.3 percent;

FIGURE 2.1 Simple Average Tariffs, South Asia, 1987–2016

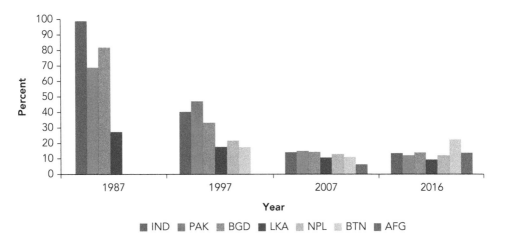

Source: Calculations based on data in Pursell 2011; WTO, ITC, and UNCTAD 2017.
Note: AFG = Afghanistan; BGD =Bangladesh; BTN = Bhutan; IND = India; NPL = Nepal; PAK=Pakistan; LKA = Sri Lanka.

East Asia and Pacific, 7.3 percent; Latin America and the Caribbean, 7.4 percent; and Sub-Saharan Africa, 11.4 percent.[5]

COMPLEXITY OF IMPORT TAXES IN SOUTH ASIA

A major complication in measuring trade protection in South Asia is that several countries make extensive use of additional taxes on imports (referred to here as paratariffs), apart from customs duties, and it is difficult to measure the associated impacts. All such taxes that are not trade neutral, that is, taxes levied on imports, but not on domestic production, can be classified as paratariffs, that is, customs duties in all but name. Among the major economies in South Asia, paratariffs are commonly used in Bangladesh, Pakistan, and Sri Lanka. They are not used in Nepal, and they are believed to be small or nonexistent in India (Pursell 2011). No data on paratariffs are available for Afghanistan, Bhutan, or Maldives.

Paratariffs significantly increase overall import duties, as well as the complexity of the tariff regime. Hence, any analysis of import duties would be incomplete and even misleading without including both tariffs and paratariffs. Although imports in other regions are usually charged customs duties and two additional taxes, the value added tax (VAT) or sales tax and the excise tax, countries in South Asia charge between four and six additional taxes, and they also have complex structures for calculating customs duties and other import taxes.

The main taxes levied on imports in selected South Asian countries are described in the following subsections. No data on import taxation in Afghanistan, Bhutan, or Maldives were collected for this analysis.

Bangladesh

Bangladesh imposes six taxes on imports.[6] In addition to customs duties, regulatory duties were introduced in fiscal year 2000/01 and are levied only on imports, mostly at 3 percent of the import value of products on which the customs duty is 25 percent. Regulatory duties are an import-specific tax levied on an annual basis, that is, a customs duty by a different name. On paper, supplementary duties and VAT are trade-neutral taxes applied on imports and domestic production. However, exemptions for some domestic products are granted through statutory regulatory orders. For example, domestic textile production is largely exempted from VAT (aside from a 2.5 percent fee); imported textiles pay the full rate of 15 percent. This nonuniform application of taxes, which increases the protection rate associated with some products, turns the VAT into a paratariff. The advance income tax is charged on the value of imports, with a corresponding adjustment when the taxpayer settles his or her income tax. The advance trade VAT applies only to commercial imports, that is, commodities imported for retail sale, and is charged on the import value, inclusive of VAT.

Pakistan

Pakistan charges six taxes on imports. In addition to customs duties, two other taxes—regulatory and additional customs duties—are charged exclusively on imports of selected products. Regulatory duties were set up originally by statutory regulatory order 482(I)2009 and covered fewer than 100 tariff lines. However, they have been expanded significantly since then and now cover 1,314 tariff lines in several sectors, including agricultural products, dairy, ceramic or tile products, and automobiles. Additional duties on the auto industry were imposed by statutory regulatory order 693(I)/2006 on 146 tariff lines that are basically components and subcomponents for automakers and assemblers; rates ranged from 15 percent to 35 percent. In November 2015, statutory regulatory order 1178(I)/2015 levied additional general duties at a rate of 1 percent for most products in the tariff schedule, presumably to raise needed fiscal revenues. Most recently, in October 2017, the Federal Board of Revenue notified significant new (137 tariff lines) or enhanced (216 tariff lines) regulatory duties, ranging from 10 percent to 30 percent; the stated purpose was to curb the imports of nonessential consumer goods.[7] Apart from these duties, a withholding tax is charged on imports only and serves as an advance income tax to be settled when the taxpayer submits his or her income tax. Sales taxes and excise duties are levied on imports and domestic production, although some domestic products are exempted from the former.

Sri Lanka

Importers in Sri Lanka face seven different taxes, some with a wide variety of rates. Under the ports and airports development levy (PAL) established in 2011, imports were charged a levy of 5 percent of their cost, insurance, and freight value. Since January 2016, the PAL rate has been increased to 7.5 percent, and some products face a reduced rate of 2.5 percent (mainly electronics). The Export Development Board Levy (cess) was introduced in 2004 and, through subsequent amendments that expanded the product scope, currently applies to 1,937 tariff lines with more than 100 rates (ad valorem, specific, and mixed) on top of customs duties. More recently, in the 2018 budget, the government removed the PAL on 970 tariff lines and the cess on 275 tariff lines (a few were revised downward).

Other import duties include the nation building tax, a VAT, a special commodity levy, and the excise duty. The building tax, VAT, and excise tax apply to imported and domestic goods; the special commodity levy combines the customs duties and paratariffs into one encompassing rate (which, however, is not equivalent to the sum of the individual tax rates) and applies largely to selected agricultural products.[8] Customs duties, the cess, and the PAL are charged only on imported goods.

Nepal

Nepal levies five taxes on imports: customs duties, a VAT, an excise tax, an agricultural reform fee, and a road construction fee. The VAT is charged at 13 percent on most imported products; only 677 tariff lines (12.4 percent of the total) are exempted. The excise tax is levied on about 350 tariff lines (6.6 percent of the total) at rates that range from NPR 3.5 a liter for fruit juices to NPR 1,868 per 1,000 for cigarettes above 85 mm, with filter. The agricultural reform fee (5 percent) is charged in lieu of customs duties for about 300 agricultural products imported from India. The road construction fee is charged on diesel and petroleum imports at NPR 2 a liter and NPR 4 a liter, respectively.

India

Before the introduction of the goods and services tax (GST) in July 2017, the customs duty had the following components. The basic customs duty was the basic or standard component of the customs duty under the Customs Act 1962. An additional customs duty—known as the countervailing duty—was equivalent to and charged in lieu of the excise duty applicable on similar goods manufactured or produced in India. The countervailing duty was typically applied at a rate of 12.5 percent on the sum of the landed value of the goods and the applicable basic customs duty. The education cess (2 percent) and the secondary and higher education cess (1 percent) were also levied on the aggregate of the customs duties paid (inclusive of the countervailing duty). A special countervailing duty was charged at 4 percent to compensate for state taxes, VAT, and local taxes, and a national calamity contingent duty was imposed on certain products, such as utility vehicles, mobile phones, and cars. After the introduction of the GST, the taxes levied on imports included the basic customs duty, an integrated GST, and a GST compensation cess on certain luxury and demerit goods.

PERVASIVENESS AND INTRICACY OF PARATARIFFS

Based on the definition of paratariffs, that is, tariffs that are levied only on imports and are therefore not trade neutral, several paratariffs have been identified in Bangladesh, Pakistan, and Sri Lanka. No evidence of significant use of paratariffs is found in India or Nepal. In the case of Nepal, the VAT and excise taxes apply to imports as well as domestic production; the road construction fee is an excise tax on fuel products by another name, applied to only two tariff lines. The agricultural reform fee is levied on imports of primary products, but only in cases where such imports are exempt from customs duties: it is applied to imports of some agricultural products from India, which are subject to zero tariffs, per the (Revised) Treaty of Trade, 2009, between India and Nepal. Thus, although the agricultural reform fee may look like a paratariff, in practice it is different from paratariffs in the rest of the region, where they are levied in addition to most-favored-nation duties. In India, there were one or two taxes that were in a gray zone; whichever way they are interpreted, their impact has been small.[9] The GST introduced in July 2017 has replaced the countervailing duties with an integrated GST. However, a few products, such as aerated water, tobacco products, and motor vehicles, would also attract the GST compensation cess levy over and above the integrated GST, though this cess is also to be levied on domestic goods and, hence, is not a paratariff. Most recently, in the 2018/19 budget, the education cess and the secondary and higher education cess were replaced by a social welfare surcharge at the rate of 10 percent of the aggregate customs duties: this may qualify as a paratariff (levied on all imports), but it will provide less than 0.4 percent of total tax revenue.[10]

Three general types of paratariffs emerge from the descriptions and table 2.1. First, there are paratariffs charged only on imports and covering the majority of tariff lines. Examples are the PAL in Sri Lanka and general additional duties in Pakistan. These taxes seem to apply in an almost blanket fashion (or at least did so until exemptions were carved out for some product groups) at relatively low and uniform rates. Second, there are taxes on imports only that are selectively applied to some sectors. Examples are regulatory duties in Bangladesh, the cess in Sri Lanka, and regulatory duties and additional duties (for automobiles) in Pakistan. Finally, there are seemingly trade-neutral taxes that end up being charged only on imports owing to exemptions on the corresponding domestic products. Examples are supplementary duties and the VAT for some products in Bangladesh. The latter type of paratariff is difficult to detect because it requires detailed data on domestic tax exemptions among products, in addition to customs data on tariff lines.[11]

Given their pervasiveness, it is not surprising that paratariffs can significantly increase the nominal protection rate. In fiscal year 2016/17, the simple average tariff in Bangladesh (13.3 percent) almost doubles to 25.6 percent, if paratariffs are taken into account, as a result of the protective effects of supplementary duties (9.2 percent) and the VAT (2 percent).[12] Similarly, the simple average tariff in Sri Lanka in 2016 (10.8 percent) more than doubles (22.4 percent) because of the protection granted by the PAL (5.8 percent) and cess (5.8 percent).[13] This can be shown through a frequency distribution of import duties (table 2.2). In Sri Lanka, for example, only 18.1 percent of

TABLE 2.1 Prevalence of Paratariffs in Bangladesh, Pakistan, and Sri Lanka

| Country, tariff | Tariff lines affected | | Rates, percent of tariff lines |
	Number	Share, %	
Bangladesh			
Regulatory duty	3,030	45.0	3 (99%), 15, 20
Supplementary duty	1,523	22.6	20 (61%), 45 (21%), 30 (5%), 10 (4%), 60 (4%), and six other rates between 100% and 500% (5%)
Value added tax	730	10.8	15 (100%)
Pakistan			
Regulatory duty	1,314	18.5	5 (30%), 10 (30%), 15 (26%), 30 (4%), and nine other rates between 2% and 60% (9.6%)
Additional duty, autos	146	2.1	15, 25, 30, 35
Additional duty, general	7,032	99.3	1 (100%)
Sri Lanka			
Ports and airports development levy	5,827	83.7	7.5 (89%), 2.5 (11%)
Cess	1,937	27.8	Ad valorem: 598 (1–70%); specific: 522 (SL Rs 4/kg to SL Rs 6,000/kg); mixed: 817 (8% or SL Rs 25/kg to 35% or SL Rs 2,000/kg)

Source: In cooperation with the Policy Research Institute of Bangladesh, calculations based on data from the National Board of Revenue (Bangladesh), Sri Lanka Customs, and the Federal Bureau of Revenue (Pakistan).
Note: The total number of tariff lines: Bangladesh = 6,739 (fiscal year 2016/17); Pakistan = 7,086 (fiscal year 2016/17); Sri Lanka = 6,965 (2016); kg = kilogram.

TABLE 2.2 Distribution of Import Duty Rates, with and without Paratariffs, Pakistan and Sri Lanka

Percent

| Country | Effective rate of import duty | | | | | | |
	0	1–9	10–19	20–29	30–39	40–49	50+
Sri Lanka (2016)							
Customs duties (CD)	64.0	3.5	14.3	3.6	13.7	0.2	0.6
CD + paratariffs	9.1	44.6	7.6	12.7	8.4	4.5	13.1
Pakistan (fiscal year 2015/16)							
Customs duties (CD)	0.5	39.3	21.4	33.1	4.3	0	1.3
CD + regulatory duty	0.5	38.9	20.6	29.0	9.6	0	1.4

Source: Calculations based on data from Sri Lanka Customs and Federal Bureau of Revenue, Pakistan.
Note: CD = customs duties.

the tariff lines are subject to customs duty rates of 20 percent or more, but this share rises to 38.7 percent of tariff lines if paratariffs are included. In Pakistan, the main impact is an increase in the number of tariff lines falling within the 30–39 percent bracket, from 4.3 percent to 9.6 percent, and a corresponding decrease in the 20–29 percent tariff bracket, from 33 percent to 29 percent of tariff lines.

Apart from increasing overall protection, paratariffs add significantly to the complexity of the tariff regime in the countries in which they are used extensively. Table 2.3 shows the number of standard customs duty rates applied in Bangladesh (six), Pakistan (eight), and Sri Lanka (three). However, because of the myriad rates imposed by paratariffs on top of customs duties, the number of possible duty rates that can be imposed rises to 49, 32, and 35, respectively. Because these paratariffs are not part of the official tariff schedule, they make the system less transparent and more open to discretionary decision making by customs officials.

Given their pervasiveness, paratariffs in these countries have undermined the process of tariff reform. For example, in Bangladesh, average customs duties declined steadily from the mid-1990s to fiscal year 2011/12. However, average paratariffs had crossed 10 percent by fiscal year 2003/04, leading to high total average protection rates (customs duties, plus paratariffs) of between 28 percent and 29 percent over fiscal year 2001 to fiscal year 2004. Since then, paratariffs have gone up, crossing average customs duties in fiscal year 2012/13, and remained at average levels of 12–15 percent over the past five years (Kathuria and Malouche 2016; World Bank 2012). In Pakistan, a 5 percent regulatory duty was introduced in fiscal year 2014/15 on 282 of the 341 products on which tariffs had been reduced from 30 percent to 25 percent. Because these

TABLE 2.3 Range of Import Duty Rates with and without Paratariffs

Country	Tariff rates, number	Standard customs duty rates, percent of TLs	Standard rates, including paratariffs
Bangladesh	6	0 (4.6%), 1 (10.2%), 5 (15.7%), 10 (23.1%), 15 (1.1%), 25 (44.5%); 47 TLs with specific rates (0.7%)	49 rates, ranging from 0% to 543%
Pakistan	8	0 (0.5%), 3 (37.7%), 11 (14.7%), 16 (7.2%), 20 (33.6%), 30 (0.5%), 35 (3.9%), 55 (0.5%)[a]; 45 TLs with specific rates (0.6%)	32 rates, ranging from 0% to 160%
Sri Lanka	3	0 (56.3%), 15 (20.9%), 30 (19%)[b]; 262 TLs with specific or mixed rates (3.8%)[c]	35 rates, ranging from 0% to 87.5%

Source: In cooperation with the Policy Research Institute of Bangladesh, calculations based on data from the National Board of Revenue (Bangladesh), Sri Lanka Customs, and the Federal Bureau of Revenue (Pakistan).
Note: TLs = tariff lines.
a. 58 TLs with more than six rates (5%–100%), 0.8% of TLs.
b. Three TLs with 75%; one TL with 85%; and five TLs with 125%.
c. 88 different rates.

282 products effectively paid the same tariff of 30 percent, the regulatory duties undermined the goals of the reform. A similar story can be told on Sri Lanka.

SECTORAL VARIATIONS IN PARATARIFFS

The protection granted by paratariffs varies by the nature of the paratariffs and the country, but some patterns have emerged. Blanket paratariffs, such as the PAL in Sri Lanka and the general additional duties in Pakistan, cover most tariff lines and charge relatively uniform, low rates across sectors (7.5 percent and 1.0 percent, respectively). The protection granted by paratariffs that target specific sectors is usually substantial, but the level and coverage of the paratariffs differ by country. For instance, figures 2.2 and 2.3 show the share of tariff lines within a sector covered by the paratariffs (horizontal axis) and the resultant additional protection (vertical axis) for two of the most important paratariffs in the region (the cess in Sri Lanka and the regulatory duty in Pakistan). On aggregate, the cess in Sri Lanka seems to cover a larger share of tariff lines and provide greater protection relative to the regulatory duty in Pakistan. However, the top three sectors with the largest share of tariff lines under paratariffs are the same in both countries (textiles and apparel, footwear, and foodstuffs), albeit with significant differences in the rates of protection in the case of the last two.

FIGURE 2.2 Prevalence and Average Additional Protection Granted by the Cess, Sri Lanka, 2016

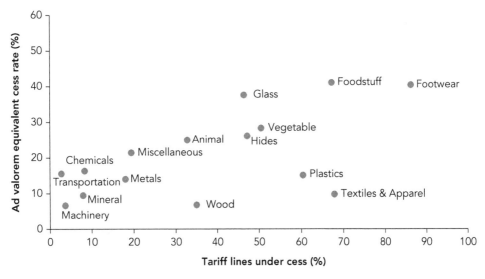

Source: Calculations based on data from Sri Lanka Customs.

FIGURE 2.3 Prevalence and Average Protection Granted by the Regulatory
Duty, Pakistan, Fiscal Year 2016/17

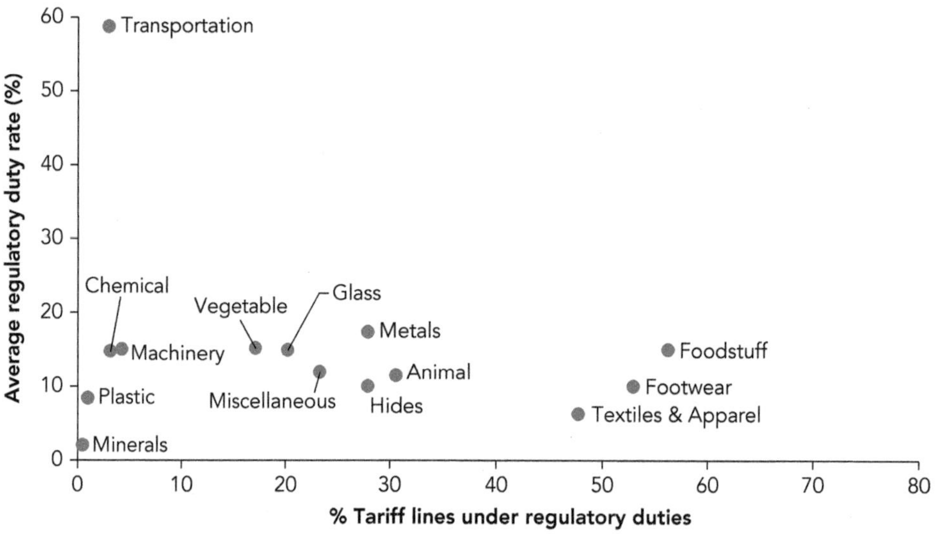

Source: Calculations based on data from the Federal Bureau of Revenue (Pakistan).

The protective effect of paratariffs is not uniform across product groups because paratariffs fall more heavily on final consumer goods. For example, the average protective effect of the cess in Sri Lanka is larger for final consumer goods (11.7 percent) compared with intermediate inputs (3.4 percent), raw materials (2.4 percent), and capital goods (0.3 percent). As a result, paratariffs increase the tariff escalation between, say, consumer and intermediate goods (from 9 percent with customs duties only to 17 percent if paratariffs are included; figure 2.4). In the case of Bangladesh, although paratariffs fall more heavily on final consumer goods, the increase in tariff escalation from intermediate to consumer goods is relatively smaller (from 8.4 percent to 12.0 percent).

This increase in the tariff wedge between intermediate and consumer goods further distorts the incentive regime in individual countries. It increases already high effective protection for consumer goods and encourages more resources to flow into that sector. In effect, this means that, even if the protection on intermediates has increased, the relative profitability of consumer goods production has risen more. This will lead to greater disparity in resource flows to consumer goods at the expense of the production of intermediate goods and prevent a meaningful domestic intermediate goods industry from emerging, which is a concern that has often been expressed in the case of Bangladesh (Kathuria and Malouche 2016).

FIGURE 2.4 The Impact of Paratariffs on Product Categories

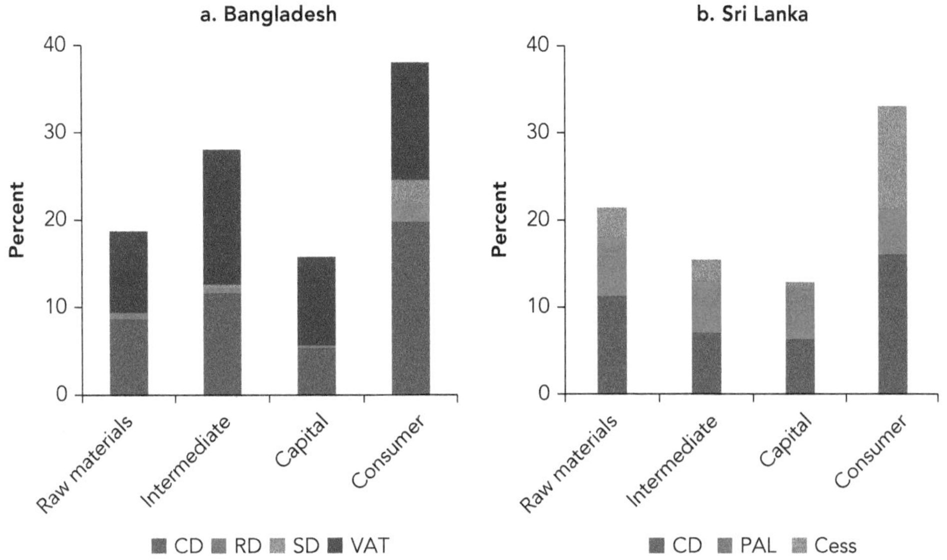

Source: In cooperation with the Policy Research Institute of Bangladesh, calculated based on data from the National Board of Revenue (Bangladesh) and Sri Lanka Customs.
Note: CD = customs duty; PAL = ports and airports development levy; RD = regulatory duty; SD = supplementary duty; VAT = value added tax.

Tariff-Related Constraints on SAFTA's Effectiveness

This section explores key reasons why SAFTA has not worked to its potential. One, there are too many exceptions to the principle of duty-free trade in SAFTA. Two, paratariffs are not a part of the phaseout program under free trade agreements, which reduces the preference margins for SAFTA partners.

SENSITIVE LISTS

A major goal of SAFTA has been to reduce the tariffs on intraregional trade among the eight South Asian Association for Regional Cooperation (SAARC) members.[14] Under SAFTA, the non–least developed country members (India, Pakistan, and Sri Lanka) were given less time to reduce tariffs compared with the least developed countries (Afghanistan, Bangladesh, Bhutan, Maldives, and Nepal). It was also agreed that India and Pakistan would reduce tariffs to 0–5 percent on all items other than those on their sensitive lists by 2012; Sri Lanka by 2013; and Bangladesh, Bhutan, Maldives, and Nepal by 2016. A two-phase approach was planned to accomplish these goals.

However, the exceptions to the liberalization program were widespread and have become entrenched. Each country is permitted to maintain a sensitive list that is exempted from the tariff liberalization program. Initially, the sensitive lists covered roughly 20 percent of the tariff lines, which meant that a substantial share of imports were not bound by tariff reductions. It has been argued that member countries created long lists of sensitive products in an effort to shield specific economic sectors from competition. In 2015, nine years after SAFTA had come into force in 2006, about 34.7 percent of intra-SAARC imports were still restricted under the sensitive lists (table 2.4).

Table 2.4 shows the current status of the sensitive lists, including updated estimates of the shares of imports and exports that were subject to sensitive lists in 2015. The estimated value of the imports from the SAARC region that is protected under SAFTA is high. The largest importers from the region, Bangladesh and Sri Lanka, also show the highest shares of import items on sensitive lists. For instance, Bangladesh has protected 45.6 percent of its imports from the SAARC region through its sensitive list; but only 2.9 percent of its exports to the region are affected by the sensitive lists of other countries. Similarly, Sri Lanka protects 44.0 percent of its imports, while 23.3 percent

TABLE 2.4 Sensitive Lists, SAFTA

Country	Products, original list	Products, revised list (phase II)	Share of trade value to South Asia subject to lists, 2015	
			Imports	Exports
Afghanistan	1,072	850	—	14.7
Bangladesh	1,233 (LDCs); 1,241 (NLDCs)	987 (LDCs); 993 (NLDCs)	45.6	2.9
Bhutan	150	156	11.6	5.6
India	480 (LDCs); 868 (NLDCs)	25 (LDCs); 614 (NLDCs)	6.2	39.1
Maldives	681	154	15.5	48.1
Nepal	1,257 (LDCs); 1,295 (NLDCs)	998 (LDCs); 1,036 (NLDCs)	36.1	0
Pakistan	1,169	936	20.2	38.8
Sri Lanka	1,042	837 (LDCs); 963 (NLDCs)	44.0	23.3

Sources: Data from UN Comtrade (United Nations Commodity Trade Statistics Database), Statistics Division, Department of Economic and Social Affairs, United Nations, New York, http://comtrade.un.org/db/; products on lists: "Agreement on South Asian Free Trade Area (SAFTA)," SAARC, Kathmandu, http://saarc-sec.org /assets/responsive_filemanager/source/Files%20for%20Areas%20of%20Cooperation/ETF/Agreement%20on%20 South%20Asian%20Free%20Trade%20Area%20(SAFTA).docx; sensitive lists: Ministry of Commerce (Bangladesh), https://www.bangladeshtradeportal.gov.bd/?r=site/display&id=121; Ministry of Commerce (Pakistan), http://www .commerce.gov.pk/about-us/trade-agreements/sensitive-list-of-safta-member-phase-ii/; Department of Commerce (Sri Lanka), http://www.doc.gov.lk/index.php?option=com_content&view=article&id=56&Itemid=183&lang=en.
Note: LDCs = least developed countries; NLDCs = non–least developed countries; SAFTA = South Asian Free Trade Area; — = not available.

of its exports are affected by the sensitive lists of other countries. India opened its market to least developed countries in 2008. It only keeps 25 temptation ("sin") products off its duty-free list for South Asian least developed countries under SAFTA (implemented in 2012), but has 614 sensitive products from the non–least developed countries on the list; it protects 6.2 percent of its South Asian imports, the lowest share in South Asia. Moreover, 39.1 percent of India's exports to South Asia are subject to the sensitive lists of the importing countries, the highest share except for Maldives. Paradoxically, Pakistan, which has the second largest number of tariff lines among non–least developed countries on its sensitive list, protects only an estimated 20.2 percent of its imports from the region, while 38.8 percent of its exports (largely textile products) do not receive concessional tariffs from other countries under SAFTA.

A critical problem in SAFTA's design (probably a conscious choice made by SAFTA countries) is that it does not provide a clear guideline for phasing out the sensitive lists. Although there is a working group to reduce the number of products on the sensitive lists, progress has been incremental and has virtually come to a halt in the two years since the working group met in Islamabad in 2015. Furthermore, although it took a good part of a decade to reduce the number of products on the sensitive lists under Phase II, the proposed agreement for Phase III reductions only narrows these lists by a maximum of 20 percent, with an unspecified timeline.[15]

HIDDEN PARATARIFFS EXCLUDED FROM FREE TRADE AGREEMENTS

The discussion in this chapter so far highlights the problem of paratariffs in some countries in the region. Paratariffs are not included in negotiations on free trade agreements. Bangladesh, Pakistan, and Sri Lanka maintain high paratariffs, which are not included in the tariff concessions that are part of their trade agreements; hence, paratariffs are charged on intraregional imports. Thus, the paratariffs virtually counterbalance the limited tariff concessions offered under SAFTA, at least for imports into these three countries. In Bangladesh, Pakistan, and Sri Lanka, tariff averages, including paratariffs, are currently more than double the customs duty averages. For many individual products and their local producers, the use of paratariffs on top of customs duties provides high protection rates, on the order of 40–80 percent above the cost, insurance, and freight charges (Pursell 2011). For example, Sri Lanka grants duty-free entry to Pakistan's exports of shelled almonds (HS 0802.1200) and pistachios (HS 0802.5200), whereas the most-favored-nation duty for these products is 30 percent.[16] The duty-free access and large preferential margin should make Sri Lanka an attractive destination for Pakistan's exports of these products. However, Sri Lanka imposes paratariffs on both products at a combined rate of about 40 percent (7.5 percent PAL and 30 percent cess), which negates the zero-duty treatment.

To the extent that paratariffs are designed to protect domestic production, they achieve the goal, even if the imposing country signs a free trade agreement. Indeed, it is the nontransparent nature of paratariffs that allows this to happen: many of the sector-specific, protective paratariffs are more difficult to unearth because their protective impact arises from myriad, scattered domestic tax exemptions. And, as in the case of Bangladesh, these duties can be widespread. Moreover, the ease with which countries such as Bangladesh, Pakistan, and Sri Lanka have been able to impose these paratariffs in recent years also means that increasing the costs of imports, should that be the objective, appears relatively simple for them.

In sum, much of the potential impact of SAFTA is lost because the use of paratariffs by a few larger countries in the region reduces or negates the limited concessions that have been put on the table.

Conclusions and Directions for Reform

The use of nontariff measures (NTMs), sensitive lists, and rules of origin (not explored in this report) to restrict liberalization in trade agreements is not new.[17] Baysan, Panagariya, and Pitigala (2006) show that the India–Sri Lanka Free Trade Agreement excludes outright many of the major sectors in which the countries had comparative advantage and imposed tariff-rate quotas and strict rules of origin to handicap the potential expansion of intraregional trade. Using the example of India in the 1990s, Bown and Tovar (2011) show that some countries substituted one form of import protection for another during a tariff liberalization episode.

It is also possible that the lack of momentum in SAFTA and its predecessor, the Agreement on SAARC Preferential Trading Arrangement, may become self-sustaining, as the incentives among countries become more aligned toward devoting relatively less of their scarce capacity to the region as a whole and focusing on bilateral or subregional trade liberalization, in some cases with deeper provisions than SAFTA. For example, the India–Sri Lanka Free Trade Agreement was signed in 1998 and became effective in 2000, with full implementation achieved in 2008; the Pakistan–Sri Lanka Free Trade Agreement was signed in 2002 and entered into force in 2005, reaching full implementation in 2010. Moreover, the number of products in the sensitive lists of these two free trade agreements is significantly lower relative to SAFTA. For instance, under the India–Sri Lanka Free Trade Agreement, India's negative list consists of 431 products (versus 614 products in SAFTA); under the Pakistan–Sri Lanka Free Trade Agreement, Pakistan's negative list has 540 products (versus 969 products under SAFTA). Additionally, countries such as Bhutan and Nepal have historically shared strong trading relations with India that predate SAFTA, and India has allowed these countries deeper and wider trade preferences.[18] Other countries, including Bangladesh and Sri Lanka, are also pursuing free trade agreements with multiple partners.

Some of the many free trade agreements could have led to erosion of effective preferences within SAFTA and, in certain cases, may even have diverted some trade away from South Asian countries. Given that South Asian regimes discriminate against each other, an appropriate response is to eliminate such discrimination and make SAFTA (and other bilateral arrangements in South Asia) as effective as possible.

The report suggests three major areas of reform to make tariff liberalization under SAFTA more meaningful. They are also relevant to bilateral or subregional free trade agreements. These suggestions should be seen within the context of open regionalism, where regional trade integration is complementary to global integration.

• *An accelerated and time-bound schedule for the reduction of sensitive lists is needed.* Downsizing sensitive lists is necessary to increase the volume of regional trade in South Asia. Although some steps have been taken in this direction, these efforts have been insufficient. For instance, none of the country offers at the third meeting of the Working Group on Reduction in the Sensitive Lists (Phase III) went beyond a 20 percent reduction, despite the large number of products in most country lists. For a genuine SAFTA to emerge, countries in the region need to agree on the timing for the complete elimination of sensitive lists, not exceeding 10 years, barring a few products of exceptional concern. In this context, India's approach of near complete liberalization in favor of least developed countries could be worth replicating among countries, such as Pakistan and Sri Lanka, at least in favor of the smaller least developed countries and Bangladesh (for other least developed countries). To begin the process, a first step could be to lower the number of products in SAFTA sensitive lists to align them with sensitive lists in bilateral South Asian agreements (the India–Sri Lanka and Pakistan–Sri Lanka free trade agreements).

• *The problem of paratariffs needs to be squarely addressed, and a schedule for elimination should be set.* Paratariffs are a critical barrier to SAFTA's functioning. Although acknowledged, the problem has not been clearly addressed in the most recent note of the SAFTA Committee of Experts. A separate subgroup of experts might address and monitor this issue with a view to eliminating paratariffs within a time period that is credible (and sufficiently ambitious) and acceptable to all parties. This approach will level the playing field between the countries that impose paratariffs and those that do not. It will also enable a greater degree of real tariff preferences within SAFTA. An obvious starting point would be the reduction and accelerated elimination of paratariffs on items not on sensitive lists, wherever applicable.

• *SAFTA members should continue their efforts to eliminate tariffs among the membership for nonsensitive items.* Although the initial plan was to achieve full trade liberalization in SAFTA by 2016 for nonsensitive items, some tariffs are still charged on member countries. The goal should be to reduce all tariffs, inclusive of paratariffs, to zero for all products on nonsensitive lists (instead of the 0–5 percent range as originally planned). If the sensitive lists are reduced over 10 years, as suggested above, the zero-tariff formula for nonsensitive items would mean that protection would only occur (at least in SAFTA trade) through the sensitive list approach.

Notes

1. See RTA-IS (Regional Trade Agreements Information System) (database), World Trade Organization, Geneva (accessed April 26, 2018), http://rtais.wto.org/UI/Public MaintainRTAHome.aspx.

2. The Southern Cone Common Market is widely referred to simply by the Spanish acronym Mercosur, which is a regional trade association of Argentina, Brazil, Paraguay, Uruguay, and República Bolivariana de Venezuela.

3. Each importing country in SAFTA places products from partner SAFTA countries that are ineligible for concessional import tariffs on its sensitive list.

4. The 2018/19 budget increased customs duties on a range of consumer goods, agroprocessed products, electronics, motorcycles, and automobile parts by 5–10 percentage points. However, the median basic customs duty rate remains at 10 percent (PwC 2018). For details on various tariff increases, see Jaitley (2018). See also the communication of customs and excise notifications by the Ministry of Finance, document D.O.F. No. 334/4/2018–TRU, Tax Research Unit, Department of Revenue, February 1, http://www.indiabudget.gov.in/ub2018 -19/cen/dojstru1.pdf.

5. The average simple tariff rates in the region in 2016 were Afghanistan, 13.6 percent; Bangladesh, 13.8 percent; Bhutan, 22.3 percent; India, 13.4 percent; Nepal, 12.1 percent; Pakistan, 12.1 percent; and Sri Lanka, 9.3 percent (WTO, ITC, and UNCTAD 2017). No data are available for Maldives.

6. For details, see "General Tariff Interpretation," Bangladesh Trade Portal, Ministry of Commerce, Dhaka, Bangladesh, https://www.bangladeshtradeportal.gov.bd/?r=site /display&id=281.

7. The notification through statutory regulatory order 1035(I)/2017, dated October 16, 2017, imposed new regulatory duties on 137 tariff lines, including new cars (less than 1,800 cubic centimeters), plastic articles, dry fruits, sunglasses, cigarette paper, tobacco, wallpaper, and so forth. Regulatory duty rates were increased on 219 tariff lines, including cosmetics, fruit juices, tiles, footwear, tires, handbags, tableware, kitchenware, air conditioners, refrigerators, and so forth. See "Levy of Duties Aimed at Reducing Import Bill, Furthering Growth," Pakcustoms.org, Press Release (October 20, 2017), http://www.pakcustoms.org /press-release.

8. The excise duty on automobiles was also modified in 2016 to act as a single encompassing rate. It replaced customs duties and paratariffs.

9. Prior to the introduction of the GST, certain charges, such as the education cess, the secondary and higher education cess, and the national calamity and contingent duty, were charged on imports. The education cesses were also levied on domestic output, but, as of March 1, 2015, were subsumed under excise duties. If one argues that the cesses are still embedded in domestic taxes (the central VAT), then they are not paratariffs. However, if they are seen to have disappeared from the central VAT, then they would count as paratariffs. The calamity duty is charged only on imports. Even if all three duties are construed as paratariffs, their overall impact is small because the education cess is levied only on customs duties and countervailing duties. In 2016–17, these three taxes represented 3.5 percent of total import duties and only 0.5 percent of total tax revenues. See "Receipt Budget, 2016–17," National Informatics Center, New Delhi, http://www.indiabudget.gov.in/ub2016-17/rec/tr.pdf.

10. Until the 2018/19 budget, the education cesses were to continue to be applied: their impact on tariff escalation was small (they are levied only on the customs duty and add a maximum of 0.3 percentage points to tariff collection rates): they could qualify as paratariffs. See "Indian Customs Gears Up for GST Roll-Out: Guidance Note for Importers and Exporters," Central Board of Excise and Customs, New Delhi, http://www.cbec.gov.in/resources//htdocs-cbec /gst/Guidance-Note-for-Importers-Exporters-v2.pdf;jsessionid=94AB5902472957A33E DAD9CBEDA86EEC. Thus, for example, the two education cesses and the calamity duty together increased the total import duty collection rate (all duties on imports, divided by the value of imports) from 7.9 percent to 8.2 percent in 2016–17. The 0.4 percent share has been calculated based on information in "Receipt Budget, 2018–19," National Informatics Center, New Delhi, https://www.indiabudget.gov.in/ub2018-19/rec/allrec.pdf. It includes the social welfare surcharge and the calamity duty.

11. This analysis has been done for Bangladesh by the Policy Research Institute of Bangladesh, one of the World Bank's collaborators in the region.

12. The simple average tariff calculated for Bangladesh is marginally different from the tariff reported in an earlier footnote citing WTO, ITC, and UNCTAD (2017).

13. The simple average tariff calculated for Sri Lanka is marginally different from the WTO, ITC, and UNCTAD (2017) tariff reported earlier. The detailed calculations on the two countries here have been performed by the Policy Research Institute of Bangladesh.

14. The eight members are Afghanistan, Bangladesh, Bhutan, India, Maldives, Nepal, Pakistan, and Sri Lanka.

15. See "Agreement on South Asian Free Trade Area (SAFTA)," SAARC, Kathmandu, http:// saarc-sec.org/assets/responsive_filemanager/source/Files%20for%20Areas%20of%20 Cooperation/ETF/Agreement%20on%20South%20Asian%20Free%20Trade%20Area%20 (SAFTA).docx.

16. See "HS Nomenclature, 2012 Edition," World Customs Organization, Brussels, http://www .wcoomd.org/en/topics/nomenclature/instrument-and-tools/hs_nomenclature_previous _editions/hs_nomenclature_table_2012.aspx.

17. Rules of origin can also affect the scope of trade liberalization. The SAFTA rules of origin stipulate that products from the non–least developed countries qualify for preferences if two criteria are met, namely, a change in tariff heading (at the 4-digit level) and 40 percent domestic value added (30 percent for least developed countries). Furthermore, regional cumulation is allowed at a minimum 50 percent of regional value (40 percent for least developed countries) and 20 percent of domestic value added in the final exporting country. Additionally, product-specific rules for 191 tariff lines have been agreed to accommodate the interests of least developed countries because of their limited natural resource base and small, undiversified industrial structures.

18. India and Pakistan have signed or are negotiating free trade agreements with many other partners. India has existing comprehensive economic partnerships, economic cooperation agreements, or free trade agreements with some 18 countries or groups of countries and is a party to negotiations on a Regional Comprehensive Economic Partnership Agreement between the 10 members of ASEAN and six of their partners in free trade agreements (Australia, China, India, Japan, the Republic of Korea, and New Zealand). India has made early announcements of negotiations with the European Union, European Free Trade Association, and the Southern African Customs Union, as well as the Bay of Bengal

Initiative on Multi-Sectoral Technical and Economic Cooperation with Bangladesh, Bhutan, Myanmar, Nepal, Sri Lanka, and Thailand. Negotiations are also ongoing with Australia, Canada, the Gulf Cooperation Council, Indonesia, Israel, and New Zealand and are being considered with the Arab Republic of Egypt and Mauritius. Pakistan has 10 free trade agreements already in force, including one with China, and has launched negotiations in seven other cases, while one signed agreement is not yet in force.

References

Baysan, Tercan, Arvind Panagariya, and Nihal Pitigala. 2006. "Preferential Trading in South Asia." Policy Research Working Paper 3813, World Bank, Washington, DC.

Bown, Chad P., and Patricia Tovar. 2011. "Trade Liberalization, Antidumping, and Safeguards: Evidence from India's Tariff Reform." *Journal of Development Economics* 96 (1): 115–25.

Jaitley, Arun. 2018. "Budget 2018–2019: Speech of Arun Jaitley, Minister of Finance." February 1, Ministry of Finance, New Delhi.

Kathuria, Sanjay, and Mariem Mezghenni Malouche, eds. 2016. *Strengthening Competitiveness in Bangladesh, Thematic Assessment: A Diagnostic Trade Integration Study*. Directions in Development: Trade Series. Washington, DC: World Bank.

Pursell, Garry. 2011. "Trade Policies in South Asia." In *Routledge Handbook of South Asian Economics*, edited by Raghbendra Jha, 219–37. Routledge Handbooks Series. London: Routledge.

PwC (PricewaterhouseCoopers). 2018. "India Budget 2018: Aiming for the Bullseye." February, PwC, Mumbai. https://www.pwc.in/assets/pdfs/budget/2018/aiming_for_the_bullseye_pwc _union_budget_2018_booklet.pdf.

World Bank. 2012. "Bangladesh Poverty Assessment: Assessing a Decade of Progress in Reducing Poverty, 2000–2010." Bangladesh Development Series Paper 29, World Bank, Washington, DC.

WTO (World Trade Organization). 2017. *World Trade Statistical Review 2017*. Geneva: WTO.

WTO (World Trade Organization), ITC (International Trade Centre), and UNCTAD (United Nations Conference on Trade and Development). 2017. *World Tariff Profiles 2017*. Geneva: WTO.

CHAPTER 3

A Granular Approach to Addressing Nontariff Barriers: India's Trade with Bangladesh and Nepal

NISHA TANEJA

Introduction

Defined as policy measures other than ordinary customs tariffs, nontariff measures (NTMs) have the potential to affect international trade in goods significantly. In a world in which tariff liberalization has generally been successful and tariffs have fallen to historically low levels, nontariff barriers are emerging as new tools of protectionism. Although NTMs are legitimate and are sanctioned by law, the general trend has been toward wider use of NTMs by developed- and developing-country governments to circumvent low tariffs and thereby protect domestic production. To understand the complex world of NTMs in South Asia, this study seeks to examine the concerns of businesses regarding measures related to sanitary and phytosanitary standards (SPS) and technical barriers to trade (TBT).

The SPS and TBT agreements of the World Trade Organization are important in that they permit members to adopt product standards to protect plant, animal, and human life. The agreements also stipulate that standards should not be applied in a trade-restrictive manner. The private sector sometimes finds complying with these technical regulations difficult because of complex requirements and administrative obstacles. Inadequate access to information about applicable measures also affects trade. Consequently, NTMs applied by partner countries can have a negative impact on market access and hinder firms from seizing trade opportunities.

Although businesses may face problems in meeting the regulatory requirements of importing countries, the United Nations Conference on Trade and Development (UNCTAD) has introduced the concept of procedural obstacles (POs), which are defined as issues that arise during the application of an NTM, rather than in the measure itself (UNCTAD 2010). Evidence suggests that POs are the main source of difficulties for exporting firms in developing countries (ITC 2011, 2012, 2014; WTO 2012). POs may be related to the arbitrary behavior of officials, delays in testing, inadequate information, and so forth. Within these, nontransparent and inadequate information is an important aspect. That SPS and TBT measures are often opaque and complex compounds these challenges and creates roadblocks for firms from other countries.

A useful way to understand NTMs is through the International Trade Centre's (ITC) business surveys, which are large surveys of companies undertaken to review the perspective of the business community on NTMs and their effects (ITC 2011, 2012, 2014). The surveys are administered to exporting and importing companies that face burdensome NTMs in a partner country. ITC uses the UNCTAD (2015) classification of NTMs and has defined NTM survey sectors as those with more than a 2 percent share in the total exports of a country. These surveys have been helpful in providing country-wise insights into cases involving NTMs and the POs faced by companies in exporting and importing goods and presenting convincing evidence on the presence of NTMs.

The objective of this chapter is to uncover patterns in the application of NTMs to enable practical and credible policy suggestions that address the difficulties faced by firms. These patterns are examined through the lens of selected products in the bilateral trade between Bangladesh and India and between India and Nepal. This process is accomplished by empirically measuring the restrictiveness of NTMs as perceived by exporting firms and identifying the POs perceived by these firms in meeting NTM requirements. To check and establish the validity of the survey findings, information received from the survey has been triangulated with an examination of the regulations and consultations with regulators in the three countries.

The rest of this chapter is organized as follows. The next section discusses the approach and the methodology used, including the criteria for product selection, the sampling frame, and the questionnaire. The following section describes the institutional structure and regulatory framework in Bangladesh, India, and Nepal for the imports and exports of the surveyed products. The subsequent section discusses the results of the survey, and the final section concludes the chapter with suggestions for policy makers.

Approach of the Chapter

This analysis of NTMs is conceptually and methodologically different from earlier studies on NTMs in intra-South Asian trade and business surveys in five ways.

First, the study is more narrowly focused on two major import-related NTMs, that is, SPS and TBT measures, that have been an important concern in regional trade. Second, it considers all categories of technical requirements (TRs) and conformity assessment measures (CAMs) laid down by the respective importing country for SPS and TBT measures. Third, it applies a rigorous filter and considers only selected products. The purpose of selecting a few products is to obtain an in-depth understanding of NTMs and how they are applied. This approach is also useful in examining NTMs in the context of the larger regulatory framework of the country. Fourth, the study examines NTMs based on a survey that has collected qualitative and quantitative information. Fifth, it triangulates information received from the survey with an investigation of the regulations and consultations with regulators in Bangladesh, India, and Nepal. This method helps in controlling for self-reporting bias in the survey and drawing inferences and recommendations.

The study uses the classification of NTMs conceived by the Multi-Agency Support Team group to support the Group of Eminent Persons on Non-Tariff Barriers established by UNCTAD. UNCTAD (2015) presents a taxonomy of all measures considered relevant in international trade. The classification is provided for imports and exports. For imports, there are two broad categories: technical measures (chapters A to C) and nontechnical measures (chapters D to O); export-related measures have a single category (chapter P) (see annexes 3A and 3B). This study focuses on the two technical measures: SPS and TBT measures.

SPS measures have six categories of TRs and one category of CAMs. TRs include prohibitions or restrictions on imports for SPS reasons; tolerance limits for residues and restricted use of substances to ensure food safety; hygiene requirements; treatment to eliminate pests and disease-causing organisms; other requirements on production or postproduction processes; and requirements for packaging, marking, and labeling. To verify that a given SPS condition has been met, CAMs include requirements for product registration, testing, certification, inspection, traceability, and quarantine.

TBT measures include TRs related to the prohibition or restriction of imports for TBT reasons; tolerance limits for substances; production or postproduction requirements; product identity requirements; product quality or performance requirements; and requirements for labeling, packaging, and marking. CAMs related to TBT measures include requirements for product registration, testing, certification, inspection, and traceability.

The study uses the classification of POs provided by UNCTAD. There are six main categories of POs: arbitrary or inconsistent behavior of government officials; discriminatory behavior of officials favoring specific producers or suppliers; inefficiency or obstruction caused by too much documentation, delays in obtaining approvals, detailed or redundant testing, and so on; nontransparent practices arising because of inadequate information on laws and regulations, unannounced changes in procedures, and so forth; legal obstacles generated by inadequate legal infrastructure, inadequate dispute resolution, or lack of enforcement; and unusually high fees or charges (annex 3C).

PRODUCT SELECTION

The study is based on a survey conducted for selected export items from Bangladesh, India, and Nepal. A questionnaire was designed and canvassed in several cities in the three countries. Exporters were selected randomly from existing databases of relevant industry and trade associations. Three export products each were selected from Bangladesh and Nepal going to India, one export item from India going to Bangladesh, and one from India going to Nepal.

The selection process for items that are traded between Bangladesh and India and between India and Nepal was based on multiple criteria. First, items having trade potential were considered using the trade possibility approach. Trade possibilities exist in items that two countries can import from each other instead of importing from elsewhere in the world. This is a simple and intuitive method and is calculated as follows: Min (SE, MI) − SE_M, where SE, MI, and SE_M are supplier's global exports, receiver's global imports, and supplier's exports to the receiver. Second, the share of exports to the South Asian partner in exports to the world was used to understand the importance of the items and their potential for bilateral trade. Third, consultations were held with industry associations, regulatory bodies, and conformity assessment bodies in the three countries to seek their views, and substantial consideration was given to these suggestions in the selection process. Fourth, product categories selected under the South Asian Regional Standards Organization for the adoption of harmonized regional standards were considered. Based on these criteria, the following export products were selected from Nepal: tea, cardamom, and medicinal and aromatic plants. The export products from Bangladesh are processed foods, ready-made garments, and jute bags.[1] The export product from India to Bangladesh is pharmaceutical raw materials (organic chemicals); from India to Nepal, it is pharmaceuticals. Table 3.1 gives a snapshot of the parameters that were used for the selection of the items (see annex 3D for the Harmonized System codes).

SAMPLING FRAME

Firms were selected randomly in Bangladesh, India, and Nepal based on a list of exporters and importers collected from respective industry associations. The survey was conducted from May to September 2014. Table 3.2 lists the number of firms that were surveyed in each country.

In the examination of NTMs, only the perceptions of exporters in each country were considered (201 respondents in all—70 exporters in Nepal and 30 exporters in India related to Nepal–India trade, and 79 exporters in Bangladesh and 22 exporters in India in case of Bangladesh–India trade). The perceptions of importers were considered only for qualitative aspects of the study.

QUESTIONNAIRE

The questionnaire used the UNCTAD classifications for SPS and TBT measures and POs (see annexes 3B and 3C).

TABLE 3.1 Parameters for the Selection of Survey Items

Item	Exports to partner in world exports of country, %	Trade potential, $ million	Exports to partner, $ million	SARSO list	Stakeholder consultations, recommended item
Nepal's exports to India					
Black tea	91.0	1.86	18.1	√	Recommended
Cardamom	100.0	0.13	45.64	x	Recommended
Medicinal and aromatic plants	35.0	8.7	4.64	x	Recommended
Bangladesh's exports to India					
Jute bags	24.0	9.13	67.35	√	Recommended
Ready-made garments	0.2	255.36	57.13	x	Recommended
Processed food	1.0	63.99	0.45	√	Recommended
India's exports to Nepal					
Pharmaceutical items	1.1	50.72	108.3	x	Recommended
India's exports to Bangladesh					
Pharmaceutical raw materials	0.4	158.91	39.3	x	Recommended

Sources: Based on 2012 trade data. Calculations based on consultations with stakeholders; data of WITS (World Integrated Trade Solution) (database), World Bank, Washington, DC, http://wits.worldbank.org/WITS/.
Note: SARSO = South Asian Regional Standards Organization; √ = yes; x = no.

A structured questionnaire was used for the survey. Qualitative and quantitative responses were obtained. In cases where perceptions on ease or difficulty in meeting standards were solicited, a Likert scale ranging from 1 to 5 was employed, where 1 indicates that the respondent finds it very easy to meet the measures, and 5 indicates that the respondent finds it very difficult. Thus, the level of restrictiveness of any measure was indicated by the score provided by the respondent on a scale of 1–5, where 1 indicated that the measure was least restrictive, and 5 that it was most restrictive (see annex 3E for the survey questionnaire).

Institutional Framework and Regulations Governing NTMs

In any regulatory framework relating to standards, the government is required to create legislation; regulatory bodies specify and enforce regulations under the appropriate

TABLE 3.2 Firms Surveyed, Bangladesh, India, and Nepal

Items	Number of firms, India survey	Items	Number of firms, Bangladesh and Nepal surveys
Indian side, Nepal survey		*Nepal survey*	
Tea	30	Tea	25
Cardamom	14	Cardamom	10
Medicinal and aromatic plants	30	Medicinal and aromatic plants	35
Pharmaceuticals	30	Pharmaceuticals	30
Total	104		100
Indian side, Bangladesh survey		*Bangladesh survey*	
Jute bags	20	Jute bags	20
Ready-made garments	35	Ready-made garments	35
Processed foods	30	Processed foods	24
Pharmaceutical raw materials, organic chemicals	22	Pharmaceutical raw materials (organic chemicals)	21
Total	107		100

legislation; standards development organizations develop the standards on which the regulations are based; conformity assessment bodies demonstrate compliance with the regulations; and an effective accreditation system ensures the competence of the conformity assessment bodies.

This section discusses the institutional structure and regulatory framework in Bangladesh, India, and Nepal for imports or exports of selected products.[2] The section also discusses specific import regulations that are relevant for the surveyed products.

COUNTRYWISE INSTITUTIONAL FRAMEWORK

India

In India, the standard-setting bodies can be segregated into voluntary standards bodies and regulatory bodies. The Bureau of Indian Standards is the national standards body, which also provides conformity assessment services. The bureau functions under the Ministry of Consumer Affairs and has developed more than 19,000 standards. It formulates the Indian standards for food and agriculture, as well as engineering, electronics, textiles, and so forth. It is a member of the International Organization for Standardization (ISO), as well as the International Electrotechnical Commission;

several Indian standards have been harmonized with the standards of these institutions to facilitate acceptance of Indian products in international markets. The Quality Council of India, under the Department of Industrial Policy and Promotion within the Ministry of Commerce and Industry, has established the national accreditation structure and promotes quality through the National Quality Campaign. It has a special wing for the accreditation of conformity assessment bodies, two of which are the National Accreditation Board for Certification Bodies and the National Accreditation Board for Testing and Calibration Laboratories (NABL). The former provides accreditation for certification bodies in India and in the South Asian Association for Regional Cooperation (SAARC) countries. The NABL provides accreditation to laboratories on assessment of their competence according to established criteria, including international standards and guidelines. The NABL is a signatory to regional and international bodies, such as the Asia Pacific Laboratory Accreditation Cooperation and the International Laboratory Accreditation Cooperation.

The National Accreditation Board for Certification Bodies accorded accreditation to the Bangladesh Standards and Testing Institution's (BSTI) product certification system in 2012 and to the Nepal Bureau of Standards and Metrology in 2014. The NABL has accredited laboratories in some foreign countries, including 15 laboratories in Bangladesh and 4 in Nepal. The NABL has accredited laboratories in Bangladesh that conduct the testing of food products such as protein-rich biscuits, wafer biscuits, edible gels, fruit drinks, chutney, pasteurized milk, flavored milk, soybean oil, edible palm oil, refined palmolein, fortified soybean oil, edible palm oil, and fortified refined palmolein. The laboratories also test textile products, including jute; plastics and resins; leather products; and cement. In Nepal, the NABL has accredited laboratories that conduct the testing of cereal products, edible oils, honey, drinking water, cosmetics, and pharmaceutical raw materials.

Several regulatory bodies lay down regulations for importing and exporting items. The Food Safety and Standards Authority of India (FSSAI) notifies regulations for the import of food items. The Directorate of Plant Protection, Quarantine, and Storage, under the Ministry of Agriculture and Farmers' Welfare notifies regulations relating to the quarantine of agricultural exports and imports. An important role that the FSSAI plays is to notify NABL-accredited laboratories that are recognized for analyzing food samples according to biological and chemical parameters. For imports into India, food samples must be tested at FSSAI-notified NABL laboratories or referral laboratories in India or the exporting country. Until recently, the FSSAI had not notified any laboratories in any foreign country. This changed in 2017, when FSSAI agreed to accept BSTI's certification for 21 food products.[3]

To support economic transactions and the use of technical regulations and standards, the government has also established the Directorate of Legal Metrology for weights and measures, including metering devices, clinical thermometers, and so forth. It is one of the separate wings under the Department of Consumer Affairs, Food, and Civil Supplies. The government enforces the Legal Metrology Act and Rules through the director at the center, who delegates power to the controllers at the state level for effective enforcement of the provisions of the acts and rules.

For exports, the government established the Export Inspection Council to ensure sound development of the country's export trade through quality control and inspection and related matters. The council sets mandatory standards for exports under the Export (Quality Control and Inspection) Act, 1963 (India, Department of Commerce 1963).

Nepal

The Nepal Bureau of Standards and Metrology is the national standards body under the Ministry of Industry, Commerce, and Supplies; it is also a member of the International Organization for Standardization. The Nepal Standards (Certification Mark) Act, 2037 (1980) governs standards, testing, and metrology activities (Nepal, Law Commission 1980). This law led to the formation of the Nepal Council for Standards, which has the main responsibility for establishing, naming, and revising national standards. The Nepal Bureau of Standards and Metrology serves as the secretariat of the Nepal Council for Standards. Effectively, the council recognizes standards established by other national bodies and international standardization institutions, and the Nepal Bureau of Standards and Metrology carries out the associated activities, such as testing facility management, calibration, laboratory accreditation services, and other administrative functions.

The Department of Food Technology and Quality Control, under the Ministry of Agriculture, Land Management and Cooperatives, is the apex organization responsible for the enforcement of the Food Act and Regulations. It has been working to implement the Feed Act and Regulations as well. Its main aim is to ensure and enhance the quality and safety of food and feed products in the country. The department, which has been designated as the contact point in Nepal for the Codex Alimentarius Commission of the Food and Agriculture Organization of the United Nations and of the World Health Organization for more than three decades, has also performed the role of National SPS Enquiry Point since 2004.

To regulate pharmaceuticals, the Nepalese government established the Department of Drug Administration (DDA) in 1979 to implement and fulfill the aims of the Drug Act 1978 (Nepal, National Parliament 1978). The department has set guidelines for the export and import of pharmaceuticals according to the Drug Act.

Bangladesh

The BSTI is the only national standards body in Bangladesh. It is entrusted with the responsibility to formulate national standards for industrial, food, and chemical products and for product quality control. The BSTI was set up through the promulgation of the Bangladesh Standards and Testing Institution Ordinance, 1985 (Bangladesh, MinLaw 1985). The BSTI is a member of the International Organization for Standardization, the Codex Alimentarius Commission, and regional organizations.

The Directorate General of Drug Administration (DGDA), under the Ministry of Health and Family Welfare, is the drug regulatory authority of the country. The DGDA, under the aegis of the Drug Act (1940), supervises and implements all prevailing drug regulations in the country and regulates all activities related to the import and procurement of raw and packing materials, the production and import of finished drugs, and the export, sales, pricing, and so forth of all kinds of medicines (Bangladesh, MinLaw 1940).

Responsible for accreditation, the Bangladesh Accreditation Board offers accreditation programs for various types of conformity assessment bodies, such as laboratories, certification bodies, inspection entities, training institutions, and individuals, in accordance with the relevant standards of the International Organization for Standardization, the International Electrotechnical Commission, and other national and international regulatory organizations. It recently signed the multilateral mutual recognition arrangement of the Asia Pacific Laboratory Accreditation Cooperation, of which it has been a full member since 2014.

MAJOR REGULATIONS GOVERNING THE SURVEYED PRODUCTS

Imports of the commodities selected for the study in Bangladesh, Nepal, and India are governed by the relevant regulations.

Food Safety and Standards Act, 2006, India

The Food Safety and Standards Act has consolidated the laws on food in India (India, Parliament 2006). It also established the FSSAI to set science-based standards and regulate the manufacture, storage, distribution, sale, and import of food items to ensure the availability of safe and wholesome food for human consumption. Four key regulations deal with the implementation of various food standards. These are related to food product standards and food additives; contaminants, toxins, and residues; labeling and packaging; and laboratory and sample analysis.

The Food Safety and Standards (Food Products Standards and Food Additives) Regulations, 2011, deal with the implementation of various food standards (A22, A41) (India, MOHFW 2011a).[4] They set detailed standards for various food products, prescribe limits for various food additives used across different food groups, and set microbiological requirements for various foods.

The Food Safety and Standards (Contaminants, Toxins, and Residues) Regulations, 2011, deal with compliance with various contaminant, toxin, and residue standards prescribed for food (A21) (India, MOHFW 2011b). They provide detailed standards for various contaminants that are naturally occurring toxic substances or residues of insecticides in various food items.

The Food Safety and Standards (Packaging and Labeling) Regulations, 2011, deal with packaging and labeling standards for food items, especially prepackaged foods

(India, MOHFW 2011c). Imported food items must meet the general requirements and the product-specific regulations for packaging and labeling (A31–A33).

The Food Safety and Standards (Laboratory and Sample Analysis) Regulations, 2011, provide a list of notified laboratories for the import functions of referral laboratories and procedures for sampling and testing (A82, A83) (India, MOHFW 2011d). The regulation states that the sample of any imported article will be sent by the authorized officer for analysis to the food analyst of any laboratory notified by the FSSAI. The regulation on procedures for sampling prescribes the approximate quantity of various food samples to be sent to the food analyst or director. A food business operator may have a food sample analyzed by any of the FSSAI-notified NABL-accredited laboratories. The FSSAI's notified list consists of private and state public health laboratories.

Until 2015, the FSSAI did not provide for any risk-based sampling of imports, and there was no distinction between high-risk and low-risk imports. Hence, 100 percent of import consignments were tested. In January 2016, the FSSAI published a notice regarding operationalization of the food import regulations. In September 2016, these were revised through the introduction of risk-based random sampling of food imports through the Single Window Interface for Facilitating Trade system, a digital interface adopted by Indian Customs in April 2016. The risk associated with a food item is determined according to three parameters: the category of the food, the source country, and the credibility of the importer and manufacturer. In September 2016, the FSSAI notified a list of 10 high-risk items.[5]

The FSSAI regulations apply to three items selected in this study: imports of tea and cardamom from Nepal and imports of processed foods from Bangladesh.

Plant Quarantine (Regulation of Import into India) Order, 2003, India

Imports of agricultural items (largely primary) are regulated by the conditions laid down in the Plant Quarantine Order (2003) (India, DAC&FW 2003). Imported items are subjected to pest risk analysis (PRA), the guidelines for which are set by the plant protection adviser and based on international standards established by the International Plant Protection Convention under the Food and Agriculture Organization of the United Nations. No import is permitted unless the PRA for the item is carried out in accordance with the guidelines. Based on the results of the PRA, the Directorate of Plant Protection, Quarantine, and Storage lists these items in the Schedules of the Plant Quarantine Order, 2003 (A86). These items are listed in Schedules V, VI, and VII of the Plant Quarantine Order, subject to the restrictions and conditions as specified in these schedules. Schedule VII consists of the items with the lowest risk, which do not require a permit from the Indian authorities. The phytosanitary certificate issued by the exporting country for schedule VII items is accepted by the Indian authorities. Schedule VI consists of items that are permitted with additional declarations and subject to special conditions laid down in the schedule. Schedule V lists items that are restricted and permissible for import only by authorized institutions with additional declarations and subject to special conditions.

For this study, imports of cardamom and medicinal and aromatic plants from Nepal are regulated by Plant Quarantine Order 2003. Both items fall under Schedule VII of the Plant Quarantine Order. Imports are permitted based on the phytosanitary certificate issued by the exporting country and the inspection conducted by the inspection authority and fumigation, if required.

Environment (Protection) Act, 1986, India

The Environment (Protection) Act provides for the protection and improvement of the environment and prevention of hazards to human beings, plants, animals, and property (India, MoEF&CC 1986).

The Ministry of Environment, Forest, and Climate Change, through a notification dated March 26, 1997 (S.O. 243 [E.]), promulgated a prohibition on handling 70 azo dyes specified in a schedule because of their cancer-causing and detrimental human health effects. The notes on import policy state that import consignments of relevant products shall be accompanied by a preshipment certificate from a textile testing laboratory accredited by the national accreditation agency of the country of origin. In this study, India's imports of jute and ready-made garments are subject to the provisions of the Environment Act (B22).[6]

Jute and Jute Textiles Control Order, 2000, India

The jute commissioner exercises regulatory powers under the Jute and Jute Textiles Control Order, 2000 (India, Ministry of Textiles 2000). The jute commissioner advises the government in all matters pertaining to the development of standards for jute and the regulation of trade in jute (B21, B31, B33, B82, B83). The primary functions of the office are to promote orderly exports through policy measures, help the Bureau of Indian Standards develop appropriate quality standards for jute, and enforce the compulsory jute packaging order in the various end user sectors covered by the Jute Packaging Materials (Compulsory Use in Packing Commodities) Act, 1987 (India, Ministry of Textiles 1987).

Foreign Trade (Development and Regulation) Act, 1992, India

The Directorate General of Foreign Trade is the nodal agency for foreign trade. Under the Foreign Trade (Development and Regulation) Act 1992, public circulars and notices of the changes in import or export procedures are notified to the public (India, Ministry of Law and Justice 2010). The Directorate General of Foreign Trade notifies the procedure to be followed for allowing imports of textile and textile articles (Public Notice 12[RE-2001]/1997–2002). All import consignments carrying a preshipment certificate from a textile testing laboratory accredited by the national accreditation agency of the country of origin must certify that the import consignment does not contain any hazardous dyes. In this study, this regulation applies to the import of jute and ready-made garments from Bangladesh.

Customs Act 1962, India

The Central Board of Excise and Customs (CBEC) is part of the Department of Revenue under the Ministry of Finance. It deals with tasks associated with the formulation of policy on customs levies, the collection of customs duties, central excise duties, and service taxes; the prevention of smuggling; and the administration of matters relating to customs under the Customs Act 1962 (CBEC 1962). Indian Customs inspects import certificates for authenticity and checks imports for physical damage or pilferage, swelling or bulging in imported items, rodent or insect contamination, and the presence of filth, dirt, and so forth, before handing over consignments to importers. Customs also inspects for compliance with marking and labeling requirements (A84, B84).

For imports of edible or food products, Customs has notified circulars from time to time providing detailed guidelines for the examination and testing of food items through port health officers prior to clearance by customs officers under the provisions of the Prevention of Food Adulteration Act, 1954, and, subsequently, under the Food Safety Standards Act, 2006. The clearance procedure for articles of food laid down in Circular 3/2011–Customs states that food items that are high risk or perishable are to be referred to the FSSAI or port health officers for testing; clearance is allowed thereafter. In the case of nonperishable goods, a test report of the FSSAI or port health officers for the first five consecutive consignments of each item is required. If the first five test reports conform to FSSAI standards, Customs would switch to random checking of 5–20 percent of the imported consignments. The guidelines also state that Customs is to rely on test reports and certificates from internationally known testing laboratories or government laboratories. At the time of the survey, tea and processed foods were classified by the CBEC as high-risk items and were therefore subject to 100 percent sampling and testing.[7]

The notifications also clarified that the risk management system module for import consignments of edible and food items does not provide for random sampling, and the system shall take the necessary steps to conform to the new requirements.

In a significant move, in April 2016, the CBEC introduced the single-window system, which enables the filing of integrated declarations for the requirements of Customs, the FSSAI, the drug controller, the Wild Life Control Bureau, the Textile Committee, and plant and animal quarantine authorities. The integration of the FSSAI into the single-window concept and FSSAI's adoption of a risk-based system through the single window have made random sample checks of up to 10 percent of consignments possible. In September 2016, the FSSAI notified a list of only 10 high-risk food items and clarified that the earlier list followed by the CBEC had to be replaced by the new list.

The CBEC has also notified the customs clearance of jute bags in consultation with the Ministry of Textiles through a circular (Circular 21/2002–Customs). The ministry has clarified that the import of bags containing jute batching oil in excess of 3 percent by weight is banned in India. Before such goods can be imported, a certificate from the authorized agency in the country of origin must be produced by the importer at the time of customs clearance. If a certificate is not produced, the goods may be cleared by customs only after the necessary testing for jute batching oil is conducted by the authorized agencies of the government of India.

Drug Act (1940), Bangladesh

The DGDA, under the Ministry of Health and Family Welfare, is the drug regulatory authority of Bangladesh. It supervises and implements all prevailing drug regulations in the country and regulates all activities related to imports, the procurement of raw and packing materials, the production and import of finished drugs, exports, sales, pricing, and so forth of all kinds of medicines, including Ayurvedic, Unani, herbal, and homoeopathic drugs and medicines. The Drug Act regulates the import, export, manufacture, distribution, and sale of drugs in Bangladesh (B14, B15, B31, B32, B33, B41, B7, B81, B82, B83, B84) (Bangladesh, MinLaw 1940).

The Drug Act (1978), Nepal

The government of Nepal promulgated the Drug Act 1978 to prohibit the misuse or abuse of drugs and allied pharmaceutical materials, as well as false or misleading information relating to the efficacy and use of drugs (Nepal, National Parliament 1978). The act also regulates and controls the production, marketing, distribution, export-import, storage, and utilization of drugs that are not safe for use by people, not efficacious, or not of standard quality (B14, B15, B31, B32, B33, B41, B7, B81, B82, B83, B84).

NTM Restrictiveness, Regulations, and Procedural Obstacles

This section provides average NTM restrictiveness scores for each NTM. The scores are based on the responses of firms engaged in exports of tea, cardamom, and medicinal and aromatic plants from Nepal to India; exports of jute bags, ready-made garments, and processed foods from Bangladesh to India; exports of pharmaceuticals from India to Nepal; and exports of pharmaceutical raw materials from India to Bangladesh. These scores measure the degree of policy distortions and represent a measure, albeit imperfect, of the degree of integration with global rules.

The average NTM restrictiveness score (*ANRscore*) for each export product (k) was calculated in three steps using simple averages at each step. At the NTM indicator (i) level, the subgroup NTM is comprised of two categories, TRs and CAMs. Firm-level responses on the scores were assigned based on the level of difficulty in meeting the NTM requirements for each indicator (i). Each score was ranked on a Likert scale of 1, very easy, to 5, very difficult.

Step1. For each product (k), the difficulty score is averaged across all respondents (n) for a specific indicator (i) within TR and CAM to provide an average indicator restrictiveness score (*AIRscore*), as follows:

$$AIRscore_k(i) = \frac{\sum_n score(n)}{N}, N = \sum n \qquad (3.1)$$

Step 2. After calculating the average restrictiveness measure at each indicator level within TR and CAM, the average subgroup restrictiveness scores (*ASRscore*) are derived by calculating a simple average of the average indicator scores within the subgroups TR and CAM, as follows:

$$ASRscore_k(TR / CAM) = \frac{\sum_i score_k(i)}{I}, I = \sum i, j \in TR / CAM \qquad (3.2)$$

Step 3. The aggregate average NTM restrictiveness score (*ANRscore*) for each product (k) is then derived using the simple average scores for TR and CAM, as follows:

$$ANRscore_k = \frac{\sum_{TR,CAM} score_k(TR / CAM)}{2} \qquad (3.3)$$

Table 3.3 provides a summary of the productwise NTM restrictiveness scores.

The average NTM restrictiveness scores for the eight selected products are highest for exports of tea from Nepal to India and lowest for exports of jute bags from Bangladesh to India. Table 3.3 also shows that, except for jute bags and pharmaceutical raw materials, the average restrictiveness scores for TRs are lower than the average restrictiveness scores for CAMs.

TEA: NEPAL TO INDIA

The survey was conducted in Ilam and Jhapa in Nepal. Five SPS measures were applicable for tea.

NTM Restrictiveness, Regulations, and POs

Testing and certification were found to be the most stringent among the applicable SPS measures (table 3.4). Because of the stringent testing and certification requirements, exporters found compliance more difficult with the CAMs than with the technical measures.

TABLE 3.3 Productwise NTM Restrictiveness Scores

Exporting country	Item	Average TR	Average CAM	Average NTM restrictiveness score
Nepal	Tea	2.96	3.84	3.40
Nepal	Cardamom	1.00	2.90	1.95
Nepal	Medicinal and aromatic plants	n.a.	2.15	2.15
Bangladesh	Processed foods	1.58	2.14	1.86
Bangladesh	Ready-made garments	1.16	1.19	1.18
Bangladesh	Jute	1.14	1.12	1.13
India	Pharmaceutical	1.62	1.44	1.53
India	Pharmaceutical raw materials	1.28	1.75	1.52

Note: CAM = conformity assessment measure; NTM = nontariff measure; TR = technical requirement; n.a. = not applicable.

TABLE 3.4 NTM Restrictiveness Score and POs Reported by Nepalese Exporters of Tea to India

Averages

NTMs	NTM restrictiveness score	POs, percent of respondents
Technical requirements		
Tolerance limits (A21)	3.32	C2 (56)
Labeling (A31)	2.60	F1 (8)
Average restrictiveness score	2.96	
Conformity assessment measures		
Testing requirements (A82)	4.04	A1 (12), A3 (56), C2 (44), C3 (8), F1 (8)
Certification requirements (A83)	4.16	C2 (80), C3 (68)
Inspection requirements (A 84)	3.32	A1 (24), A3 (16), D6 (8)
Average restrictiveness score	3.84	
Average NTM restrictiveness score	3.40	

Note: See annexes 3A, 3B, and 3C for the classification of NTMs and POs. NTM = nontariff measure; POs = procedural obstacles; Numbers in brackets indicate the percentage of respondents who reported that the POs were strict. Blank cells (other than for average scores) indicate that exporters reported no problems in meeting the requirements of the particular NTM.

Tolerance limits for residues or contamination by certain (nonmicrobiological) substances (A21). The regulations on tolerance limits for residues or contamination by certain substances for tea relate to limits of iron filings and the guidelines in the Plant Protection Code. All regulatory requirements are set by the FSSAI. In 2012, the FSSAI set a temporary limit of 150 milligrams per kilogram (mg/kg) of iron filings. The temporary limit was more stringent than the earlier limit of 250 mg/kg. In 2016, the FSSAI revised the limit back to 250 mg/kg.

The survey showed that 56 percent of the respondents felt that the tolerance limit standards are too strict (C2) because the use of pesticides had to be decreased substantially to meet the current standard (see table 3.4). The exporters also anticipated that Indian standards would become stricter in the future.

Labeling requirements (A31). The FSSAI regulation on labeling and packaging requires that the details regarding date of manufacture, batch number, and best before date are to be labeled on the packaged product. Labeling requirements are to be written not only in any foreign language, but also in English. A circular of the Tea Board of India dated May 7, 2014, requires any bulk packaging of tea to bear a label stating that the shelf life is nine months.

The respondents did not perceive any major POs related to the labeling of tea products. Only 8 percent of the respondents felt that the cost of meeting the labeling requirements was high (F1).

Testing requirements (A82). According to the guidelines provided by the FSSAI regulations, testing must be undertaken at the time of import to ensure that the imported item is safe for consumption. The cost of testing is Rs 3,000 per sample. The quantity of the tea sample to be sent for analysis is 200 grams.

In Nepal, 44 percent of the respondents mentioned that the testing requirements were too strict or too detailed (C2); 12 percent felt that the behavior of customs officials was arbitrary (A1); and 56 percent felt that testing of consignments was carried out in an arbitrary manner in deciding whether every consignment had to be checked or random checks had to be conducted (A3). In some cases, Customs checked every consignment; in other cases, however, if the first five consignments were found satisfactory, then, in the following consignments, samples were drawn from 5 percent to 20 percent of the consignments. Among the respondents, 8 percent mentioned that the time taken by the Central Food Laboratory in Kolkata for testing was substantial because samples had to be sent all the way to that city (15–30 days) (C3). Another 8 percent found that the fees and charges for testing were high (F1).

Certification requirements (A83). In Nepal, 80 percent of the respondents mentioned that the certification requirements were too strict or too detailed because it was mandatory to obtain a test certificate from the Central Food Laboratory (C2); 68 percent mentioned that the time taken to obtain certification was substantial (15–30 days) (C3). Moreover, the exporters complained about the duration of the validity of the certificate, which was usually only six months.

Inspection requirements (A84). As set by the Customs Manual of the Customs Act, customs officials physically check consignments for any damage. Of the respondents, 20 percent stated that the behavior of the customs officials is arbitrary or inconsistent (A1). The discriminatory behavior of the officials in applying certain rules and regulations was a concern among 16 percent of the respondents (A3). Another 8 percent said that the customs officials asked for informal payment to clear the consignments (D6).

Inferences and Recommendations

India imposes the same standards for domestic products and imports; therefore, these are not discriminatory measures. However, the expectation of stricter domestic standards in India in the future has raised concerns among tea exporters in Nepal. The tea exporters feared that the domestic standards in India would be raised continuously, and it may become more difficult for them to meet the requirements. Contrary to the expectations of Nepalese exporters, India increased the permissible limit of iron filings.

Because there are no testing facilities at the border, too much time is wasted in sending samples to Kolkata for testing. An observation that was made during the survey was that all samples were sent to only one laboratory, the Central Food Laboratory in Kolkata, although there are several private laboratories in Kolkata that are FSSAI-notified and NABL-accredited. Discussions with regulators and government officials in Kolkata and New Delhi revealed that, historically, because there were no laboratories catering to the needs of border trade, all samples were sent to the Central Food Laboratory. The dependence on the laboratory has continued, although several new government and private accredited laboratories notified by the FSSAI have emerged since 2011. Samples from the Kolkata seaport are sent to FSSAI-notified, NABL-accredited laboratories, private and public, but the land port continues to depend only on the Central Food Laboratory in Kolkata. The dependence on one laboratory causes delays and leads to inefficiencies and rent seeking.

The NABL has accredited laboratories in Nepal for testing tea. However, these laboratories have not been notified by the FSSAI. At the time of the survey, the CBEC classified tea as a high-risk item; hence, every consignment had to be tested. However, there was ambiguity about whether tea was a perishable or nonperishable item because Customs does not provide a definition of perishable items. Hence, the lack of clarity in the regulations has resulted in the arbitrary behavior of officials.

At the time of the survey, the FSSAI did not make any distinction between high-risk, perishable, or nonperishable items and had a set of vertical standards for imports of all food items, which required every consignment to be tested for all food items.[8] Lack of clarity on the regulations and lack of coordination among agencies left the traders confused and have also been a reason for the arbitrary behavior of officials. In 2016, the FSSAI issued a list of high-risk food items, which does not include tea, implying that tea would only be subjected to random sampling for testing.[9]

The single window introduced by Customs integrates the FSSAI with other agencies and facilitates a coordinated approach to adopting a risk-based system for importing food items. However, the innovation is available only at customs stations that have an electronic data interchange system.

The following actions are recommended for tea:

• Electronic data interchange should be installed at border points so that risk management systems can become operational through single windows. This will ensure coordination among agencies.

• The FSSAI should notify NABL-accredited laboratories in Nepal. This will enable random checks at the border.[10] Once notified, authorities in India, in cooperation with Nepal, should monitor the system and take corrective steps, as needed, to ensure that only random checks are being conducted.

• Enforcement rules should ensure that different ports interpret given regulations in a standard manner so that there is consistency. This will reduce the arbitrary behavior of customs officials.

• Traders and customs officials on both sides of the border need to be made aware that there are several private and public laboratories in India, in addition to the Central Food Laboratory in Kolkata, that are FSSAI notified and NABL accredited. The list of these laboratories is published by the FSSAI.

CARDAMOM: NEPAL TO INDIA

The survey on NTMs for exports of cardamom was undertaken in Jhapa in Nepal. All the respondents who were interviewed exported cardamom consignments through the Biratnagar–Jogbani border point at the India–Nepal border, and not through the Kakarvita–Panitanki border point, which is closer to the cardamom growing areas of Nepal.

NTM Restrictiveness, Regulations, and POs

Five SPS measures are applicable for cardamom. Testing and certification were found to be the most stringent for the exporters. Hence, compliance was more difficult with CAMs than with the TRs (table 3.5).

Tolerance limits for residues or contamination by certain (nonmicrobiological) substances (A21). The FSSAI has set limits on the quantity used of various insecticides for cardamom: Endosulfan (residues are measured as the total of Endosulfan A and B) not to exceed 1.0 mg/kg; Monocrotophos not to exceed 0.5 mg/kg; Quinolphos not to exceed 0.01 mg/kg; and Fosetyl-A1 not to exceed 0.2 mg/kg (India, Parliament 2006).

No problems were reported by exporters in Nepal with meeting tolerance limits.

TABLE 3.5 Scores for NTMs and POs Reported by Nepalese Exporters of Cardamom to India

Averages

NTMs	NTM restrictiveness score	POs, percent of respondents
Technical requirements		
Tolerance limits (A21)	1.00	
Conformity assessment measures		
Testing requirements (A82)	3.90	A3 (10), C2 (100)
Certification requirements (A83)	3.50	A1 (10), C2 (50)
Inspection requirements (A 84)	3.00	C3 (20), D6 (70)
Quarantine requirements (A86)	1.20	F1 (10)
Average restrictiveness score	2.90	
Average NTM restrictiveness score	1.95	

Note: See annexes 3A, 3B, and 3C for classification of NTMs and POs. NTM = nontariff measure; POs = procedural obstacles. Blank cells (other than for average scores) indicate that exporters reported no problems in meeting the requirements of the particular NTM.

Testing requirements (A82). Cardamom is listed under Schedule VII of India's Plant Quarantine Order, which classifies cardamom as a low-risk item. Hence, the phytosanitary certificate issued by Nepalese authorities is accepted by India.

The FSSAI has stipulated that the sample required to test cardamom for permissible tolerance limits is 500 grams per consignment. At the time of the survey, the FSSAI did not differentiate between low- and high-risk items; therefore, all consignments had to be tested. The CBEC has classified cardamom as a low-risk item and therefore stipulated that, if the first five consignments are found satisfactory, then, in the following consignments, samples should only be drawn from 5 percent to 20 percent of the consignments.

In Nepal, all the respondents claimed that the testing requirement for tolerance limits is too strict or redundant (C2), mainly because testing had to be performed by the FSSAI in India for every consignment even though the CBEC did not classify cardamom as a high-risk item. Additionally, 10 percent of the respondents stated that the nonuniformity of rules and regulations in different ports in different states of India is a problematic issue faced by exporters (see table 3.5). The state of West Bengal requires testing for each consignment, whereas, if the consignments are sent to the state of Bihar through the Biratnagar–Jogbani customs station, no testing is required. Therefore, although the cost of transport rises if exporting via Bihar, exporters prefer that route instead of exporting through the Kakarbhitta–Panitanki Customs.

Certification requirements (A83). For cardamom, the exporter must provide a phytosanitary certificate issued by the national Plant Protection Authority. A test certificate certifying that the product is free of toxins and contaminants must be issued by an authorized laboratory.

Of the exporters who were interviewed, 50 percent felt that the certification requirement related to the test analysis was redundant (perceiving cardamom to be low risk), not realizing that two different certificates, a phytosanitary certificate and a test analysis certificate, are needed (C2). Of the respondents, 20 percent stated that Indian authorities take up to 30 days to issue a test certificate (C3). Another 10 percent reported that the validity of the certificate issued by Indian authorities was determined arbitrarily as it could be valid from one to three months (A1).

Inspection requirements (A84). Customs is required to inspect the goods physically for possible damage. Of the exporters, 50 percent reported that inspection is carried out arbitrarily by customs officials (A1), while 70 percent said that they must make informal payments; otherwise, every bag is inspected (D6).

Quarantine requirement (A86). Cardamom requires a plant quarantine clearance. The phytosanitary certificate issued in Nepal is accepted for cardamom, and only a no-objection certificate is required from the plant quarantine authority in India. The exporters did not face any problems in meeting the plant quarantine requirements.

Inferences and Recommendations

Testing procedures are ad hoc and inconsistent and vary at different customs locations. Exporters perceive that testing requirements are more stringent in West Bengal than in Bihar. Testing facilities are not available at Jogbani or Panitanki. Kolkata is the nearest testing facility for Panitanki, and Patna is the nearest for Biratnagar–Jogbani.

NABL-accredited laboratories in Nepal have not been accredited for cardamom. Hence, according to FSSAI regulations at the time, with no distinction between high- and low-risk items, or between perishables and nonperishables, 100 percent testing must be conducted for cardamom. This changed in September 2016, because cardamom is not included in the list of high-risk items notified by the FSSAI, which makes it permissible to import with random checks, provided the NABL accredits laboratories in Nepal for cardamom, and FSSAI notifies the NABL-accredited laboratories in Nepal.

The following actions are recommended in the case of cardamom:

- The NABL should accredit laboratories in Nepal to test cardamom. The FSSAI should notify NABL-accredited laboratories in Nepal. This will enable random checks at the border.

- Enforcement rules should ensure that different ports interpret given regulations in a standard manner so that there is consistency. This would reduce the arbitrary behavior of customs officials.

- Electronic data interchange should be installed at border points so that risk management systems can become operational through single windows. This will ensure coordination among agencies.

- Traders need to be made aware that, in addition to the Central Food Laboratory in Kolkata, several private and public laboratories in India are notified by the FSSAI and accredited by the NABL. The list of these laboratories is published by the FSSAI.

MEDICINAL AND AROMATIC PLANTS: NEPAL TO INDIA

To identify NTMs in the trade of medicinal and aromatic plants, the respondents were interviewed in Nepalgunj in Nepal. All the respondents mentioned that Nepalgunj–Rupedia is the main land customs station for the trade in medicinal and aromatic plants between India and Nepal.

NTM Restrictiveness, Regulations, and POs

Four SPS measures are applicable to exports of medicinal and aromatic plants, all related to conformity assessment (table 3.6). Among the CAMs, the inspection requirement was reported to exhibit the highest level of difficulty for compliance.

Testing and certification requirements (A82, A83). Imports of medicinal and aromatic plants in India are governed by Plant Quarantine Order, 2003. Of the medicinal and aromatic plants produced in Nepal, 17 are under Schedule VII of the order, which classifies them as low-risk items and permits their import on the basis of a phytosanitary certificate issued by the exporting country. Nepal produces 61 additional medicinal plants, but these are not on any schedule of the Plant Quarantine Order because a PRA has not been conducted on them. A list of the 61 items is provided in annex 3F.

Although testing and certification for the phytosanitary certificate are conducted in Nepal, a no objection certificate is issued by the plant quarantine office in India on the basis of the phytosanitary certificate for the 17 items under Schedule VIII.

TABLE 3.6 Scores for NTMs and POs Reported by Nepalese Exporters of Medicinal and Aromatic Plants to India

Averages

SPS particulars	NTM restrictiveness score	POs, percent of respondents
Testing requirement (A82)	1.88	
Certification requirement (A83)	1.88	
Inspection requirement (A 84)	3.34	A1 (51), A3 (34), D6 (49)
Quarantine requirement (A86)	1.51	
Average NTM restrictiveness score	2.15	

Note: See annexes 3A, 3B, and 3C for classification of NTMs and POs. NTM = nontariff measure; POs = procedural obstacles; SPS = sanitary and phytosanitary standards. Blank cells indicate that exporters reported no problems in meeting the requirements of the particular NTM.

Most of the exporters reported that they faced no problems in exporting the medicinal plants listed under Schedule VII of the Plant Quarantine Order. Because the phytosanitary certificate for these medicinal herbs is supplied by Nepalese quarantine offices, all the exporters agreed that there was no problem in testing the medicinal plants and obtaining the phytosanitary certificate.

Inspection requirements (A84). Physical and visual inspection is performed by customs officials (as specified in the Customs Manual) to assess whether there is any damage.

The survey found that 49 percent of the respondents stated that inspection officials demand significant informal payments at multiple inspection points for products not listed on Schedule VII (D6). Moreover, 51 percent of the exporters complained that there is no particular pattern of inspection because the inspection is carried out at the discretion of the inspection officer (A1). Furthermore, 34 percent said that the inspectors can exercise discretionary power to unload products, which increases loading and unloading costs (A3) (see table 3.6).

Quarantine requirements (A86). Medicinal and aromatic plants require a plant quarantine clearance from the plant quarantine authorities in India. The respondents did not face any problem in obtaining clearance from the Plant Quarantine Department.

Inferences and Recommendations

The key inference from the survey on medicinal and aromatic plants is that exporters do not face any problem with regard to the 17 items listed in Schedule VII that are allowed into India on the basis of a phytosanitary certificate issued by Nepal's Plant Protection Authority. However, Nepal has 61 other medicinal plants that are not permitted in the Indian market because no PRAs have been conducted on these plants. Most of them find their way into India illegally. The incidence of substantial bribery derives from the illegal transborder trade in medicinal and aromatic plants.

The following actions are recommended for medicinal and aromatic plants:

- Exporters and importers in the two countries should be made aware of the regulatory regimes in the two countries. They need to be informed that, unless the Plant Quarantine Department in India conducts PRAs on Nepal's 61 other products, the products cannot be legally imported into India. The PRAs can be performed only if an importer or the national plant protection organization of the exporting country makes a demand. (See annex 3F for a list of the 61 items.)

- Items on which Nepal's national plant protection organization or importers in India have demanded that PRAs should be brought under the South Asian Free Trade Area (SAFTA) process and fast-tracked. The ministries of commerce and agriculture in both countries should work together to ensure that PRAs are conducted on the additional items and that those items are subsequently added to the schedules of the Plant Quarantine Order.

TABLE 3.7 Scores for NTMs and POs Reported by Bangladeshi Exporters of Processed Foods to India

Averages

NTMs	NTM restrictiveness score	POs, percent of respondents
Technical requirements		
Tolerance limits (A21)	1.46	
Restricted use of certain substances (A22)	1.41	C2 (58)
Labeling (A31)	1.58	A (46), C2 (33)
Marking (A32)	1.29	
Packaging (A33)	1.88	
Microbiological criteria (A41)	1.88	C2 (13)
Average restrictiveness score	1.58	
Conformity assessment measure		
Testing requirement (A82)	2.54	A1 (42), C2 (54), C3 (42), D2 (21), F (4)
Certification requirement (A83)	2	
Inspection requirement (A 84)	1.89	C2 (13), D6 (21)
Average restrictiveness score	2.14	
Average NTM restrictiveness score	1.86	

Note: See annexes 3A, 3B, and 3C for the classification of NTMs and POs. NTM = nontariff measure; POs = procedural obstacles. Blank cells (other than for average scores) indicate that exporters reported no problems in meeting the requirements of the particular NTM.

- These recommendations could be applied to all of Nepal's agricultural products that have the potential for export. Given that agricultural exports are extremely important for Nepal, PRAs for items with large potential can help the country increase its overall agricultural exports to India.

PROCESSED FOODS: BANGLADESH TO INDIA

Firms exporting processed foods were interviewed in Chittagong and Dhaka in Bangladesh.

NTM Restrictiveness, Regulations, and POs

The survey results indicate that firms found it easier to meet TRs than to meet CAMs (table 3.7).

Tolerance limits for residues or contamination by certain (nonmicrobiological) substances (A21). Imports of processed foods into India are governed by the regulations laid down by the FSSAI on the standards for various contaminants, toxins, and residues in food items. No POs were reported on meeting tolerance limits.

BOX 3.1 Xanthan Gum Case Study

Bangladeshi manufacturers use xanthan gum as a preservative in fruit juices and drinks. This preservative is accepted in several countries, but it is not accepted in India, where the regulations prescribe only the use of pectin as a preservative. Other countries to which Bangladesh exports fruit juices have not raised this issue. The use of pectin instead of xanthan as a preservative is an additional condition that must be met in the Indian market.

BOX 3.2 Packaging Information Case Study

In the case of candies and lollipops, wrappers often do not offer sufficient space to display all the required information. The rules are implemented more rigorously on imported products than on domestically produced goods in this instance. This is a common situation across countries because it is administratively much easier for authorities to check imported products rather than conduct checks in numerous locations within their own countries.

Restricted use of substances in foods and feeds and their contact materials (A22). The FSSAI regulations require that food business operators comply with permissible limits of various additives to be used in individual food products. Of the respondents, 58 percent felt that the regulation prescribing only pectin as a preservative in fruit juices and drinks for imported goods was too strict and posed an additional burden (box 3.1).

Microbiological criteria for the final product (A41). The FSSAI regulations require food products to comply with the microbiological standards for various food products. Of the respondents, 13 percent reported that the requirements were too detailed.

Labeling, marking, and packaging (A31, A32, A33). The labeling, marking, and packaging requirements are laid down in the Food Safety and Standards (Labeling and Packaging) Regulations, 2011. Of the respondents, 33 percent (all of whom were exporting candy) stated that the labeling requirement was too detailed for the surface area of the candy wrapper. Another 46 percent felt that the behavior of customs officials was arbitrary (box 3.2).

Testing and certification requirements (A82, A83). India's NABL has accredited 15 laboratories in Bangladesh. However, none of these had been notified by the FSSAI at the time of the survey.[11] While the surveyed products were being tested at NABL-accredited laboratories in Bangladesh, they were subjected to 100 percent checks of consignments in India since the laboratories had not been notified by the FSSAI.

Of the respondents, 42 percent felt that there were substantial delays in testing. Delays of up to a month were reported by the respondents. Another 54 percent felt that the testing of every consignment was a redundant requirement, and 42 percent felt that the behavior of customs officials in drawing samples was arbitrary. Of the respondents, 21 percent reported that the regulations on sampling and testing were not transparent.

Inspection requirements (A84). Customs officials check the certificates and conduct a physical examination for damaged goods.

Of the respondents, 13 percent stated that the inspections are redundant because 100 percent of the consignments are tested anyway. Another 21 percent stated that they had to make informal payments at the time of inspection.

Inferences and Recommendations

Although some firms reported that meeting the standards was difficult because the requirements were too detailed, they did not report any discrimination between national and foreign firms in the standards that were applicable to both. However, they reported discrimination in the enforcement of the labeling standards; enforcement was reportedly weaker for domestic products compared with imports, and they perceived this requirement to be a nontariff barrier for Bangladeshi exporters. Hence, although domestic standards and standards for imports are not discriminatory, implementation differs. The nonrecognition of a Codex-approved preservative (xanthan) by Indian authorities was also perceived as a nontariff barrier by Bangladeshi exporters.

All the surveyed firms mentioned that tests were conducted by the Central Food Laboratory in Kolkata. None of the firms was aware that there were several other government and private laboratories that were accredited by the NABL and notified by the FSSAI.

Some processed food items with food dyes and food additives were classified by the CBEC as high-risk items. All processed food items containing food additives therefore require 100 percent testing.

It was widely perceived by the Bangladeshi exporters and BSTI officials that 100 percent testing was being unfairly conducted even for products that were tested by NABL-accredited laboratories in Bangladesh. The exporters perceived this as evidence of the presence of nontariff barriers. There was no awareness among the exporters or regulatory authorities in Bangladesh that, unless the FSSAI notifies the NABL-accredited laboratories, random testing cannot be conducted on imports.

The following actions are recommended for processed foods:

- The FSSAI should notify NABL-accredited laboratories in Bangladesh to enable random checks at the border.

- Enforcement rules should ensure that different ports apply the same interpretation of given regulations so that there is consistency and to reduce the arbitrary behavior of customs officials.

- Electronic data interchange should be installed at border points so that risk management systems can become operational through single windows. This will ensure coordination among agencies.

- Traders need to be made aware that, in addition to the Central Food Laboratory in Kolkata, several private and public laboratories are FSSAI notified and NABL accredited. The list of these laboratories is published by the FSSAI.

READY-MADE GARMENTS: BANGLADESH TO INDIA

The survey respondents in Bangladesh were in Chittagong, Dhaka, and Gazipur. The most important land customs station used for exports of ready-made garments was Benapole–Petrapole.

NTM Restrictiveness, Regulations, and POs

Exporters of ready-made garments find meeting the technical and conformity assessment requirements easy. Meeting the labeling requirements was reportedly relatively more difficult (table 3.8).

Restricted use of substances (B22). The main TR for imports of ready-made garments is that the products should be free of azo dyes. India recognizes the azo dye certification provided by the BSTI. Hence, imports accompanied by a preshipment certificate issued by a BSTI-recognized laboratory are accepted by the Indian authorities.

No problems were reported in the survey related to meeting this TR.

TABLE 3.8 Scores for NTMs and POs Reported by Bangladeshi Exporters of Ready-Made Garments to India

Averages

NTMs	NTM restrictiveness score	POs, percent of respondents
Technical requirements		
Restricted use of substances (B22)	1.00	
Labeling requirements (B31)	1.36	C2 (20)
Marking requirements (B32)	1.11	
Average restrictiveness score	1.16	
Conformity assessment measures		
Testing requirement (B82)	1.11	
Certification requirement (B83)	1.17	
Inspection requirement (B84)	1.29	C2 (57), D6 (31)
Average restrictiveness score	1.19	
Average NTM restrictiveness score	1.18	

Note: See annexes 3A, 3B, and 3C for classification of NTMs and POs. NTM = nontariff measure; POs = procedural obstacles. Blank cells (other than for average scores) indicate that exporters reported no problems in meeting the requirements of the particular NTM.

Labeling requirements (B31). There are no mandatory labeling and marking requirements, but voluntary standards have been specified in a draft by the Textiles Department of the Bureau of Indian Standards.[12] According to the draft standards, ready-made garments must satisfy requirements relating to length, width, mass, blend composition, shrink resistance, color-fastness ratings, fire resistance, environmental labeling, and care labeling.

Although the labeling requirements were easy to meet, 20 percent of the respondents felt that the requirements were too detailed.

Marking requirements (B32). Marking requirements for ready-made garments include the manufacturer's name or trademark if any, month and year of manufacture, country of origin, and any other information as required by law.

The survey reported no problems related to meeting the marking requirements.

Testing and certification requirements (B82, B83). Testing and certification are associated with the presence of azo dyes. Testing is performed to check for the presence of azo dyes, and certificates are issued to certify their absence.

Because preshipment certificates issued by BSTI-accredited laboratories are accepted by India, no testing is required at the border at the time of import.

No obstacles were reported in the acceptance of preshipment certificates certifying the absence of azo dyes.

Inspection requirements (B84). Inspection largely consists of customs officials checking the labeling requirements, based on draft standards. Inspection is also performed to check for any physical damage to goods (box 3.3). Of the respondents, 57 percent said that inspection was redundant, and 31 percent stated that they had to make informal payments at the inspection point to obtain clearance for the consignments.

Inferences and Recommendations

The Bangladeshi exporters did not face any problems in acceptance of the test results from NABL-accredited laboratories in Bangladesh. The only problem they faced was related to labeling requirements. Customs officials insist that products should comply with the draft standards set by the Textiles Department. In principle, the voluntary draft standards set by the Bureau of Indian Standards cannot be applied to imports or domestically manufactured goods. Information asymmetry has led to some inefficiencies at the border and to rent seeking. While most firms were able to meet these requirements quite easily, it should be made clear to border inspection agents that such voluntary standards are not part of their inspection duties.

BOX 3.3 Labeling and Packaging Case Study: Ready-Made Garments

Consignments are inspected rigorously, and customs officials insist on labeling and packaging requirements, although they are set by buyers and are not mandatory regulatory requirements. Bribes must be paid to clear consignments if labeling requirements have not been met.

TABLE 3.9 Scores for NTMs and POs Reported by Bangladeshi Exporters of Jute Bags to India

Averages

NTMs	NTM restrictiveness score	POs, percent of respondents
Technical requirements		
Tolerance limits for residues (B21)	1.00	
Restricted use of certain substances (B22)	1.00	
Labeling requirements (B31)	1.55	B1 (25)
Marking requirements (B32)	1.00	A1 (25), C2 (25), D1 (20)
Average restrictiveness score	1.14	
Conformity assessment measures		
Testing requirement (B82)	1.00	
Certification requirement (B83)	1.30	
Inspection requirement (B84)	1.05	C2 (60)
Average restrictiveness score	1.12	
Average NTM restrictiveness score	1.13	

Note: See annexes 3A, 3B, and 3C for classification of NTMs and POs. NTM = nontariff measure; POs = procedural obstacles. Blank cells (other than for average scores) indicate that exporters reported no problems in meeting the requirements of the particular NTM.

JUTE: BANGLADESH TO INDIA

Most of the survey respondents in Bangladesh for jute were in Chandpur, Dhaka, Faridpur, Gazipur, Khulna, Kishorganj, Narshingdhi, Nowapara, and Sithakunda. The main land customs station was at Benapole. Note that the survey was conducted in May–September 2014, prior to the 2017 imposition of antidumping duties on Bangladesh's jute bags exported to India.[13] The focus here, however, is solely on NTMs, and, hence, this subsection does not analyze the issue of antidumping duties.

NTM Restrictiveness, Regulations, and POs

The average ranks for the TRs and CAMs reveal that it is not difficult to meet the regulations. However, labeling requirements were flagged by the exporters as relatively difficult (table 3.9).

Tolerance limits (B21). Under the Jute and Jute Textiles Control Order, products containing jute batching oil in excess of 3 percent by weight should not be permitted in domestic manufacture or imports. Jute batching oil is used in the manufacture of jute bags to make the jute fibers pliable. India accepts preshipment certificates issued by a BSTI-recognized laboratory certifying that the product has permissible limits of jute batching oil.

The survey did not report any problems because the preshipment certificates were accepted by the Indian authorities.

Restricted use of substances (B22). For jute bags, the use of azo dyes is restricted according to the provisions of the Environment (Protection) Act. India accepts preshipment certificates issued by a textile testing laboratory accredited by the Bangladesh Accreditation Board. For jute batching oil, India accepts certificates from a BSTI-accredited laboratory.

No problems were reported because the preshipment certificates were accepted by the Indian authorities.

Testing and certification requirements (B82, B83). No testing is required at the border because preshipment certificates certifying the absence of azo dyes and permissible limits of jute batching oil are accepted by the Indian authorities. Preshipment certificates from laboratories accredited by the requisite authorities is accepted by the Indian authorities.

No problems were reported in the survey related to the acceptance of preshipment certificates.

Labeling requirements (B31). The Office of the Jute Commissioner requires every jute bag to be labeled "Jute Bag Made in Bangladesh." Of the respondents, 25 percent felt that this requirement was put in place to favor domestic manufacturers. Indian importers were reluctant to buy bags with this label because the bags were used to pack goods made in India.

Marking requirements (B32). The Office of the Jute Commissioner requires every imported bale containing raw jute or jute product to be marked "Made in Bangladesh" and include the names and addresses of the importers/traders of jute and jute textile.

About 25 percent of the respondents felt that the marking requirements were redundant; 20 percent felt that the regulation on marking requirements was not clear.

Inspection requirements (B84). Customs inspects the certificates and checks the goods for any physical damage. The survey showed that 60 percent of the respondents felt that the inspection was redundant.

Inferences and Recommendations

The problem faced by the Bangladeshi exporters of jute bags is related to the labeling and marking of jute bags with information on the country of origin.

India could consider revoking this requirement for labeling and marking jute bags because it poses unnecessary problems for exporters and importers. India might instead adopt a regulatory requirement such as the one in the United States, which requires importers to indicate the country of origin of the jute bags on the container (CBP 2004).

PHARMACEUTICALS: INDIA TO NEPAL

The survey for this product was undertaken in Ahmedabad, Hyderabad, and Mumbai in India. The main land customs station that the respondents used for trade in pharmaceutical items with Nepal was Birganj (Nepal)–Raxaul (Bihar, India).

TABLE 3.10 Scores for NTMs and POs Reported by Indian Exporters of Pharmaceuticals to Nepal

Averages

NTMs	NTM restrictiveness score	POs, percent of respondents
Technical requirements		
Authorization requirements(B14)	2.71	C2 (27), C3 (60)
Labeling requirements (B31)	1.52	
Marking requirements (B32)	1.12	
Packaging requirements (B33)	1.23	
TBT regulations on production processes (B41)	2.15	C2 (67), F1 (10)
Product quality or performance requirement (B7)	1.00	
Average restrictiveness score	1.62	
Conformity assessment measure		
Product registration requirement (B81)	2.74	C3 (73)
Testing requirement (B82)	1.00	
Certification requirement (B83)	1.00	
Inspection requirement (B84)	1.00	
Average restrictiveness score	1.44	
Average NTM restrictiveness score	1.53	

Note: See annexes 3A, 3B, and 3C for the classification of NTMs and POs. NTM = nontariff measure; POs = procedural obstacles; TBT = technical barriers to trade. Blank cells (other than for average scores) indicate that exporters reported no problems in meeting the requirements of the particular NTM.

NTM Restrictiveness, Regulations, and POs

The exporters found it more difficult to meet TRs than CAMs because of the complex regulations pertaining to authorization requirements and TBT regulations on production processes (table 3.10).

Authorization requirement (B14). For authorization to export, the exporter must register the company with the DDA, Nepal. For registration, the company must pay NPR 50,000 to the DDA, Nepal.

Of the respondents, 27 percent felt that the requirements were too detailed; 60 percent felt that there were substantial delays in obtaining authorization from the DDA (box 3.4).

Labeling, marking, and packaging requirements (B31, B32, B33). According to the Drug Act 1978, manufacturing includes packaging and labeling. According to the requirements for the registration of the foreign pharmaceutical manufacturer to export their products to Nepal, all GMP regulations of the World Health Organization on product packaging and labeling are applicable. All products should thus be labeled in English. The label on each container should at least include the international nonproprietary name or generic name, the batch number, a dosage form, information on the strength, the name of the manufacturer, the quantity in the container, storage conditions, and expiry date. The weight per carton should not exceed 50 kilograms, and the product should not be mixed with other products in the same carton.

No obstacles were reported related to labeling, marking, and packaging.

TBT regulations on the production process (B41). The GMP guidelines of the World Health Organization must be followed by manufacturers exporting pharmaceutical products to Nepal. To ensure this is addressed, DDA inspectors visit the site factory in India; Indian exporters must pay US$1,500 for such a visit.

Of the respondents, 67 percent felt that the DDA requirements were too detailed. Another 10 percent felt that the fee required for the site visit was too high.

Product quality or performance requirement (B7). The DDA requires all manufacturers exporting to Nepal to follow the GMP guidelines of the World Health Organization for pharmaceutical products.

The survey did not report any problems related to following the World Health Organization guidelines for manufacturing pharmaceuticals.

Product registration requirement (B81). The Drugs Registration Rules, 1981, require product registration of drugs, including imported drugs, before any sale (Nepal, Law Commission 1981). According to the Requirements for Registration of Modern Medicines, under the DDA, the fee levied on product registration is NPR 2,400; an additional fee of NPR 300 must be paid to acquire the import recommendation letter.

In the survey, 73 percent of the exporters reported that there was too much delay in getting products registered with the DDA (see box 3.4).

BOX 3.4 Case Study: Import Requirements for Pharmaceuticals

It is difficult to comply with the requirements set for import authorization and product registration, given that the regulations are strict, and the process for obtaining approvals from several entities is complex (see table B3.4.1). According to the importer, the various documents required from the exporter in India include the up-to-date manufacturing license, list of products, dosage forms intended to be registered, and the latest Good Manufacturing Practice (GMP) internal audit report of the manufacturer. These have to be submitted to the DDA to obtain the authorization. After the documents are submitted to the DDA, the manufacturing company in India can be registered with the DDA. The exporting company will then be audited. Respondents felt that the requirement of registering every individual product separately and renewing the registration yearly is an unnecessary process.

TABLE B3.4.1 Time Taken to Obtain Approvals for Pharmaceutical Exports from India to Nepal

Requirement	Time taken
Registration of the manufacturing company with the DDA	6–12 months
Company audit for manufacturing company by the DDA	1–2 weeks
Product registration for each product with the DDA	4–6 months
Product renewal for each product, each year	2–3 hours

Note: DDA = Department of Drug Administration.

Testing requirement (B82). Prior to the registration of a pharmaceutical product, a test report from any recognized laboratory is required in Nepal (Nepal, Law Commission 1981). Thereafter, the DDA conducts a test of the pharmaceutical product prior to giving permission for registration and sales. The Department of Customs is also entitled to conduct any tests on pharmaceutical raw materials.[14]

No obstacles were reported related to testing.

Certification requirement (B83). Manufacturers of pharmaceutical products must present a certificate issued by the DDA that specifies that the manufacturer (exporter) has followed the GMP of the World Health Organization (Nepal, Law Commission 1981).

No obstacles were reported related to issuing certificates.

Inspection requirement (B84). Section 19 and chapter 17 of the Customs Act 2007 permit physical inspection (visual and physical examination) as required. According to the Drug Act, the DDA is authorized to inspect any product at any time or place during storage, distribution, or sales, to check that the product is safe for public consumption, or whether there is any contravention against any rules and regulations.

No problems related to inspection were reported in the survey.

Inferences and Recommendations

The process for obtaining authorization and product registration is time-consuming, and there are substantial delays. The Nepalese authorities can conduct only a limited number of inspections of manufacturing facilities in a year because the funding is inadequate. They also conduct a detailed inspection of the GMP followed by Indian manufacturing firms, which is time-consuming.

The Nepalese authorities recognize pharmaceutical products produced in countries that are members of the Pharmaceutical Inspection Convention (PIC) and the Pharmaceutical Inspection Co-operation Scheme (PIC Scheme), which, together, are known as the PIC/S. The Nepalese authorities do not conduct any tests of manufacturing facilities or processes associated with products from PIC/S member countries. Because India is not a member of the PIC/S, the authorities in Nepal conduct inspections of manufacturing facilities. The PIC/S is an instrument agreed among countries and pharmaceutical inspection authorities to promote GMP. The aim of the PIC/S is global harmonization of health and regulatory inspection procedures through the establishment of common GMP standards and the provision of training opportunities for inspectors.

Although exporters in India have expressed their view that the Indian Department of Pharmaceuticals should apply for membership in the PIC/S, government officials are concerned about the ability of small and medium manufacturers to upgrade their facilities to meet PIC/S GMP standards. It would be in the interest of the Indian pharmaceutical industry for the Department of Pharmaceuticals to apply for accession to the PIC/S because this would help India not only in seeking global markets, but also in implementing global best practices in the domestic pharmaceutical market.

The following actions are recommended for pharmaceuticals:

- Registration and authorization requirements should be made simpler, more efficient, and less time-consuming.

- India should become a member of the PIC/S. This would allow India to export to Nepal without the need for the DDA Nepal to conduct inspections and tests of Indian manufacturing facilities. It would also help India export to other countries.

- India should apply for the Pre-Accession Procedure under the PIC/S (which precedes the accession procedure). The advantage would be that the procedure involves carrying out a preassessment by an auditor, which would include a gap analysis, after which a recommendation on the readiness of the applicant country's inspectorate to apply for membership is provided. This process would help the Indian government identify the compliance requirements and associated costs.

PHARMACEUTICAL RAW MATERIALS: INDIA TO BANGLADESH

In India, the survey of pharmaceutical raw material exporters was conducted in Ahmedabad, Delhi, and Hyderabad.

NTM Restrictiveness, Regulations, and POs

Indian exporters found it more difficult to meet CAMs than to meet TRs (table 3.11).

Labeling, marking, and packaging (B31, B32, B33). The DGDA Bangladesh requires importers to follow labeling, marking, and packaging requirements according to international standards. No obstacles were reported by the Indian exporters in meeting these requirements.

TBT regulations on production processes and product quality and performance (B41, B7). TBT regulations on production processes and product quality or performance requirements for active pharmaceutical ingredients are maintained following the internationally accepted GMP standards of the World Health Organization guidelines. These rules must be strictly followed in the production of pharmaceutical raw materials if the products are to be accepted as imports by the DGDA and Bangladesh Customs.

Product registration (B81). In the case of product registration requirements, exporter registration with the DGDA is mandatory for block list approval.

In the survey, 67 percent of the exporters felt that there were substantial delays in obtaining approvals.

Testing requirements (B82). Testing at the port by Bangladesh Customs is mandatory. In addition, to ensure the quality and content of the active pharmaceutical ingredients, drug manufacturers in Bangladesh often conduct tests of the raw materials at their production facilities.

In the survey, 67 percent of the exporters felt that there were substantial delays in obtaining test results.

Inspection requirement (B84). Inspection for physical damage or pilferage is carried out by Customs at the port. No POs at inspection were reported by the respondents.

Inference and Recommendation

The only problem perceived by the Indian exporters of pharmaceutical raw materials to Bangladesh was related to delays in product registration by the DGDA.

TABLE 3.11 Scores for NTMs and POs Reported by Indian Exporters of
Pharmaceutical Raw Materials to Bangladesh
Averages

NTMs	Average score	POs, percent of respondents
Technical requirements		
Labeling requirements	1.29	
Packaging	1.67	
TBT regulations on production processes (B41)	1.00	
Product quality or performance requirement (B7)	1.15	
Average restrictiveness score	1.28	
Conformity assessment measures		
Product registration requirement (B81)	1.95	C3 (67)
Testing requirement (B82)	2.00	C3 (67)
Inspection requirement (B84)	1.30	
Average restrictiveness score	1.75	
Average NTM restrictiveness score	1.52	

Note: See annexes 3A, 3B, and 3C for classification of NTMs and POs. NTM = nontariff measure;
POs = procedural obstacles; TBT = technical barriers to trade. Blank cells (other than for average scores) indicate
that exporters reported no problems in meeting the requirements of the particular NTM.

The following action is recommended for pharmaceutical raw materials: the DGDA should take steps to make the procedures for product registration less time-consuming.

Conclusion and Policy Recommendations

Based on a survey of firms, this study assesses NTM restrictiveness confronting exporting firms and identifies the POs faced by exporters in meeting the NTM requirements of the importing country in eight selected products in the context of bilateral trade between Bangladesh–India and India–Nepal. Tea, cardamom, and medicinal and aromatic plants were selected as export items from Nepal to India; processed foods, ready-made garments, and jute bags were selected as export products from Bangladesh to India; pharmaceuticals were selected as the export item from India to Nepal; and pharmaceutical raw materials were selected as the export item from India to Bangladesh. For a deeper understanding of the application of NTMs as perceived by exporters, information received from the field survey was triangulated with an examination of the regulatory framework and consultations with regulators in the three countries.

Based on the analysis, the study suggests possible actions to address the obstacles faced by exporters in meeting the requirements of the NTMs of the partner country markets. A summary of the key regulations governing each product, NTM restrictiveness scores, major obstacles in meeting NTM requirements, key impediments, and key recommendations for each product is provided in annex 3G.

The key recommendations can be grouped under three categories, as follows.

INFORMATION FLOWS

Initiate information campaigns and workshops to reduce information asymmetry.
For example, spread awareness about the need for and procedures relating to PRAs for
agricultural products, including medicinal and aromatic plants, to enable imports of
such products into India. Annex 3F provides a list of relevant items pertaining to Nepal
for which PRAs are needed. Requests for PRAs by exporters in India and importers in
Bangladesh and Nepal could be fast-tracked under SAFTA and bilateral forums. This
would also apply to other SAFTA countries.

***Spread awareness about all available public and private accredited laborato-
ries in India.*** India, as well as partner countries, could spread awareness among exporters, importers, and regulators about all of the available public and private accredited
laboratories in India. There has been historical dependence in India on only one public
laboratory, namely, the Central Food Laboratory in Kolkata. This dependence continues to date because it is not widely known in Bangladesh, India, and Nepal that several laboratories in India now are accredited by the NABL and notified by the FSSAI.
Governments can develop marketing and communication strategies to familiarize traders with the various NABL-accredited and FSSAI-notified laboratories

PROCEDURES AND INFRASTRUCTURE

***Establish a bilateral institutional mechanism to coordinate and expedite the FSSAI's
notification of the partner country laboratories accredited by the NABL.*** It is not well
known among traders and regulatory authorities in Bangladesh, India, and Nepal that
test reports for food products issued by NABL-accredited laboratories in Bangladesh
and Nepal are not accepted by Indian authorities unless these laboratories are also notified by the FSSAI.[15] It is therefore recommended that an institutional mechanism be
established bilaterally between the concerned countries so that recognition by the FSSAI
of NABL-accredited laboratories can be coordinated and expedited. This would help
ensure that food products imported into India are tested only on a random basis and
help catalyze food trade, particularly agricultural trade, among countries in the region.

***Introduce electronic data interchange, risk management systems, and single win-
dows at more border points to enable realization of potential gains from coordination
and efficiency.*** So far, electronic data interchange is operational between India and Nepal
on one corridor along Kolkata to the Nepal border (Jogbani and Raxaul), while coordinated risk management has been introduced at the Bangladesh–India border (Petrapole/
Benapole). Single-window systems at national levels have enabled greater coordination
among agencies, thereby reducing transaction costs for traders. The FSSAI has been
included in the single-window system and has introduced risk profiling to enable the system
to identify high-risk consignments electronically. In general, electronic data interchanges
can enhance risk profiling and are a prerequisite for single-window systems. Thus, if the

goal is to achieve expedited clearance of food imports (with valid exporting-country test certificates recognized by India), electronic data interchange facilities need to be extended to other major land ports, such as Panitanki. Eventually, to realize their efficiency gains fully, national single windows need to be interoperable between countries. Interoperability allows traders to submit all import, export, and transit information required by regulatory agencies through a single electronic gateway. This is a longer-term goal.

Streamline import procedures for pharmaceutical raw materials in Bangladesh and Nepal. Currently, product registration and requisite authorization processes, which are mandatory for pharmaceutical imports, are cumbersome and time-consuming in both countries. The DGDA Bangladesh should work to streamline the process of product registration and reduce the time taken for registering products and obtaining requisite approvals. The pharmaceutical industry in Bangladesh would also benefit from this, given its heavy dependence on imports of pharmaceutical raw materials. Similarly, streamlining the process in Nepal would also benefit the local pharmaceutical industry.

Ensure that regulations and procedures are followed consistently at all border points in India. The study finds that different rules and procedures are applied at different border points. For greater transparency and to reduce arbitrariness and rent seeking, there must be harmonization of rules and regulations across the borders, and all ports should follow the same rules and regulations. This will help speed the crossborder flow of goods. To foster more vibrant crossborder trade, simplification of trade processes and procedures—along with the harmonization of trade transaction data and documents across the borders—is needed.

HARMONIZATION

Become a member of the PIC/S convention (India). India should become a member of the PIC/S convention. The PIC/S is a nonbinding, informal cooperative arrangement among regulatory authorities on the GMP for medicinal products for human or veterinary use. It is open to any authority having a comparable GMP inspection system. Currently, the PIC/S comprises 49 participating authorities from all over the world. It is useful in harmonizing inspection procedures worldwide by promoting the development of common standards in manufacturing and providing training opportunities to inspectors. Because Nepal recognizes PIC/S members and does not conduct testing at the manufacturing facilities of exporting countries that are members of the PIC/S, India and Nepal would benefit if India became a member. Indeed, India's pharmaceutical exports would benefit significantly if India became a member of the PIC/S.

Change the labeling requirement for jute bag imports into India. The requirement by India to have the country of origin labeled on every jute bag and marked on every bale is considered trade restrictive. This problem can be overcome by having the label bear the country of origin on the full load of cargo in the container. This practice is followed in many developed countries, including the United States.

Annex 3A: Classification of Nontariff Measures by Chapter

TABLE 3A.1 Classification of Nontariff Measures, by Chapter

Category	Chapter, measure
Imports: technical measures	A Sanitary and phytosanitary measures
	B Technical barriers to trade
	C Preshipment inspection and other formalities
Imports: nontechnical measures	D Contingent trade-protective measures
	E Nonautomatic licensing, quotas
	F Price-control measures
	G Finance measures
	H Measures affecting competition
	I Trade-related investment measures
	J Distribution restrictions
	K Restrictions on postsale services
	L Subsidies (excluding export subsidies under P7)
	M Government procurement restrictions
	N Intellectual property
	O Rules of origin
Exports	P Export-related measures

Source: UNCTAD 2015.
Note: P7 Export subsidies: Financial contribution by a government or public body, or via government entrustment or direction of a private body (direct or potential direct transfer of funds, for example, grant, loan, equity infusion, guarantee; government revenue foregone; provision of goods or services or purchase of goods; payments to a funding mechanism); or income or price support, which confers a benefit and is contingent in law or in fact upon export performance (whether solely or as one of several conditions), including measures illustrated in annex I of the Agreement on Subsidies and Countervailing Measures and measures described in the Agreement on Agriculture.

Annex 3B: Sanitary and Phytosanitary Measures and Technical Barriers to Trade

TABLE 3B.1 Sanitary and Phytosanitary Measures and Technical Barriers to Trade

Sanitary and phytosanitary measures	Technical barriers to trade
A1 Prohibitions/restrictions of imports for SPS reasons	*B1 Prohibitions/restrictions of imports for objectives set out in the TBT agreement*
Temporary geographic prohibitions for SPS reasons (A11)	Prohibition for TBT reasons (B11)
Geographical restrictions on eligibility (A12)	Authorization requirement for TBT reasons (B14)
Systems approach (A13)	Registration requirement for importers for TBT reasons (B15)
Special authorization requirement for SPS reasons (A14)	
Registration requirements for importers (A15)	
A2 Tolerance limits for residues and restricted use of substances	*B2 Tolerance limits for residues*
Tolerance limits for residues or contamination (A21)	Tolerance limits for residues of or contamination by certain substances (B21)
Restricted use of certain substances (A22)	Restricted use of certain substances (B22)
A3 Labeling, marking, and packaging requirements	*B3 Labeling, marking, and packaging requirements*
Labeling (A31), marking (A32), and packaging (A33)	Labeling requirements (B31), marking requirements (B32)
	Packaging requirements (B33)
A4 Hygienic requirements	*B4 Production or postproduction requirements*
Microbiological criteria for the final product (A41)	TBT regulations on production processes (B41)
Hygienic practices (A42)	TBT regulations on transport and storage (B42)
A5 Treatment for elimination of plant and animal pests and disease-causing organisms in the final product	
Cold/heat treatment, irradiation, and fumigation	
A6 Other requirements on production or postproduction processes	*B6 Product identity requirement*
Plant-growth processes (A61), animal-raising or -catching processes (A62), and food and feed processing (A63)	
Storage and transport conditions (A64)	
	B7 Product quality or performance requirement
A8 Conformity assessment related to SPS	*B8 Conformity assessment related to TBT measures*

table continues next page

TABLE 3B.1 Sanitary and Phytosanitary Measures and Technical Barriers to Trade
(continued)

Sanitary and phytosanitary measures	Technical barriers to trade
Product registration requirement (A81)	Product registration requirement (B81)
Testing requirement (A82), Certification requirement (A83) and inspection requirement (A 84)	Testing requirement (B82)
Traceability requirements (A85) and quarantine requirement (A86)	Certification requirement (B83)
	Inspection requirement (B84)
	Traceability information requirements (origin, processing, and distribution) (B85)
A9 SPS measures, n.e.s.	*B9 TBT measures, n.e.s.*

Source: UNCTAD 2015.
Note: n.e.s. = not elsewhere specified; SPS = sanitary and phytosanitary; TBT = technical barrier to trade.

Annex 3C: Classification of Procedural Obstacles

TABLE 3C.1 Classification of Procedural Obstacles

Chapter	Description
A	*Arbitrary or inconsistent behavior*
A1	Behavior of customs officials or any other government official
A2	With regard to how your product has been classified or valued
A3	The manner in which procedures, regulations, or requirements have been applied
B	*Discriminatory behavior favoring specific producers or suppliers*
B1	Favoring local suppliers or producers in destination markets
B2	Favoring suppliers or producers from other countries
B3	Favoring large (or small) companies in destination markets
C	*Inefficiency or cases of outright obstruction*
C1	Too much documentation or forms to be supplied or completed
C2	Too strict, too detailed, or redundant testing/certification or labeling requirement
C3	Substantial delays in obtaining authorization/approval
C4	Complex clearing mechanism, such as a need to obtain approval from several entities
C5	Short submission deadlines to supply information

table continues next page

TABLE 3C.1 Classification of Procedural Obstacles *(continued)*

Chapter	Description
C6	Outdated procedures, such as lack of automation
C7	Lack of resources, such as understaffing or scarce equipment in destination market
D	*Nontransparent practices*
D1	Inadequate information on laws/regulations/registration
D2	Unannounced change of procedure, regulation, or requirement
D3	No focal point for information
D4	Opaque government bid or reimbursement processes
D5	Opaque dispute resolution process
D6	Request for an informal payment
E	*Legal obstacles*
E1	Lack of enforcement in breaches of patents, copyrights, trademarks, and so forth
E2	Inadequate dispute resolution or appeals mechanisms and processes
E3	Inadequate legal infrastructure
F	*Unusually high fees or charges*
F1	Fees or charges are unusually high (for example, fees for stamp, testing, or other services)

Annex 3D: Harmonized System Codes, Selected Items

TABLE 3D.1 Harmonized System Codes, Selected Items, Bangladesh and Nepal

Country, item	Harmonized system code
Bangladesh	
Jute bags	6305
Ready-made garments	61, 62
Processed foods	1704, 19, 20, 21
Organic chemicals	29
Nepal	
Tea	090240
Cardamom	090830
Medicinal and aromatic plants	121190
Pharmaceutical items	30

Annex 3E: Questionnaire for the NTM Survey: India and Nepal

TABLE 3E.1 Questionnaire, NTM Survey, India and Nepal

Sr. No.					Trade Flow: ☐ Export ☐ Import

Product: HS Code:

Section 1: General information

1.1 Please fill out the following	
Name of the firm	
Name of the respondent and designation	
Address of firm	
Location	

1.2 Type of respondent (Please tick the option applicable to you.)	
Exporter (trader)	Importer (trader)
Exporter + manufacturer	Importer + manufacturer
Freight forwarder	Clearing agent
Freight forwarder + clearing agent	
Others (please specify)	

1.3 Profile for the year 2012–13FY						
Please answer the following (trade with India):						
(unit in NR Lakh)		World	India		World	India
Value of exports	☐ 2009–10 ☐ 2012–13			☐ 2012/13 FY		
Value of imports	☐ 2009–10 ☐ 2012/13 FY:			☐ 2012/13 FY		
Total turnover[a]	☐ 2009–10			☐ 2012/13 FY		

a. Firm's annual sales turnover.

1.4 List of trading partners in India

1.5	Product traded with India	2012–13	
		Exports	Imports
	Number of commodities traded		
	List of commodities traded, name and HS code[a]	Exports (HS Code)	Imports (HS Code)
	Commodity 1—(Name)[b]		
	Commodity 2—(Name)		
	Commodity 3—(Name)		
	Commodity 4—(Name)		
	Commodity 5—(Name)		
	Commodity 6—(Name)		

Note: HS = Harmonized System.
a. HS Codes to be added by investigator.
b. Selected commodity.

1.6	Modes of transport for the selected product							
	Exports				Imports			
	Mode	Commodity	Please tick the option applicable	Proportion, %	Mode	Commodity	Please tick the option applicable	Proportion, %
	Sea				Sea			
	Air				Air			
	Rail				Rail			
	Road				Road			
	IWT				IWT			

Note: IWT = Inland Waterway Transport.

1.7 List of land customs stations/border check-post used for trading with India for the selected product

	Land customs station 1	Land customs station 2	Land customs station 3	Land customs station 4
Export				
Import				

Section 2: Non-tariff measures[a]

For products traded between India/Nepal, please rank the difficulty of meeting the standard for imports: 1 (very easy); 2 (easy); 3 (average); 4 (difficult); 5 (very difficult).

2.1a. SPS (Agricultural Commodities Standards) (A1)

Regulations	Yes/no	Rank difficulty 1 easy— 5 difficult	Procedural obstacles (explain in detail)
A1: Prohibitions/restrictions of imports for SPS reasons			
Temporary geographic prohibitions for SPS reasons (A11)			
Geographical restrictions on eligibility (A12)			
Systems approach (A13)			
Special authorization requirement, SPS (A14)			
Registration requirements, importers (A15)			
A2: Tolerance limits for residues and restrictive use of substance			
Tolerance limits for residues of or contamination by certain (nonmicrobiological) substances (A21)			
Restricted use of certain substances in foods and feeds and their contact (A22)			
A3: Labeling, marking, and packaging requirements			
Labeling (A31)			
Marking (A32)			
Packaging (A33)			
A4: Hygienic requirements			
Microbiological criteria, final product (A41)			
Hygienic practices during production (A42)			
A5: Treatment to eliminate plant and animal pests and disease-causing organisms in the final product			
Cold/heat treatment (A51)			
Irradiation (A52)			
Fumigation (A53)			
A6: Other requirements on production or postproduction processes			
Plant-growth processes (A61)			
Animal-raising or -catching processes (A62)			
Food and feed processing (A63)			
Storage and transport conditions (A64)			
A8: Conformity assessment related to SPS			
Product registration requirement (A81)			
Testing requirement (A82)			
Certification requirement (A83)			
Inspection requirement (A84)			
Traceability requirements (A85) (origin, processing, and distribution)			
Quarantine requirement (A86)			
Conformity assessment related to SPS, n.e.s. (A89)			

2.1b. Other measures not specified elsewhere

a. Surveyors will bear in mind that this information pertains specifically to (a) the product selected, and (b) the experience of trading with India and Nepal.

2.1c. Have you encountered a situation in which you have been asked to meet regulatory requirements that are not specified in the official procedures? If yes, please explain.

☐ Yes ☐ No

2.2a. TBT (Manufactured Goods)—Standards

	Yes/no	Rank difficulty 1 easy— 5 difficult	Procedural obstacles (explain in detail)
B1: Prohibitions/restrictions of imports for objectives set out in the TBT agreement			
Prohibition for TBT reasons (B11)			
Authorization requirement, TBT reasons (B14)			
Registration requirement for importers for TBT reasons (B15)			
B2: Tolerance limits for residues and restrictive use of substances			
Tolerance limits for residues of or contamination by certain substances (B21)			
Restricted use of certain substances (B22)			
B3: Labeling, marking, and packaging requirements			
Labeling requirements (B31)			
Marking requirements (B32)			
Packaging requirements (B33)			
B4: Production or postproduction requirements			
TBT regulations on production processes (B41)			
TBT regulations, transport and storage (B42)			
Product identity requirement (B6)			
Product quality or performance requirement (B7)			
B8: Conformity assessment related to TBT measures			
Product registration requirement (B81)			
Testing requirement (B82)			
Certification requirement (B83)			
Inspection requirement (B84)			
Traceability information requirements (origin, processing, and distribution) (B85)			
Conformity assessment related to TBT, n.e.s. (B89)			

2.2b. Measures not elsewhere specified

2.2c Have you encountered a situation in which you have been asked to meet regulatory requirements that are not specified in the official procedures? If yes, please explain.

☐ Yes   ☐ No

Note: NTM = nontariff measures; SPS = sanitary and phytosanitary standards; TBT = technical barriers to trade.

Annex 3F: Plant Material in Nepal Requiring Pest Risk Analysis

TABLE 3F.1 Plant Material Requiring Pest Risk Analysis, Nepal

Number	Botanical name	Local name
1	Aconitum palmatum	Bikhma
2	Aconitum heterophyllum	Atees
3	Aconitum spicatum	Bikh
4	Acacia rugata	Shikakai
5	Aegle marmelos	Bael
6	Amomum subulatum	Badi elaichi
7	Andrographics paniculata	Kalmegh
8	Asparagus racmoscus	Satawar
9	Bacopa moniersi	Pakhanved
10	Berginia ciliate	Jal bramhi
11	Cassia occidentalis	Kasondi
12	Chlorophytum esculentum	Seta musli
13	Coleus barbatus	Sajaino, Bajradanti
14	Corydalis gevaniana	Bhootkesh
15	Curculigo orchoides	Kalo musli
16	Delphinium himalayai	Nirmasi
17	Elaeocarpus sphaericus	Rudrasksha
18	Emblica officianalis	Amla
19	Embelia ribes	Via-vidang
20	Ephedra gerardiana	Somlata
21	Hibiscus abelmoschus	Lata kasturi
22	Hollarhena Antidysentrica (seeds)	Inderjau
23	Jurinea dolomaicea	Dhoopjadi
24	Lycipodium clavatum (powder)	Negbeli dhulo

table continues next page

TABLE 3F.1 Plant Material Requiring Pest Risk Analysis, Nepal *(continued)*

Number	Botanical name	Local name
25	Morchella esculenta	Gucchi chyau
26	Mucuna pruriens (seeds)	Kauso, Kauncha beej
27	Nardostachys grandiflora	Jatamnsi
28	Orchis obcordata	Kaladana, Salammishri
29	Otochillus porrectus	Jiwanti
30	Paris polyphylla	Satuwa
31	Phyllanthus niruri	Bhumi amala
32	Podophyllum hexndrum	Laghupatra
33	Polypodium vulgare	Bisfez
34	Panaxpseudo gingseng	Banmula
35	Parmelia nepalense	Chharila
36	Rheum australe (root)	Padamchal, dolu
37	Rheum australe (leaf stalk)	Amalaved
38	Rhododndrom anthopogon	Sunpati
39	Sida cordifolia	Bala
40	Swertia aspera	Chiraita
41	Taraxum officinale	Tukiphool
42	Terminalia arjuna	Arjun
43	Terminali belerica	Barro
44	Terminalia chebula	Harro
45	Tribulus terrestris	Gokharu
46	Trichosanthes palmata	Indrayani
47	Woodfordia fruiticosa (flower)	Dhawa phool
48	Allium wallichii	Ban lahsun
49	Bassia Butyracea	Bhorlapat
50	Bauhinia Aristata	Bhorla bokra
51	Betula utilis	Bhoj patra
52	Cinnamomum ceciododaphne	Sugandha kokila
53	Cordyceps sinensis	Yarsa gumba
54	Entada phaseoloides	Pangra/pangro
55	Juglans regia	Okhar
56	Myrica esculenta	Kaiphal
57	Piper Lingum	Kakara singhi
58	Polypodium vulgare	Bisfez
59	Rauvolfia serpentina	Carpaghanda
60	Smilax aspera	Chobchini
61	Tinospora cordifolia	Gurjo

Annex 3G: Summary of NTM Findings

TABLE 3G.1 Exports of Tea from Nepal to India

Regulation	Measure	Rank	Procedural obstacles, percent of respondents	Regulatory impediment	Recommendations
FSS Act	Tolerance limit	3.32	C2 (56)	Lack of coordination between regulatory agencies	Introduce electronic data interchange and risk management at border land customs stations
FSS Act	Labeling	2.60	F1 (8)	Delay in testing and certification	
FSS Act, Customs Act	Testing	4.04	A1 (12), A3 (56), C2 (44), C3 (8), F1 (8)	Testing and certification done only by public laboratories	Spread awareness on FSSAI-notified NABL-accredited private and public laboratories in India
FSS Act	Certification	4.16	C2 (80), C3 (68)	Different testing methods were	FSSAI should notify NABL-accredited laboratories in Nepal
Customs Act	Inspection	3.32	A1 (24), A3 (16), D6 (8)	applied at different ports	The same rules should apply to all ports

Note: FSS = food safety standard.

TABLE 3G.2 Exports of Cardamom from Nepal to India

Regulation	Measure	Rank	Procedural obstacles, percent of respondents	Regulatory impediment	Recommendation
FSS Act	Tolerance limit	1.0	nil	Lack of coordination between regulatory agencies	Introduce electronic data interchange and risk management at border land customs stations
FSSAI/ PQO/ Customs	Testing	3.9	A3 (10), C2 (100)	Delay in testing and certification	Spread awareness on FSSAI-notified NABL-accredited private and public laboratories in India
FSSAI/PQ Order	Certification	3.5	A1 (10), C2 (50)	Testing and certification done only by public laboratories	FSSAI should notify NABL-accredited laboratories in Nepal
Customs Act	Inspection	3.0	C3 (20), D6 (70)	Different testing methods were	
PQ Order	Quarantine	1.2	F1 (10)	applied at different ports	Enforcement of same rules at all ports

Note: FSS = food safety standard; FSSAI = Food and Safety Standards Authority of India; NABL = National Accreditation Board for Testing and Calibration Laboratories; PQO = plant quarantine order.

TABLE 3G.3 Exports of Medicinal and Aromatic Plants from Nepal to India

Regulation	Measure	Rank	Procedural obstacles, percent of respondents	Regulatory impediment	Recommendation
PQ Order	Testing	1.88		Large informal trade in items not on permissible list of imports	Increase awareness on regulatory requirements under PQO
PQO/ Customs Act	Certification	1.88		Lack of information on request procedure to	Encourage importers and exporters to make a demand for PRA
Custom Act	Inspection	3.34	A1 (51), A3 (34), D6 (49)	include more items under permissible imports list.	for items not on the permissible list
PQ Order	Quarantine	1.51		Lack of information on PRA requirement for items not included in Schedule VII of PQO	Bilateral or SAFTA mechanism should be used for rapid risk clearance of items for which a PRA is requested

Note: NABL = National Accreditation Board for Testing and Calibration Laboratories; PQO = plant quarantine order; SAFTA = South Asian Free Trade Area. Blank cells indicate that exporters reported no problems in meeting the requirements of the particular NTM.

TABLE 3G.4 Exports of Processed Food from Bangladesh to India

Regulation	Measure	Rank	Procedural obstacles, percent of respondents	Regulatory impediment	Recommendation
FSS Act	Tolerance limit	1.46		Codex recognized additive not recognized by India	Internationally recognized additive could be added to the list of permissible additives
FSS Act	Restricted use of substances	1.41	C2 (58)	No testing facility at border	
FSS Act	Labeling	1.58	A1 (46), C2 (33)	Products certified by NABL-accredited labs in Bangladesh undergo testing of every consignment	Introduce electronic data interchange and risk management at border land customs stations
FSS Act	Marking	1.29			
FSS Act	Packaging	1.88			
FSS Act	Microbiological criteria	1.88	C2 (13)	Inconsistent regulation at different ports	Spread awareness on FSSAI-notified NABL-accredited private and public laboratories in India
FSS Act	Testing	2.54	A1 (42), C2 (54), C3 (42), D2 (21), F (4)	Testing and certification done only by one public laboratory	FSSAI should notify NABL-accredited laboratories in Nepal
FSS Act	Certification	2.00			Enforcement of same rules at all ports
Customs Act	Inspection	1.89	C2 (13), D6 (21)		

Note: FSS = food safety standard; FSSAI = Food and Safety Standards Authority of India; NABL = National Accreditation Board for Testing and Calibration Laboratories. Blank cells indicate that exporters reported no problems in meeting the requirements of the particular NTM.

TABLE 3G.5 Exports of Ready-Made Garments from Bangladesh to India

Regulation	Measure	Rank	Procedural obstacles, percent of respondents	Regulatory impediment	Recommendation
Environment Protection Act/Foreign Trade Act)	Restricted use of substances	1.00		Labeling requirements are checked rigorously although these are private standards	Better information on regulatory requirements
	Labeling	1.36	C2 (20)		
Draft Regulation	Marking	1.11			
	Testing	1.11			
	Certification	1.17			
	Inspection	1.29	C2 (57), D6 (31)		

Note: Blank cells indicate that exporters reported no problems in meeting the requirements of the particular NTM.

TABLE 3G.6 Exports of Jute Bags from Bangladesh to India

Regulation	Measure	Rank	Procedural obstacles, percent of respondents	Regulatory impediment	Recommendation
	Tolerance limit	1.00		Requirement to label jute bags with country of origin was found to be restrictive	Labeling requirement of country of origin on bags can be replaced with the label on the container
	Restricted use of substances	1.00	B1 (25)		
	Labeling	1.55	A1 (25), C2 (25), D1 (20)	Requirement for marking jute bales containing jute bags was found to be restrictive	
	Marking	1.00			
	Testing	1.00			
	Certification	1.30	C2 (60)		
	Inspection	1.05			

Note: Blank cells indicate that exporters reported no problems in meeting the requirements of the particular NTM.

TABLE 3G.7 Exports of Pharmaceuticals from India to Nepal

Regulation	Measure	Rank	Procedural obstacles, percent of respondents	Regulatory impediment	Recommendation
Drug Act (1978)	Authorization	2.71	C2 (27), C3 (60)	Delays in approvals Limited funds for audit Rigorous system in place because India is not a member of PIC/S	Registration and authorization requirements should be made simpler, more efficient, and less time consuming in Nepal India should become a member of PIC/S
	Labeling	1.52			
	Marking	1.12			
	Packaging	1.23			
	TBT regulations on production processes	2.15	C2 (67), F1 (10)		
	Product-quality requirement	1.00			
	Product registration	2.74	C3 (73)		
	Testing	1.00			
	Inspection	1.00			

Note: PIC/S = Pharmaceutical Inspection Convention and Pharmaceutical Inspection Co-operation Scheme; TBT = technical barriers to trade. Blank cells indicate that exporters reported no problems in meeting the requirements of the particular NTM.

TABLE 3G.8 Exports of Pharmaceutical Raw Materials from India to Bangladesh

Regulation	Measure	Rank	Procedural obstacles, percent of respondents	Regulatory impediment	Recommendation
Drug Act (1940)	Labeling	1.29	C3 (67), F1 (13)	Delays in approvals from DGDA for product registration	DGDA should take steps to make the procedures for product registration less time consuming
	Packaging	1.67	—		
	TBT regulations on production processes	1.00			
	Product-quality requirement	1.15	—		
	Product registration	1.95	C3 (67)		
	Testing	2.00	C3 (67)		
	Inspection	1.30			

Note: DGDA = Directorate General of Drug Administration; TBT = technical barriers to trade. Blank cells indicate that exporters reported no problems in meeting the requirements of the particular NTM.

Notes

1. At the time of the survey in 2014, jute bags were one of the major export items from Bangladesh to India. However, in January 2017, India imposed antidumping duties on jute bags exported by Bangladesh, which significantly reduced Bangladesh's jute bag exports to India.

2. Bangladesh, India, and Nepal have mandated export regulations. The countrywise regulations discussed here are not exhaustive because the study considers the respective trade flows (import or export) for the selected commodities.

3. In April 2017, FSSAI issued a notification authorizing the BSTI to issue certificates of test analysis for 21 food products. This means that BSTI certificates are now recognized for the import of these food products into India, which will now be subjected to only random testing if the consignment is accompanied by a BSTI certificate. The survey for this study was conducted prior to the notification. See "Orders and Guidelines on Imports of Food Articles," Food Safety and Standards Authority of India, New Delhi, http://fssai.gov.in/home/imports /order-guidelines.html.

4. Chapter "A" covers SPS measures that are applied to protect human or animal life from risks arising from additives, contaminants, toxins, or disease-causing organisms in their food; to protect human life from plant- or animal-carried diseases; to protect animal or plant life from pests, diseases, or disease-causing organisms; to prevent or limit other damage to a country from the entry, establishment, or spread of pests; and to protect biodiversity. See annex 3B for descriptions of the NTM classification for SPS and TBT measures and annex 3C for descriptions of POs.

5. The high-risk items are infant formula, milk powder, condensed milk, infant milk food, milk cereal–based weaning foods, cocoa butter, meat and meat products, fish and fish products, egg and egg products, and fats except edible vegetable oil.

6. Chapter "B" includes TBT measures relating to technical regulations as well as procedures for the assessment of conformity with technical regulations and standards, excluding measures covered by the SPS agreement.

7. High-risk items include edible oils and fats, infant formula, pulses and pulse products, food dyes, cereals and cereal products, food additives, milk powders, natural mineral water, condensed milk, packaged drinking water, infant milk food, tea and coffee, milk cereal–based weaning foods, and cocoa butter.

8. A standard is vertical if it covers all regulations relating to a product or a specific category of products. As of April 2016, the singe window operationalized by Customs incorporates a risk module on food products. Single windows are operational at all ports that are on the electronic data interchange system.

9. These products include meat and meat products, fish and fish products, egg and egg products, milk powders, condensed milk, milk cereal–based weaning foods, infant milk food, infant formula, fats in any form except edible vegetable oil, and cocoa butter equivalent or substitute. See "FAQs on Imports," Food Safety and Standards Authority of India, New Delhi, http://www.fssai.gov.in/home/imports/FAQs-on-Imports.html.

10. Random checks would reduce the number of consignments requiring testing to only 5–10 percent of total import consignments.

11. In April 2017, the FSSAI authorized the BSTI to issue test analysis certificates for 21 food products.

12. See "Draft Indian Standard: Textiles, Requirements for Labeling and Marking of Consumer Textiles, Specification," Bureau of Indian Standards, New Delhi, http://www.bis.org.in/sf /txd/TX31(900).pdf.

13. Antidumping duties were imposed on jute bags exported by Bangladesh in January 2017, with a subsequent amendment in April 2017, based on a petition filed by the Indian Jute Mills Association, followed by an antidumping investigation by the government of India. See "Final Findings," Directorate General of Anti-Dumping and Allied Duties, Department of Commerce, Ministry of Commerce and Industry, New Delhi, http://www.dgtr.gov.in /sites/default/files/Jute_FF_NCV_20.10.16.pdf. For the amended notification, see the website of the Central Board of Indirect Taxes and Customs, India, at http://www.cbec.gov.in /resources/htdocs-cbec/customs/cs-act/notifications/notfns-2017/cs-add2017/csadd11 -2017.pdf.

14. See "Frequently Asked Questions (FAQs)," Department of Customs, Ministry of Finance, Kathmandu, Nepal, http://www.customs.gov.np/en/faq.html.

15. In April 2017, the FSSAI authorized the BSTI to issue certificates of test analyses on 21 food products. See "Orders and Guidelines on Imports of Food Articles," Food Safety and Standards Authority of India, New Delhi, http://fssai.gov.in/home/imports/order-guidelines.html

References

Bangladesh, MinLaw. 1940. "The Drugs Act, 1940 (Act No. XXIII of 1940)." Legislative and Parliamentary Affairs Division, Ministry of Law, Justice, and Parliamentary Affairs, Dhaka. http://bdlaws.minlaw.gov.bd/pdf_part.php?id=188.

———. 1985. "The Bangladesh Standards and Testing Institution Ordinance, 1985 (Ordinance No. XXXVII of 1985)." Legislative and Parliamentary Affairs Division, Ministry of Law, Justice, and Parliamentary Affairs, Dhaka. http://bdlaws.minlaw.gov.bd/pdf_part.php?id=689.

CBEC (Central Board of Excise and Customs). 1962. *Customs Act, 1962.* CBEC, Department of Revenue, Ministry of Finance, New Delhi. http://www.cbec.gov.in/htdocs-cbec/customs /cs-acts-botm#.

CBP (U.S. Customs and Border Protection). 2004, "Marking of Country of Origin on U.S. Imports: Acceptable Terminology and Methods for Marking." CBP Publication 0000-0539 (December), Special Classification and Marking Branch, Office of Regulations and Rulings, CBP, Washington, DC. https://www.ams.usda.gov/sites/default/files/media/CBP%20Markings%20 Document%20on%20Imports.pdf.

India, DAC&FW (Department of Agriculture Cooperation and Farmers Welfare). 2003. *Plant Quarantine (Regulation of Import into India) Order, 2003.* November 18. New Delhi: DAC&FW, Ministry of Agriculture and Farmers Welfare. http://plantquarantineindia.nic.in /pqispub/pdffiles/PQorder2015.pdf.

India, Department of Commerce. 1963. "The Export (Inspection and Quality Control) Act, 1963 (No. 22 of 1963)." August 24, Department of Commerce, Ministry of Commerce and Industry, New Delhi. http://www.eicindia.gov.in/Knowledge-Repository/Legal/act-rules1963-1964.pdf.

India, Ministry of Law and Justice. 2010. "Foreign Trade (Development and Regulation) Amendment Act, 2010." *Gazette of India* 33 (August 20), New Delhi. http://dgft.gov.in /exim/2000/Foreign_Trade_(Development_&_Regulations)_Amendment_Act,_2010.pdf.

India, Ministry of Textiles. 1987. "The Jute Packaging Materials (Compulsory Use in Packing Commodities) Act, 1987 No. 10 of 1987." *Gazette of India* 13 (May 11), New Delhi. http:// www.jutecomm.gov.in/acts1.htm.

———. 2000. "Jute and Jute Textiles Control Order of 19th April, 2000." *Gazette of India* 276 (April 19), New Delhi. http://www.jutecomm.gov.in/orders1.htm.

India, MoEF&CC (Ministry of Environment, Forest, and Climate Change). 1986. "Environment (Protection) Act, 1986: No. 29 of 1986." May 23, MoEF&CC, New Delhi. http://envfor.nic.in /legis/env/env1.html.

India, MOHFW (Ministry of Health and Family Welfare). 2011a. *Food Safety and Standards (Food Products Standards and Food Additives) Regulations, 2011.* August 1. New Delhi: MOHFW. http://www.old.fssai.gov.in/Portals/0/Pdf/Food%20safety%20and%20standards% 20(Food%20product%20standards%20and%20Food%20Additives)%20regulation,%202011 .pdf.

———. 2011b. "Food Safety and Standards (Contaminants, Toxins, and Residues) Regulations, 2011." August 1, MOHFW, New Delhi. http://www.old.fssai.gov.in/Portals/0/Pdf/Food% 20safety%20and%20standards%20(contaminats,%20toxins%20and%20residues)%20 regulation,%202011.pdf.

———. 2011c. "Food Safety and Standards (Packaging and Labeling) Regulations, 2011." August 1, MOHFW, New Delhi. http://www.old.fssai.gov.in/Portals/0/Pdf/Food%20Safety%20and%20 standards%20(Packaging%20and%20Labelling)%20regulation,%202011.pdf.

———. 2011d. "Food Safety and Standards (Laboratory and Sample Analysis) Regulations, 2011." August 1, MOHFW, New Delhi. http://www.old.fssai.gov.in/Portals/0/Pdf/Food%20Safety%20 and%20Standards%20(Laboratory%20and%20sampling%20analysis)%20regulation,%20 2011%20(.pdf.

India, Parliament. 2006. "The Food Safety and Standards Act, 2006: Act No. 34 of 2006." August 23, Ministry of Health and Family Welfare, New Delhi. http://lawmin.nic.in/ld/P-ACT/2006 /The%20Food%20Safety%20and%20Standards%20Act,%202006.pdf.

ITC (International Trade Centre). 2011. "Sri Lanka: Company Perspectives." Document MAR-11-207.E, International Trade Centre Series on Non-Tariff Measures, ITC, Geneva.

———. 2012. "Malawi: Company Perspectives." Document MAR-12-222.E, International Trade Centre Series on Non-Tariff Measures, ITC, Geneva.

———. 2014. "Kenya: Company Perspective." Document MAR-14-248.E, International Trade Centre Series on Non-Tariff Measures, ITC, Geneva.

Nepal, Law Commission. 1980. "Nepal Standards (Certification Mark) Act, 2037 (1980)." September 11, Law Commission, Kathmandu. http://www.lawcommission.gov.np/en /documents/2015/08/nepal-standards-certification-mark-act-2037-1980.pdf.

———. 1981. "Drugs Registration Rules, 2038 (1981)." August 3, Law Commission, Kathmandu. http://apps.who.int/medicinedocs/documents/s18830en/s18830en.pdf.

Nepal, National Parliament. 1978. "Drug Act, 2035 (1978)." October 25, Department of Drug Administration, Kathmandu. http://apps.who.int/medicinedocs/documents/s18829en /s18829en.pdf.

UNCTAD (United Nations Conference on Trade and Development). 2010. *Non-Tariff Measures: Evidence from Selected Developing Countries and Future Research Agenda; Developing Countries in International Trade Studies.* Report UNCTAD/DITC/TAB/2009/3. Geneva: UNCTAD.

———. 2015. "An International Classification of Non-Tariff Measures: 2012 Version." Document UNCTAD/DITC/TAB/2012/2/Rev.1, UNCTAD, Geneva.

WTO (World Trade Organization). 2012. *World Trade Report, Trade and Public Policies: A Closer Look at Non-Tariff Measures in the 21st Century.* Geneva: WTO.

CHAPTER 4

Reducing Connectivity Costs: Air Travel Liberalization between India and Sri Lanka

SANJAY KATHURIA, MAURO BOFFA, NADEEM RIZWAN,
RAVEEN EKANAYAKE, VISVANATHAN SUBRAMANIAM, AND JANAKA WIJAYASIRI

Introduction

The commercial aviation market between India and Sri Lanka has become progressively more integrated with each modification to the first air services agreement (ASA) signed by India and Sri Lanka in 1948. Both countries were committed to opening their civil aviation markets progressively to facilitate travel, thereby encouraging firm competition, easing logistics, and stimulating trade. The beneficial impact of air services liberalization can be traced from the early amendments in the 1990s to the major amendment of the ASA in 2003 and, further, to the major liberalization push in 2011.

The objective of this chapter is to survey the evolution of the commercial aviation market between India and Sri Lanka and draw lessons for South Asia. On the qualitative side, the study looks at the historical development of the ASA between India and Sri Lanka, focusing on how successive amendments made the agreement more open. The chapter also compares the agreement with similar ASAs around the world. The historical perspective is complemented with information obtained through in-depth, face-to-face interviews with key stakeholders in India and Sri Lanka. The stakeholders included senior representatives of the Civil Aviation Authority of Sri Lanka, former members of the Sri Lankan air services negotiation team, senior representatives of various airlines operating between India and Sri Lanka, freight forwarders, and reputable travel agents. The face-to-face interviews were conducted in March and April 2015, with updates in 2017, and helped frame the background and highlight the binding constraints in the aviation market; they also underscored the importance of persistence with respect to the key goals of liberalization. On the quantitative side, the study uses data from the Data In, Intelligence Out (DIIO) database for econometric analysis based on a difference in differences approach to assess the impact of the 2011 amendment to the ASA on air connectivity between the two countries.

The study finds that a substantial part of the improvement in air connectivity between India and Sri Lanka post-2011 in the greater number of flights per week and in the available seats per week can be attributed to the amendment. The 2011 reforms translated into 16 more flights and 2,442 more seats a week. Both the 2003 and 2011 reforms also had positive impacts on competition and pricing. The impacts could have been deeper; however, structural weaknesses constrained the ability of the domestic airlines in the two countries to supply more air services on routes between India and Sri Lanka, particularly in the face of competing demand for air services to other global destinations. Nonetheless, the reforms had a significant impact on bilateral air services, which grew rapidly in number of flights and seat capacity over 2004–17 and even more rapidly over 2010–17 after the end of the civil war in Sri Lanka.

The reforms likewise stimulated cargo volumes, but this growth was less pronounced and robust compared with the growth in passenger traffic. The economic impact of air services liberalization reached far beyond the aviation industry because improved air connectivity facilitated more people-to-people contacts and enhanced the scope for trade, investment, and tourism links to be forged and deepened. The tourism industry benefited in both countries, but even more in the case of Sri Lanka. India had become the largest source of foreign tourists to Sri Lanka by 2005, enabling the Sri Lankan tourism industry to weather a turbulent recession. The flow of Sri Lankan tourists to India also continued to grow steadily.

The rest of the chapter is structured as follows. The next section reviews the types of ASAs in force around the world and the development of the ASA between India and Sri Lanka. The subsequent section evaluates the status of regional air connectivity in South Asia and describes the civil aviation markets in India and Sri Lanka. The section thereafter assesses the impacts of the 2003 and 2011 amendments to the bilateral ASA on total traffic between the two countries. The penultimate section discusses the impacts of air services liberalization on market composition and competition. The final section summarizes the findings and suggests some policy options.

Air Services Agreements

AIR SERVICES AGREEMENTS AROUND THE WORLD

The International Civil Aviation Organization defines air connectivity as an indicator of a network's concentration and its ability to move passengers from their origin to their destination seamlessly (ICAO 2013). Enhancing air connectivity is often seen as a vital component of a broader strategy to unleash a country's economic growth potential. In addition to its direct, indirect, and induced impacts on aggregate output, the commercial aviation industry has a much wider catalytic (spin-off) impact on the economy (Morphet and Bottini 2014). Air connectivity is an infrastructural asset. It allows business travelers to meet existing and new customers, thereby expanding markets and generating economies of scale and scope. It opens opportunities for businesses to access the best sources of supply around the world for high-value added materials, components, skills, and ideas (ICAO 2012).

Although the benefits of air connectivity are clear, public policy and regulation can work to facilitate or hinder air connectivity. Traditionally, the aviation industry has been highly regulated, dominated by national flag carriers and state-owned airports. Since World War II, air services between countries have operated under the terms of bilateral ASAs negotiated between countries. The commercial rights of airlines on international routes are governed by a complex web of more than 10,000 bilateral ASAs. ASAs regulate a wide range of conditions related to the provision of international air services (Fu, Oum, and Zhang 2010). Bilateral ASAs are structured around provisions that grant partial or total access to freedoms of the air (box 4.1).

BOX 4.1 Freedoms of the Air

The freedoms of the air were formulated in 1944 at an international gathering held in Chicago (known as the Chicago Convention) to establish uniformity in world air commerce. The freedoms are defined as follows:

1. *First freedom:* The right or privilege of an airline from country A to fly across the territory of country B without landing.

2. *Second freedom:* The right or privilege of an airline from country A to land for nontraffic purposes, such as refueling (commonly referred to as a technical stop), in another country B.

3. *Third freedom:* The right or privilege of an airline from country A to deliver revenue passengers or cargo from its home country to country B.

4. *Fourth freedom:* The right or privilege of an airline from country A to carry passengers or cargo from another country B to its home country.

5. *Fifth freedom:* The right or privilege of an airline from country A to take passengers or cargo from its home country, deposit them at destinations in country B, and then pick up and carry passengers or cargo to destinations in other countries C. (This freedom is sometimes referred to as beyond rights.)

6. *Sixth freedom:* The right or privilege of an airline from country A to carry passengers or cargo between two foreign countries (B and C), provided the aircraft touches down in the airline's home country. (This freedom is a combination of the third and fourth freedoms.)

7. *Seventh freedom:* The right or privilege of an airline from country A to carry on flights that originate in a country B, bypass its home country, and deposit the passengers or cargo at another international destination C.

> **BOX 4.1 Freedoms of the Air** *(continued)*
>
> 8. *Eighth freedom:* The right or privilege of an airline from country A to carry passengers or cargo from one point in the territory of a country B to another point within the same country on a flight that originates in the airline's home country A. (This freedom is also known as cabotage and is extremely rare outside Europe.)
>
> 9. *Ninth freedom:* The right or privilege of an airline from county A to originate a flight in a foreign country B and carry passengers or cargo from one point to another within that country B. (This freedom is also known as stand-alone cabotage. It differs from the aviation definition of true cabotage in that it does not connect flights to the home country.)
>
> *Source:* Based on ICAO 2004.

Bilateral ASAs continue to be the instrument of choice for the liberalization of international air services in most countries. More than 1,000 bilateral ASAs (including amendments and memorandums of understanding [MOUs]) have been concluded over the past decade; a majority of the agreements and amendments has involved some form of liberalized arrangements, such as expanded traffic rights (covering the third, fourth, and, in some cases, fifth freedoms of the air), no limitations on capacity, a free-pricing regime, and broadened criteria of airline ownership and control (ICAO 2016). As the airline business has evolved, some of the most recent bilateral ASAs have grown to encompass computer reservation systems, airline code-sharing, leasing of aircraft, and intermodal transport. A notable development is the considerable expansion in the number of bilateral open skies agreements (OSAs) (Fu, Oum, and Zhang 2010).

In addition to bilateral ASAs, most countries have specific rules on foreign ownership of operating airlines. Thus, the development of international air services has been as much a function of government policy as of economic and commercial considerations (InterVISTAS-EU 2009).

Since 1979, the United States has actively pursued OSAs with other countries; to date, the United States has signed more than 100 OSAs. These agreements are seen as the most liberal form of ASAs. Although there is no single accepted definition of open skies, such agreements create a liberal aviation market between the two signatory nations. They allow any number of airlines from either country and unlimited rights to fly between any city pair involving the two countries, without significant restrictions on capacity, frequency, or price. Typically, they also include traffic rights up to the fifth freedom of the air. They permit cooperative marketing arrangements, such as code-sharing, and liberal all-cargo operations. The open skies policy rejects the traditional practice of highly restrictive ASAs protecting national flag carriers.

OSAs are becoming increasingly popular around the globe. More and more countries are negotiating more liberal ASAs, including OSAs (ICAO 2012). At the time of the Fifth Worldwide Air Transport Conference, in 2003, there were only 87 OSAs involving

70 countries, 59 of which included the United States as one of the signatory parties. As of September 2016, more than 300 OSAs had been signed, involving 150 states, but 119 still included the United States as one of the parties (ICAO 2016).

The U.S. OSAs grant unrestricted first through sixth freedom traffic rights to airlines of the signatory parties and often seventh freedom all-cargo rights, including provisions that eliminate government interference in the commercial decisions of airlines on capacity and pricing. Many of the OSAs signed by other countries grant only unrestricted first to fourth freedoms of the air. However, the granting of cabotage rights (eighth and ninth freedoms of the air) is still an exception, registered only within the European Union and by a few other countries in other regions (ICAO 2012).

In addition to the increasing popularity of OSAs, more recently, following the experience of the European Union, several regional groupings across Africa, Asia, and the Middle East have adopted intraregional liberalization programs, including open market access commitments. For instance, the member countries of the Association of Southeast Asian Nations (ASEAN) concluded an agreement to achieve a single open skies market by 2015; other liberal agreements have been concluded by South Pacific Island States, the Caribbean Community, and members of the Latin American Civil Aviation Commission (ICAO 2012).

DEVELOPMENT OF THE INDIA–SRI LANKA ASA

Commercial aviation between India and Sri Lanka can be traced to 1948, when the first ASA between the two countries was signed. This ASA was essentially modeled on the United States–the United Kingdom Bermuda Agreement of 1946. The provisions in the agreement covered pricing, capacity, air rights, and designated airlines that were granted air rights. Several amendments have been made to the ASA in subsequent years (table 4.1).

In its original form, the agreement granted traffic rights pertaining to the first, second, third, and fourth freedoms of the air to both countries. Traffic was restricted to four Indian destinations (Madras, Mumbai, Trichy, and Trivandrum) and two Sri Lankan destinations (Colombo and Kankesanthurai). In addition, the agreement granted rights to operate flights between the two countries only to the two national flag carriers, Air India and Air Lanka (later renamed SriLankan Airlines). The price of tickets was regulated, and any modifications had to be approved by the two governments. The capacity and frequency of flights were regulated by the number of seats per week and the type of aircraft that could service the routes. However, at the time of signing the agreement, no limits on seating or aircraft type were specified.

Several provisions have been liberalized from time to time through amendments to the original agreement. Negotiations through the 1990s resulted in enhancement of the capacity limit. Designated airline(s) in both countries were allowed to operate a maximum of 2,250 seats a week in each direction prior to the signing of the MOU in 1991; that limit had been gradually increased to 4,020 seats a week by 1997. New destinations

TABLE 4.1 **Timeline of Developments in the Bilateral ASA between India and Sri Lanka**

Year	Developments
1948	ASA signed between India and Sri Lanka
	Traffic rights granted to both countries pertaining to the first, second, third, and fourth freedoms of the air
	Traffic restricted to four Indian destinations (Madras, Mumbai, Trichy, and Trivandrum) and two Sri Lankan destinations (Colombo and Kankesanthurai)
	Air rights granted only to the two national flag carriers: Air India and Air Lanka (renamed SriLankan Airlines)
	Prices of tickets were to be regulated and any modifications to be approved by the two governments
	Capacity and frequency of flights were to be regulated by number of seats per week and types of aircraft that were allowed to be operated to service these routes
1991	Agreement reached to increase maximum number of seats per week allowed in each direction by each designated airline from the existing 2,250 to 2,500 by April 1992, 2,600 by April 1993, and 2,700 by April 1994
	Agreement reached to raise capacity limits, within the overall entitlement, for Trichy and Trivandrum, for seats per week, from the existing 500 and 625, respectively, to 500 and 690 by April 1992 and 500 and 780 by April 1993; Air Lanka was allowed to operate 780 seats per week to and from Trivandrum as and when it operated all its flights to the city using A320 aircraft or equivalent
1993	Consensus reached to allow Air Lanka to use any vacant seating capacity of designated Indian carriers for service routes between Colombo and Chennai and between Colombo and Trivandrum
1994	Agreement reached to raise capacity limit to 3,050 seats per week by April 1994 and to 3,350 seats per week by July 1994
	Indian Airlines also designated to operate flights between India and Sri Lanka
1997	Capacity limit increased to 4,020 seats per week in each direction with aircraft of any type
	Capacity limits on Trichy and Trivandrum raised to 440 and 870 seats a week, respectively
	Designated airline(s) of each side permitted to use unutilized capacity entitlement of the other side subject to commercial agreement between the designated airlines and permission of the civil aviation authorities of both countries
2000	Kolkata and Varanasi opened
	Capacity limits to Trichy and Trivandrum raised to 600 and 1,050 seats a week, respectively
2002	Bangalore and Bodh Gaya added as destinations
2003	Price determination left to market forces
	Private scheduled airlines of India—Air Sahara and Jet Airways—allowed to operate between India and Sri Lanka
	Capacity limits established as flights per week, instead of seats per week; SriLankan Airlines allowed to fly up to seven flights a week between Colombo and six Indian metropolitan cities (Bangalore, Chennai, Delhi, Hyderabad, Kolkata, and Mumbai) and unlimited flights to 18 secondary cities
	Designated SriLankan Airlines to serve Delhi and Gaya, as well as Goa and Kochi, on the same flight, without any cabotage rights between the two destinations
	Designated airlines from both countries granted traffic rights pertaining to the fifth freedom, allowing them to operate flights beyond the other country to other South Asian Association of Regional Cooperation (SAARC) countries
	Existing requirement of commercial agreements between designated airlines of the two countries for asymmetrical operations eliminated
2011	Further relaxation of capacity constraints (raised to 112 flights a week), and Coimbatore and Madurai added to the list of metropolitan cities
	Any type of aircraft allowed to operate, but with capacity not exceeding that of a Boeing 747 (that is, 467 seats)
	For cargo, granted full traffic rights pertaining to the third, fourth, and fifth freedoms of the air to all designated airlines

Source: Information from the Civil Aviation Authority, Sri Lanka.
Note: ASA = air services agreement.

were opened—Kolkata and Varanasi in 2000 and Bangalore and Bodh Gaya in 2002—
primarily with the objective of facilitating travel to Buddhist pilgrimage sites. Indian
Airlines was designated to operate flights between India and Sri Lanka in 1994.

In the early 2000s, in the face of dwindling passenger volumes from traditional destinations in the West, as well as East and Southeast Asia, the initial thrust for liberalizing
the ASA between India and Sri Lanka came from the Sri Lankan side. Stakeholders in
Sri Lanka looked at liberalization as an opportunity to revive the country's ailing tourism and aviation sectors, with India as a key partner, given the latter's dynamic and
growing middle class. By this time, SriLankan Airlines had already managed to become
established in the Indian aviation market, servicing several key routes between the two
countries.

Initially, the Sri Lankan negotiation team wanted to liberalize air services completely
between the two countries along the lines of a full-fledged OSA. However, India's policies for private domestic carriers was evolving, and it was about to allow domestic
Indian carriers to fly international routes. The Indian delegation preferred gradual, progressive steps toward liberalization.

Nonetheless, in October 2003, extensive amendments were made to the ASA in prices,
competition, capacity, and new routes. Regulations governing pricing were dismantled,
and price determination was left to market forces. In line with developments related to
the deregulation of the domestic Indian aviation industry, private Indian airlines—Air
Sahara and Jet Airways—were allowed to operate between India and Sri Lanka. The
requirement that there be commercial agreements between designated airlines of both
countries for asymmetrical operations was also eliminated. Most importantly, the seats
per week concept of capacity was replaced by flights per week. SriLankan Airlines was
allowed to fly up to seven flights a week from Colombo to six Indian metropolitan cities
(Bangalore, Chennai, Delhi, Hyderabad, Kolkata, and Mumbai) and unlimited flights
to 18 tourist destinations in India (Ahmedabad, Amritsar, Aurangabad, Bhubaneswar,
Calicut, Cochin, Gaya, Goa, Guwahati, Jaipur, Khajuraho, Lucknow, Patna, Port Blair,
Thiruvananthapuram [erstwhile Trivandrum], Tiruchirapalli [or Trichy], Varanasi, and
Vishakhapatnam). Further liberalization of the provisions included allowing the designated SriLankan Airlines to serve Delhi and Gaya, as well as Goa and Kochi, on the
same flight, without any cabotage rights between the two destinations. Designated airlines in both countries were also granted traffic rights pertaining to the fifth freedom,
allowing them to operate beyond the other country to other South Asian countries.

In March 2004, Air Sahara became the first private Indian carrier to operate on international routes, with the commencement of its first-ever international flight between
Chennai and Colombo. Jet Airways began international operations in April 2004 by
launching its inaugural flight between Chennai and Colombo. In addition to two daily
flights between Chennai and Colombo, it launched daily flights between Colombo and
Delhi, as well as Colombo and Mumbai in 2008. Today, Jet Airways only operates direct
flights between Colombo and Mumbai. In March 2007, Air India Express, the low-
cost subsidiary of Air India, commenced daily flights between Chennai and Colombo;

Air India Express continues to operate this route. In addition, Indian low-cost carrier Spice Jet started operations to Colombo, its second international destination after Kathmandu, in October 2010. Sri Lanka introduced its low-cost carrier, Mihin Lanka, in October 2007.[1] Mihin Lanka began serving three Indian destinations—Bodhgaya, Trichy, and Trivandrum—but subsequently terminated operations to Trichy and Trivandrum. In 2016, it operated only one regular flight a week to Bodhgaya and Varanasi and five flights a week seasonally to Varanasi. By 2007, with 94 flights a week to India, SriLankan Airlines was the largest foreign airline serving India; 42 percent of its revenue was derived from Indian operations (Kelegama and Mukherji 2007).[2]

In May 2011, India and Sri Lanka further liberalized bilateral air services. Designated airlines on both sides were allowed to operate 112 flights a week from and to Indian metropolitan cities, including Coimbatore and Madurai. With this enhancement, frequency entitlement saw a sixfold increase (from 7 to 42 flights a week) for Chennai; a doubling (from 7 to 14 flights a week) for Bangalore, Delhi, and Mumbai; and remained the same (at 7 flights a week) for Hyderabad and Kolkata. Coimbatore and Madurai were added to the list of metropolitan cities, with an entitlement of seven flights a week. To accommodate the greater frequency of flights and traffic growth, the two countries decided to allow any type of aircraft to operate, but with capacity not exceeding that of a Boeing 747 (that is, 467 seats). For cargo, the countries granted full traffic rights pertaining to the third, fourth, and fifth freedoms of the air to all designated airlines.

India–Sri Lanka have subsequently finalized a new ASA, which came into force on September 2013. Furthermore, in December 2016, during International Civil Aviation Organization negotiations, India and Sri Lanka signed an MOU allowing airlines from Sri Lanka unlimited flights to six metropolitan airports in India (Bengaluru, Chennai, Delhi, Hyderabad, Kolkata, and Mumbai), in line with India's National Civil Aviation Policy 2016 (India, Ministry of Civil Aviation 2016).[3]

Sri Lanka's ASAs with other South Asian neighbors, except for Maldives, are relatively restrictive compared with the ASA with India. For example, according to the Civil Aviation Authority of Sri Lanka data, Sri Lanka's ASAs with Bangladesh, Nepal, and Pakistan are restricted to 28, 14, and 36 weekly flights, respectively, while, with Maldives, Sri Lanka has an OSA. Outside South Asia, Sri Lanka's ASAs are a mixed bag, with OSAs with countries such as Malaysia, Singapore, Switzerland, and the United States and restricted access to countries such as Germany (10 flights per week), Qatar (21 per week), the United Kingdom (14 per week), and so on.[4]

Evolution of the Regional Market for Air Services

AIR CONNECTIVITY IN SOUTH ASIA

The status of regional air connectivity in South Asia in 2015 is shown in tables 4.2 and 4.3, which show, respectively, the number of bilateral flights per week between any country pair in South Asia and the number of air routes covered by these bilateral flights.

TABLE 4.2 Bilateral Connectivity in South Asia, by Number of Flights per Week

Country	Sri Lanka	India	Pakistan	Bangladesh	Maldives	Nepal	Afghanistan	Bhutan
Sri Lanka	n.a.	147	10	6	30	0	0	0
India	147	n.a.	6	67	32	71	22	23
Pakistan	10	6	n.a.	10	0	1	6	0
Bangladesh	6	67	10	n.a.	1	5	0	2
Maldives	30	32	0	1	n.a.	0	0	0
Nepal	0	71	1	5	0	n.a.	0	14
Afghanistan	0	22	6	0	0	0	n.a.	0
Bhutan	0	23	0	2	0	14	0	n.a.

Source: Compiled using data obtained from the websites of various South Asian airlines, June 2015.
Note: n.a. = not applicable.

TABLE 4.3 Bilateral Connectivity in South Asia, by Number of Air Routes

Country	Sri Lanka	India	Pakistan	Bangladesh	Maldives	Nepal	Afghanistan	Bhutan
Sri Lanka	n.a.	11	2	1	1	0	0	0
India	11	n.a.	3	5	4	4	1	6
Pakistan	2	3	n.a.	1	0	1	1	0
Bangladesh	1	5	1	n.a.	1	1	0	1
Maldives	1	4	0	1	n.a.	0	0	0
Nepal	0	4	2	1	0	n.a.	0	1
Afghanistan	0	1	2	0	0	0	n.a.	0
Bhutan	0	6	0	1	0	1	0	n.a.

Source: Compiled using data obtained from the websites of various South Asian airlines, June 2015.
Note: n.a. = not applicable.

India, which has land borders with all non-island countries except Afghanistan, has the maximum number of flights in the region; several major cities in India—including Bengaluru, Chennai, Hyderabad, Kolkata, Mumbai, and New Delhi—act as hubs for Indian and regional traffic. Bangladesh and Sri Lanka have good connectivity with some South Asian countries. Afghanistan and Pakistan are the least connected in the region; Afghanistan has flights only to and from India and Pakistan. In bilateral connectivity, India and Sri Lanka are the most well connected. Indian and Sri Lankan carriers operate a total of 147 flights a week between the two countries, covering a total of 11 bilateral routes between 11 destinations in India (Bengaluru, Chennai, Delhi, Gaya, Kochi, Kolkata, Madurai, Mumbai, Trichy, Trivandrum, and Varanasi) and one in Sri Lanka (Colombo).

Among the airlines operating in the region, the bulk of air traffic, with the exception of traffic between India and Nepal and between Bangladesh and India, is carried by the national flag carriers, namely, Air India, Biman Bangladesh Airlines, Druk Air (Bhutan),

TABLE 4.4 Routes and Frequencies between India and Sri Lanka, by Carrier
Flights per week

Route	SriLankan Airlines	Spice Jet	Jet Airways	Mihin Lanka	Air India Express	Total
Chennai–Colombo	28	7			7	42
Bangalore–Colombo	11					11
Delhi–Colombo	14					14
Mumbai–Colombo	14		14			28
Kolkata–Colombo				3		3
Varanasi–Colombo				1		1
Cochin–Colombo	14					14
Gaya–Colombo				1		1
Madurai–Colombo		5		7		12
Trichy–Colombo	14					14
Trivandrum–Colombo	7					7
Total	102	12	14	12	7	147

Source: Compiled from data obtained from the websites of the respective airlines, June 2015.
Note: Commercial air connectivity between Colombo and three Indian destinations—Coimbatore, Hyderabad, and Visakhapatnam—started in July 2017.

Maldivian (Maldives), Pakistan International Airlines, and SriLankan Airlines. India is home to the largest number of budget airlines or low-cost carriers operating in the region, namely, Air India Express, Indigo, and Spice Jet. However, their operations are limited to weekly flights covering Colombo, Kabul, Kathmandu, and Malé. Sri Lanka's state-owned low-cost carrier, Mihin Lanka, flies to four Indian destinations, namely, Bodh Gaya, Kolkata, Madurai, and Varanasi, as well as Dhaka, Lahore, and Malé (table 4.4).[5] Sri Lankan carriers—SriLankan Airlines and Mihin Lanka—account for the majority of the flights (about 80 percent of total bilateral flights per week) between India and Sri Lanka.

The state of connectivity in South Asia is evolving. Traffic within and between countries has picked up significantly. Despite progress, connectivity among capitals in South Asia is still inadequate. For example, there are no direct flights for Colombo–Islamabad, Colombo–Kabul, Colombo–Paro, and Dhaka–Kabul. There are no direct flights between Sri Lanka and Afghanistan, Bhutan, or Nepal, although interline connections are available.[6] Similarly, there are no direct connections between Maldives and Afghanistan, Bhutan, or Nepal.

That regional connectivity in South Asia still has a long way to go can be seen by comparing it with regional connectivity in ASEAN.[7] Figure 4.1 compares annual flights between five of the most well connected country pairs in ASEAN with the three most well connected pairs in South Asia. There are about 30,914, 26,691, and 26,317 annual flights, respectively, from Indonesia to Malaysia, Singapore to Indonesia, and Singapore to Malaysia, compared with about 7,594, 4,128, and 3,967, respectively, from India to Sri Lanka, India to Nepal, and India to Bangladesh.[8]

FIGURE 4.1 Air Connectivity between Selected Country Pairs in ASEAN and South Asia, 2017

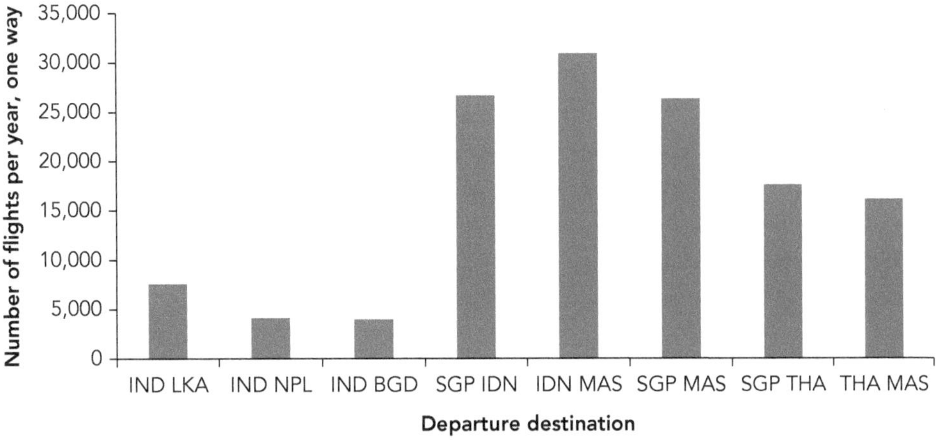

Source: Based on data from DIIO (Data In, Intelligence Out) (database), Diio, LLC, Reston, VA (accessed August 2017), https://www.diio.net/products/index.html.
Note: ASEAN = Association of Southeast Asian Nations; IND = India; LKA= Sri Lanka; BGD = Bangladesh; SGP = Singapore; IDN = Indonesia; MAS = Malaysia; THA = Thailand.

GROWTH OF THE SRI LANKAN AVIATION MARKET

The history of civil aviation in Sri Lanka in the past few decades has been marred by civil war. A brief period of peace followed a ceasefire agreement signed in February 2002; the armed conflict resumed in 2005/06, adversely impacting passenger traffic into Sri Lanka and the aviation industry there. The end of the conflict in 2009 and the ushering in of peace provided a major opportunity for the development of Sri Lanka's civil aviation sector.

Currently, Sri Lanka has bilateral ASAs with close to 75 countries, of which more than 10 are OSAs with Malaysia, Singapore, the United States, and other countries. Additionally, 22 foreign airlines, including Air India, Jet Airways, and Spice Jet in India, operate scheduled flights on international routes to and from Sri Lanka.[9] Sri Lanka's own domestic carriers—SriLankan Airlines and Mihin Lanka—also operate on international routes.

SriLankan Airlines, the country's flag carrier, has been in operation since 1979. From 1998 to 2008, the airline operated under a 10-year management contract with Emirates Airlines, combined with their equity participation (44 percent at the time of a buyback by the government of Sri Lanka in 2010). As of March 2016, the carrier was flying to 30 destinations in 17 countries across the Indian subcontinent, the Far East, the Middle East, and Europe; through code-share, it was serving another 71 destinations in 31 countries across Africa, Australia, Central Asia, Europe, and North America (SriLankan Airlines 2016). As of March 2016, the airline was operating 250 scheduled flights a week on 29 routes. Nine routes covered Southeast Asia; nine were regional routes; seven were to the Middle East; and four to European destinations (SriLankan Airlines 2016). In addition to SriLankan Airlines, the government also owned and operated Mihin Lanka, a low-cost carrier, which commenced commercial operations in 2007 and was taken over by SriLankan Airlines in October 2016. While in operation, Mihin Lanka operated flights to 10 destinations spread across India, Indonesia, Pakistan, the Seychelles, and the United Arab Emirates and served 15 other international destinations through code-share partnerships with SriLankan Airlines.

Since the end of the conflict in 2009, Sri Lanka has seen substantial growth in international passenger traffic and cargo volumes. International passenger traffic almost doubled in five years, standing at 7.8 million in 2014 (figure 4.2). International cargo volume has also grown, albeit at a slower pace (figure 4.3). Sri Lanka has two airports servicing international destinations, Bandaranaike International Airport and Mattala Rajapaksa International Airport; the bulk of air traffic is handled by the former.

GROWTH OF THE INDIAN AVIATION MARKET

India's civil aviation industry is on a high-growth trajectory. This growth has been driven by the deregulation of the domestic aviation industry, which opened domestic skies to private airlines and subsequently allowed them to operate on international routes; the push for better infrastructure during the 1990s and into the 2000s, involving airport modernization and the development of greenfield airports; and increased foreign direct investment (FDI) limits on airlines and other subsectors of the industry, such

FIGURE 4.2 International Passenger Traffic, Sri Lanka, 2006–14

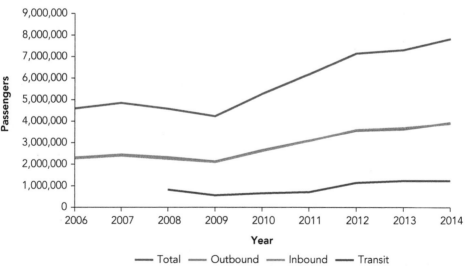

Source: Compiled using data from the Civil Aviation Authority, Sri Lanka.

FIGURE 4.3 International Cargo Volumes, Sri Lanka, 2006–14

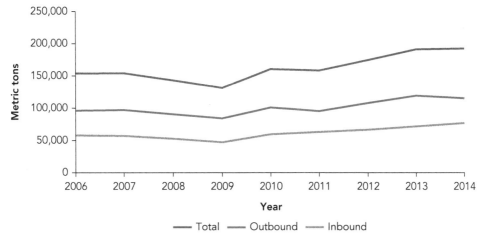

Source: Compiled using data from the Civil Aviation Authority, Sri Lanka.

as airports, air cargo, aircraft ground handling, and so forth. At the same time, India has also provided greater access to foreign carriers, signing close to 100 bilateral ASAs.

As of March 2017, more than 80 foreign carriers and five Indian carriers were operating scheduled flights on international routes to and from India.[10] The five Indian carriers operating on international routes included Air India, the flag carrier of the country; Air India Express, Air India's low-cost subsidiary; and three private airlines, Indigo, Jet Airways, and Spice Jet.

Air India operates flights to 90 domestic and foreign destinations; it accounted for 11 percent of international passenger traffic and 7 percent of cargo volume to and from India in 2015–16.[11] Air India has two wholly-owned subsidiaries, Air India Express and Alliance Air. Air India Express, launched in 2005, operates short-haul flights to 15 international destinations in South Asia (Dhaka), Southeast Asia (Kuala Lumpur and Singapore), and the Middle East from 15 cities in India.[12] Alliance Air, founded in 1996, flies to 37 destinations in India.[13]

India deregulated the domestic aviation market in 1992, allowing private players to operate domestic air services. This initially saw Air Deccan, Air Sahara, and Jet Airways commence domestic operations. In 2004, India allowed private operators who had served the domestic market for five years or more and possessed a fleet of 20 aircraft or more to operate on international routes. Initially, these operations were restricted to markets in South Asia; however, this restriction was removed in December 2004 (India, Ministry of Civil Aviation 2005). In 2015–16, there were 11 scheduled private airlines operating domestic flights in India: Air Asia, Air Costa, Air Pegasus, Blue Dart, Go Air, Indigo, Jet Airways, Jetlite, Spice Jet, Trujet, and Vistara.[14]

International passenger traffic and cargo volumes have seen significant growth in India. Passenger traffic more than quadrupled, and cargo volumes have trebled since fiscal year 2000/01 (figures 4.4 and 4.5). India currently has 21 international airports.[15]

FIGURE 4.4 International Passenger Traffic, India, Fiscal Year 2000/01 to 2016/17

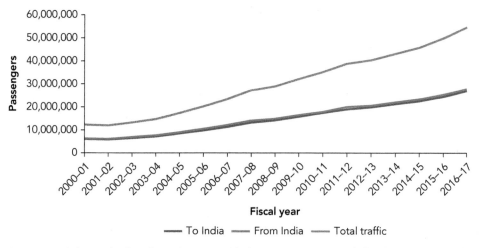

Source: Compiled using data from the DGCA Statistics (database), Directorate General of Civil Aviation, New Delhi, http://dgca.nic.in/reports/stat-ind.htm.

FIGURE 4.5 International Cargo Volumes, India, Fiscal Year 2000/01 to 2016/17

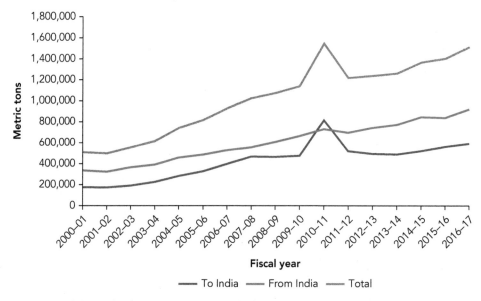

Source: Compiled using data from the DGCA Statistics (database), Directorate General of Civil Aviation, New Delhi, http://dgca.nic.in/reports/stat-ind.htm.

Impact of Air Services Liberalization on Traffic between India and Sri Lanka

EVOLUTION OF AIR TRAFFIC BETWEEN INDIA AND SRI LANKA

The impact of the amendments of 2003 and 2011 on bilateral air services between India and Sri Lanka can be seen in the increase in the number of flights and seats between the two countries (figures 4.6 and 4.7). During 2004–17, air services between India and

FIGURE 4.6 Growth in Flights between India and Selected Countries, 2004–17

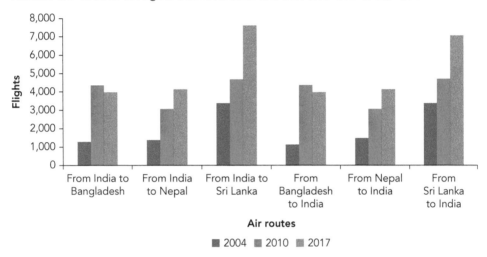

Source: Based on data from DIIO (Data In, Intelligence Out) (database), Diio, LLC, Reston, VA (accessed August 2017), https://www.diio.net/products/index.html.

FIGURE 4.7 Growth in Airline Seats Available between India and Selected Countries, 2004–17

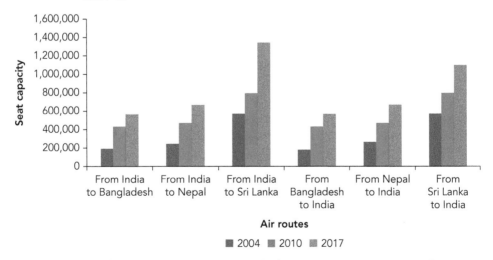

Source: Based on data from DIIO (Data In, Intelligence Out) (database), Diio, LLC, Reston, VA (accessed August 2017), https://www.diio.net/products/index.html.

FIGURE 4.8 Passenger Traffic between India and Sri Lanka, Fiscal Year 2000/01 to 2016/17

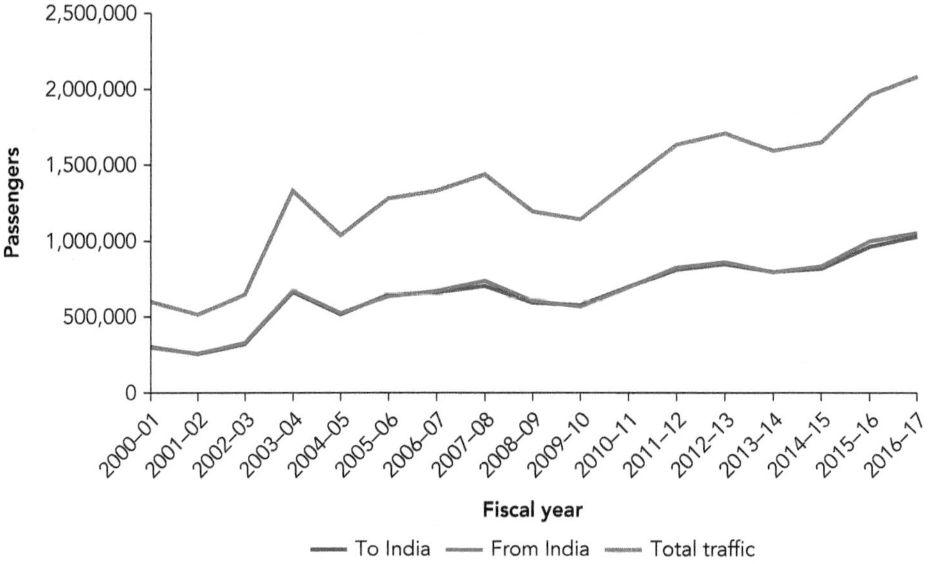

Source: Compiled using data from the DGCA Statistics (database), Directorate General of Civil Aviation, New Delhi, http://dgca.nic.in/reports/stat-ind.htm.

Sri Lanka, in flights and seats, grew at a compound annual growth rate of 6.1 percent and 6.0 percent, respectively. This bilateral air connectivity picked up pace after the end of the civil war in Sri Lanka in 2009: flights grew at an annual average compound rate of 6.6 percent, and seats grew at 6.3 percent, over 2010–17. This post-2009 growth was also more rapid than air connectivity growth between India and Nepal and between Bangladesh and India, the second and third most well connected country pairs in South Asia after India–Sri Lanka, despite this last's higher base. During 2010–17, flights and seats grew at compound annual growth rates of 4.3 percent and 5.1 percent, respectively, in the case of India-Nepal and –1.3 percent and 3.9 percent, respectively, in the case of Bangladesh–India. In 2017, air services between India and Sri Lanka continued to exceed, by a large margin, the services between the other two country pairs.

Based on data on bilateral passenger traffic, as opposed to seating capacity, prior to the 2003 liberalization, figure 4.8 shows that, in addition to the upward spurt in passenger volumes after fiscal year 2009/10, there was a similar upward trend over fiscal year 2002/03 to fiscal year 2007/08, except for a sharp dip in fiscal year 2004/05.

The improvement in air services between India and Sri Lanka emerges not only in the increased flights and seats between the two countries but also in the new destinations in India. The 1948 ASA had allowed bilateral flights to only four Indian destinations: Chennai, Mumbai, Trichy, and Trivandrum. In the early 2000s, bilateral flights were also allowed to Bangalore, Bodh Gaya, Kolkata, and Varanasi. The 2003 agreement allowed air services to six metropolitan Indian cities—Bangalore, Chennai,

Delhi, Hyderabad, Kolkata, and Mumbai—and 18 secondary destinations. Thus, bilateral air services started delivering air traffic to Indian cities, such as Madurai, that were not associated with large international airports at the time (See also Wijesinha and de Mel 2012.). A beneficiary of this rising trend in passenger traffic was the tourism industry in both countries (box 4.2).

BOX 4.2 Impact of Air Service Liberalization on Tourism, India and Sri Lanka

The initial thrust of the major amendments to the ASA between Sri Lanka and India in 2003 came from the Sri Lankan side, with a view to generating increased tourist traffic from India. Traditionally, the tourism industry in Sri Lanka flourished on the back of tourist arrivals from the Western Hemisphere, notably, the United Kingdom, and the rest of Western Europe. The worsening security situation in Sri Lanka following the terrorist attack on Bandaranaike International Airport in Katunayake in July 2001, and the turbulence in the global aviation industry after the September 2001 terrorist attacks in the United States, saw a substantial decline in tourist arrivals from Sri Lanka's traditional sources. Because of its geographical proximity, growing middle class, and a population relatively less alarmed by the security situation in Sri Lanka, India was considered the ideal market to tap. The 2003 liberalization of the ASA coincided with the granting of visas on arrival to Indian tourists. It also coincided with a brief period of peace in Sri Lanka. There was a lull in the civil war when Sri Lanka embraced a peace deal in December 2002, brokered by the Norwegian government. The resultant improvement in the security situation was critical to enhancing the country's tourism prospects.

During the early 2000s, India was the third major source of tourist arrivals in Sri Lanka, after the United Kingdom and Germany. By 2004, India had jumped to second place; by 2005, India had become the top source, surpassing the United Kingdom by as much as 20 percent in tourist arrivals. Since then, India has been the top source of tourist arrivals in Sri Lanka.

It was expected that the negotiated peace deal, together with the liberalization of the air services and visa regime, would lead to a sizable rise in tourist arrivals in Sri Lanka. Between 2003 and 2006, it was business rather than recreation travelers that accounted for most of the increase in Indian tourist arrivals (figure B4.2.1). The resumption of the armed conflict in 2005/06 saw a sharp drop in the number of tourists, but, with the end of the civil war in May 2009, there was again a surge, particularly of recreation travelers.[a] The end of the civil war also witnessed an uptick in tourist arrivals from the West, and, more recently, Eastern European countries. However, tourist arrivals from India continued to play a crucial role. The peak tourist season for European tourists runs from September to January, which coincides with the winter months in the Western Hemisphere. The peak season for Indian tourists runs from March to April and June to August, which coincide with school holidays and the summer season in India. Thus, tourist arrivals from India support the tourism industry in Sri Lanka during the lean season between February and August each year.

In 2002 and 2003, Sri Lanka was the third-largest source of tourist arrivals in India, preceded only by the United States and the United Kingdom. By 2013, Sri Lanka had been overtaken by Bangladesh, dropping to fourth place. Despite the fall in market share, the number of Sri Lankan tourists arriving in India has grown steadily since 2003 (figure B4.2.2).

box continues next page

BOX 4.2 Impact of Air Service Liberalization on Tourism, India and Sri Lanka *(continued)*

FIGURE B4.2.1 Arrival Statistics by Purpose of Travel, Indian Visitors to Sri Lanka

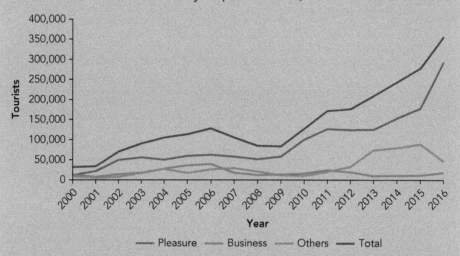

Source: Data from the Tourism Research and Statistics (database), Sri Lanka Tourism Development Authority, Colombo, Sri Lanka, http://www.sltda.lk/statistics.

FIGURE B4.2.2 Arrival Statistics by Purpose of Travel, Sri Lankan Visitors to India

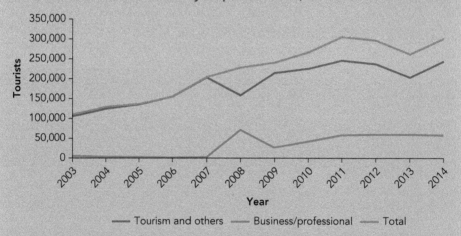

Source: Compiled from Market Research and Statistics (database), Ministry of Tourism, New Delhi, http://tourism.gov.in/market-research-and-statistics.

Since 2009, the number of business travelers arriving in India has also risen, which is an indication of the growing trade and investment ties of Sri Lankan entrepreneurs in the India market; Chennai, in particular, has been a popular destination for Sri Lankan business travelers, especially traders.

box continues next page

> **BOX 4.2 Impact of Air Service Liberalization on Tourism, India and Sri Lanka** *(continued)*
>
> Closer inspection of the composition of Sri Lankan tourist arrivals in India based on data available from the Ministry of Tourism suggests that, in addition to tourists for recreation and tourists visiting friends and family, there has been notable growth in the number of Sri Lankans traveling to India for medical treatment and education, an indication that India is quickly emerging as a popular destination for educational and medical services within South Asia.
>
> Overall, the liberalization of the India–Sri Lanka ASA has improved air connectivity and greatly facilitated increased people-to-people contacts, laying the foundations for greater trade and investment in coming years. The liberalization has benefited the services sectors of the two countries the most, and tourism has been the largest beneficiary. Mounting evidence suggests that, with further improvements in air connectivity, there is much potential for enhanced trade in health care and education.
>
> *Source:* Ekanayake 2016.
> a. The available data do not permit disaggregation of Indian tourists to Sri Lanka by origin in India.

A closer analysis of the routewise frequency of flights suggests that the major expansion in passenger traffic after the 2003 reforms may be attributed to the additional capacity generated in destinations that were already established—such as Chennai, Mumbai, Trichy, and Trivandrum—because of the greater frequency of flights, as opposed to additional traffic created by newly opened routes (Ekanayake 2016).

Cargo volumes also received a stimulus from the 2003 reforms and again after the 2011 reforms, but growth was less pronounced and robust than in the case of passenger traffic (figure 4.9). Cargo volume contracted throughout much of fiscal year 2005/06 to fiscal year 2009/10. The full cargo traffic rights pertaining to the third, fourth, and fifth freedoms of the air granted in 2011 were followed by a sharp rise in cargo volumes, fueled essentially by greater volumes from India, while there was only a modest increase in volumes from Sri Lanka.

Anecdotal evidence on cargo volumes suggests there has been no major change in the composition of goods ferried between the two countries by air. Perishable agricultural items, such as spices, betel leaves, other horticultural produce, processed foods, and, to some extent, apparel, figure most prominently in the basket of goods shipped to India by air. Pharmaceutical products appear most prominent in inbound air cargo from India. According to industry experts, most of the goods traded between India and Sri Lanka comprise low value-to-weight or bulk items, such as bulk tea, petroleum and petroleum-based products, sugar, onions, electrical cables, automobile tires, cement, automobiles, and automobile parts and components. It is not feasible or profitable to use air freight for transporting these items. The lack of regional production networks in high value-to-weight products, such as electronics, electronic appliances, and electronic components, as experienced in East and Southeast Asia, is another reason for the unchanging composition of goods transported between the two countries.

FIGURE 4.9 Cargo Volumes between India and Sri Lanka, Fiscal Year 2000/01 to 2016/17

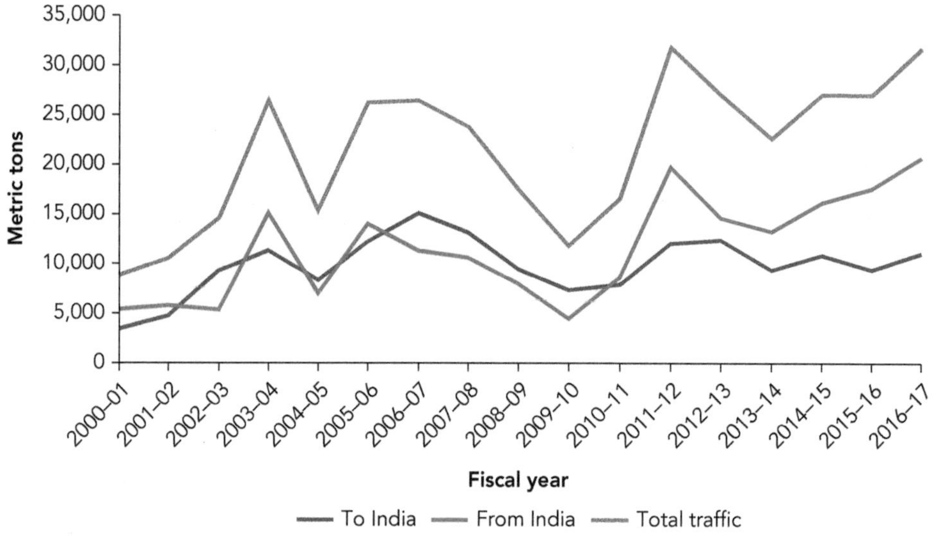

Source: Compiled using data from the DGCA Statistics (database), Directorate General of Civil Aviation, New Delhi, http://dgca.nic.in/reports/stat-ind.htm.

Industry experts also note that the bulk of air cargo volume (close to 60 percent) between India and Sri Lanka consists of couriered cargo or personal baggage; these include transshipment of goods of Indian migrant workers based in the Middle East into India via Colombo. The experts believe that this is because the passenger traffic on inbound flights into Colombo from Middle Eastern destinations is often low, prompting airlines operating the Middle East–Colombo routes to charge lower air freight rates. Compared with shipping cargo directly to India from the Middle East, freight forwarders consider transshipping air cargo via Sri Lanka as a cheaper option. Most of the air cargo between the two countries is carried between Colombo and Chennai, which utilize wide-bodied aircraft; other routes from Colombo to Indian destinations employ narrow-bodied aircraft (A320) with limited cargo capacity.

DIFFERENCE IN DIFFERENCES ANALYSIS OF BILATERAL AIR SERVICES LIBERALIZATION

One of the most popular tools in economic research to estimate the impact of a policy change is the difference in differences approach (Ashenfelter and Card 1985). The idea behind the method is straightforward. To test the effect of a policy (a treatment), a proper counterfactual is needed. In an ideal situation, the same country or group in both conditions, that is, treated and untreated, would need to be observed. However, in the absence of this, a counterfactual (control group) is used, assuming that it is similar to the untreated country under study, to assess the impact of the policy change on various outcome variables.

This study employs the difference in differences approach, adapted from Ashenfelter and Card (1985) and Meyer (1995), to quantify the impact of the amendment to the bilateral ASA between India and Sri Lanka, which was agreed in 2011. The liberalization episode is evaluated through the impact on three outcome variables: flights per week, seats per week, and aircraft capacity (number of seats per flight). The Bangladesh–India aviation market is used as the control group because the trends in bilateral air traffic in that market and in the India–Sri Lanka aviation market were similar prior to the amendments in the India–Sri Lanka ASA.[16] Bangladesh did not experience any significant liberalization in air services with India or Sri Lanka during the period under focus.

The estimation equation follows the traditional difference in differences approach, as in Ashenfelter and Card (1985):

$$y_{it} = \beta_0 + \beta_1 dB_i + \delta_0 d2_t + \delta_1(d2_t{}^* dB_i) + \varepsilon_{it} \qquad (4.1)$$

$$i = INDBGD, INDLKA; \; t = 2004jan - 2015dec$$

where:

- y = outcome variable (number of flights per week, seats per week, seats per flight)
- i = India–Bangladesh aviation market ($INDBGD$); India–Sri Lanka aviation market ($INDLKA$)
- β_0 = average outcome for the control group before the treatment
- $\beta_0 + \beta_1$ = average outcome for the treatment group before the treatment
- dB_i = dummy variable, taking the value of 1 if the observation belongs to the aviation market that was subject to the policy change (the treatment group) and 0 otherwise
- δ_0 = coefficient that evaluates the difference in the outcome variable between the control group and the treatment group, before the policy change
- δ_1 = coefficient that evaluates the effect of the policy, taking into account the changes in the control group that would have occurred irrespective of the policy change, after the policy change
- $d2_t$ = treatment period dummy variable, taking the value of 1 if the policy was in place and 0 otherwise (takes the value of 1 starting with the air liberalization of 2011 and 0 otherwise)

The baseline equation is estimated to assess the impact of the 2011 amendments to the ASA between India and Sri Lanka on three outcome variables: the number of roundtrip flights per week, the number of seats available per week, and the capacity

TABLE 4.5 Effects of the 2011 Liberalization

Variable	(1) Flights per week	(2) Seats per week	(3) Seats per flight
Diff-in-diff	16.45***	2,442***	2.622
	(3.863)	(521.6)	(3.107)
Observations	288	288	288
R-squared	0.743	0.864	0.625
Mean control t(0)	53.71	6,898	135.5
Mean treated t(0)	103.8	17,515	168.7
Diff t(0)	50.05	10,616	33.14
Mean control t(1)	61.40	7,606	125.8
Mean treated t(1)	127.9	20,665	161.6
Diff t(1)	66.51	13,058	35.76

Source: Based on data from DIIO (Data In, Intelligence Out) (database), Diio, LLC, Reston, VA (accessed August 2017), https://www.diio.net/products/index.html.
Note: Robust standard errors are in parentheses. The traffic between Bangladesh and India is used as the control group. The treatment period corresponds to all the months after January 1, 2011. t(0) and t(1) refer, respectively, to the pretreatment and treatment periods. *$p < 0.1$ **$p < 0.05$ ***$p < 0.01$.

of the plane measured as the number of seats per flight. The results are shown in table 4.5. For each outcome variable, the table indicates the average value of the variable for the treatment group (India–Sri Lanka aviation market) and the control group (Bangladesh–India aviation market) before and after the intervention. The table shows the mean treated $t(0)$ and $t(1)$ for the treatment group and the mean control $t(0)$ and $t(1)$ for the control group, where $t(0)$ refers to the period before the implementation of the policy changes, and $t(1)$ refers to the period after the implementation.

The estimates obtained from the difference in differences approach (see table 4.5) indicate that, of the total increase of 24 flights per week between India and Sri Lanka, an increase of 16 flights per week can be attributed directly to the liberalization of 2011. Similarly, an increase in 2,442 weekly seats can be attributed to the 2011 amendments. However, the policy changes of 2011 did not have any statistically significant impact on the average seat capacity of planes, which is not surprising because introducing larger planes requires substantial investment.

The difference in differences approach takes into account market trends before the policy reforms through the control group. The estimated increase is therefore less than the actual increase in flight frequency, seats, and flight capacity because some of the increase would have occurred even in the absence of a policy change. The methodology also enhances the credibility of the results because it goes beyond the simple comparison of outcomes before and after policy changes.

Changes in Competition and Market Composition

Two major developments in competition and pricing took place in 2003. With respect to competition, India allowed two of its private carriers, Air Sahara and Jet Airways, to operate between India and Sri Lanka. Flexibility was granted to market forces to determine prices. In the absence of historical pricing data, anecdotal evidence collated from industry representatives suggests that, in the immediate aftermath of the entry of private Indian carriers in the market, ticket prices on routes with competition, namely, Chennai–Colombo, and Colombo–Mumbai, and Delhi–Colombo, experienced a sharp downward revision ranging from 20 percent to 40 percent. Industry experts believe that this downward revision in prices cannot be attributed primarily to the additional capacity created as a result of competition; instead, it derived from price undercutting by the new entrants to gain and consolidate market share.

Some evidence suggests that the price impact of the liberalization episodes has not been insignificant. First, in the absence of historical data on prices, one may observe that the market share of low-cost carriers seems to have been widening, which intuitively should imply lower average ticket fares. Table 4.6 shows that, after 2011, the number of flights and seats rose by 67 percent and 64 percent, respectively, among low-cost carriers, compared with 19 percent and 14 percent, respectively, among other alliances. If this trend continues, implying growing low-cost competition for the other alliances, it could create downward pressure on prices.

Second, a price comparison on two major routes in South Asia offers insights. Table 4.7 shows that one-way (nonstop) economy class fares on flights from New Delhi to Colombo are typically cheaper (by 15–40 percent in three of four cases) than corresponding fares on flights from New Delhi to Dhaka, despite the flying times, which are a third less in the case of Delhi–Dhaka.

Anecdotal evidence also suggests that the price competition was not sufficiently strong. Since the early days of liberalization, the exit or scaling-back of operations by Indian carriers has allowed Sri Lankan carriers to account for almost 80 percent of overall supply capacity. Of the 10 routes currently being operated between India

TABLE 4.6 India–Sri Lanka: Growth in Seats and Flights, Low-Cost Carriers, and
　　　　　　Other Alliances
Average number per month

Carrier type	Flights			Seats		
	2004–11	2011–16	Difference, %	2004–11	2011–16	Difference, %
Other alliances	401	475	19	69,273	79,084	14
Low-cost carriers	51	85	67	6,956	11,430	64

Source: Data from DIIO (Data In, Intelligence Out) (database), Diio, LLC, Reston, VA (accessed August 2017), https://www.diio.net/products/index.html.

TABLE 4.7 Cheapest One-Way Nonstop Economy Class Fare on Select Routes, South Asia
Indian rupees

Period	New Delhi to Colombo, flight time: 3 hours 35 minutes	New Delhi to Dhaka, flight time: 2 hours 15 minutes
August 10 (1 week out)	Rs 9,035	Rs 10,780
August 17 (2 weeks out)	Rs 9,035	Rs 7,945
August 24 (3 weeks out)	Rs 9,035	Rs 14,428
August 31 (4 weeks out)	Rs 9,035	Rs 12,646

Source: MakeMyTrip (travel portal) website (accessed August 3, 2017), https://www.makemytrip.com/.

and Sri Lanka, SriLankan Airlines and Mihin Lanka face competition (on a limited scale) on only three routes. Industry experts believe limited competition has essentially allowed the two Sri Lankan carriers to enjoy a near-monopoly position in the markets in which they operate. As a result, ticket prices have partially scaled back up.

Thus, the impression among some industry experts in Sri Lanka seems to be that, although the liberalization of air services has had a positive impact on pricing post-2003, the impact on competition, capacity, and pricing could have been much greater but for the structural weaknesses of the airlines operating in the region. For example, SriLankan Airlines currently possesses a small fleet, around 25 aircraft, on which there is competing demand from traffic from and to destinations in East and Southeast Asia. It had to terminate operations to Hyderabad in 2009 and is unable to operate on other profitable Indian routes because of lack of aircraft. Also, SriLankan Airlines and Mihin Lanka are state-owned enterprises and are heavily subsidized. Since 2008, SriLankan Airlines has accumulated losses of over SL Rs 100 billion. In the financial year ending in 2014, it incurred a net loss of about SL Rs 32.4 billion. Mihin Lanka became financially troubled soon after it was set up in 2007 and lost more than SL Rs 15 billion (Wijayasiri 2015); Mihin Lanka ceased to exist in October 2016, and its operations were merged into SriLankan Airlines. The subsidization of the operations of these two airlines could have dampened competition from other airlines on the same routes, and this needs to be explored. Several Indian private airlines as well as the flag carrier, Air India, have been grappling with financial problems, too; their financial constraints, along with competing demand from traffic to and from other destinations, could have resulted in lower capacity increases on India–Sri Lanka routes than would otherwise have been observed.

In short, the liberalization of the ASA had a positive impact on competition, capacity, and pricing. Industry insiders, however, feel the impact could have been far greater in the absence of factors that tend to dampen competition, such as government subsidies to flag carriers and the financial constraints faced by airlines.

Conclusion

Regional air connectivity within South Asia is restricted, and connectivity is poor between capitals. For example, there are no direct connections between Colombo and Islamabad, Colombo and Kabul, Colombo and Paro (the site of Bhutan's only international airport), and Dhaka and Kabul. Moreover, there are no direct connections between some countries (for instance, Afghanistan–Nepal and Bhutan–Maldives). Bilateral air connectivity is the best between India and Sri Lanka, which is a result of the progressive liberalization of air services between the two countries.

Through decades of discussions, negotiations, and amendments, the first bilateral ASA between India and Sri Lanka, signed in 1948, has become progressively more liberal. Although the agreement has not reached the status of a truly open skies arrangement, bilateral air services between India and Sri Lanka have been significantly liberalized, particularly after the extensive amendments that were made to the ASA in 2003 and in 2011.[17] The 2003 and 2011 amendments created a freer market by allowing prices to be determined by the market, allowing private airlines to operate flights on routes between India and Sri Lanka, easing capacity limits and redefining them in flights per week as opposed to seats per week, and opening new destinations to bilateral air services.

This study finds that the liberalization episode in 2011 had a positive effect on air connectivity between the two countries. The quantitative analysis, based on a difference in differences approach, shows that a large part of the increase in flights per week and in available seats per week between India and Sri Lanka after the 2011 amendments can be attributed to the policy changes; the 2011 reforms translated into increases of 16 flights a week and 2,442 seats a week. The 2003 reforms probably also had a substantial impact, but the econometric results are not highlighted in this report because the relevant data are only available since 2004.

Cargo volumes also received a stimulus from the 2003 and 2011 reforms, but growth was less pronounced and robust compared with passenger traffic growth. This finding can be partly explained by the domination of bilateral trade between India and Sri Lanka by low value-to-weight products, which typically are not transported by air freight.

The reforms also had a positive impact on competition and pricing. The study could not quantify the effects on airfares in the absence of historical pricing data. However, interviews with stakeholders have confirmed that prices fell, initially by as much as 20–40 percent on routes where there was competition, but the declines were rolled back partially after the exit or scaling-back of operations by Indian carriers left SriLankan Airlines and Mihin Lanka with 80 percent of the supply capacity. Another indication of the decline in airfares is that the market share of low-cost carriers in seats and flights has been rising, which suggests that average fares should decline. Similarly, fares on the New Delhi-to-Colombo route are typically much cheaper than those on another comparable major route, New Delhi-to-Dhaka, despite the fact that the flying time on the latter route is one-third less. Overall, while the impact on competition and prices has been positive, it could have been greater. Structural weaknesses in the domestic airlines of India and Sri Lanka have constrained the ability of the airlines to supply more air services on the routes between the two countries, especially in the face of competing demand for air services to destinations in other parts of the world.

Several other events have shaped the demand for air services between India and Sri Lanka. The end of the civil war in Sri Lanka in 2009 was key to enhancing the prospects for aviation and tourism. Two other developments have also been significant: the visa-on-arrival scheme, introduced for Indian tourists to Sri Lanka in 2003, and the implementation of the India–Sri Lanka Free Trade Agreement in 2000. Combined with the 2003 and 2011 air services liberalization, these events have meant that India–Sri Lanka flights and seat capacity continued to exceed the Bangladesh–India and India–Nepal traffic significantly.

The aviation industry, especially in Sri Lanka, has been a big beneficiary of the air services liberalization. By 2007, SriLankan Airlines was the largest foreign airline operating in India in flights per week (94 flights a week). Its expansion into the Indian market came at a critical juncture for the airline: the global tourism and aviation industry was in disarray following the September 2001 terrorist attacks in the United States; it was facing dwindling demand from its traditional sources in the West because of the civil war; and it had lost 3 of the 12 commercial aircraft in its fleet in the July 2001 terrorist attack on Bandaranaike International Airport in Katunayake, Sri Lanka.

The economic impact of air services liberalization has reached far beyond the aviation industry. Improved air connectivity has facilitated more people-to-people contacts and enhanced the scope for deeper trade, investment, and cultural and religious links. The tourism industry has benefited in both countries, more so in the case of Sri Lanka. Because of the liberalized bilateral air services, along with the visa-on-arrival authorization for Indian tourists in Sri Lanka, India had moved up from third place on the list of largest source countries of foreign tourists in Sri Lanka in the early 2000s to the top position by 2005. Although Sri Lanka had fallen from third place on the list of the largest sources of foreign tourists in India in 2002 and 2003 to fourth place by 2013, there has been steady growth in the number of Sri Lankan tourists arriving in India since 2003, including notable growth in the number of Sri Lankans traveling to India for medical treatment and education.

Overall, the gains from air services liberalization between India and Sri Lanka have been substantial and can be increased by spurring more competition on the routes between the two countries. Other countries in South Asia can learn from this experience and strive for deeper air services liberalization with each other at the bilateral or regional level. The study suggests that policy makers remain agnostic about the relative impact of liberalization on specific airlines, irrespective of country of origin, because they should focus on bigger prizes, including the benefits to consumers of more choice in flights and airlines, better customer service, and lower prices, which could encourage deeper trade and investment.

A key lesson among policy makers in South Asia is the understanding that a gold standard such as an OSA is not necessary to begin liberalization. An alternative is to adopt an incremental approach, as has been done by India and Sri Lanka, toward the goal of freeing up air services. Such an incremental approach may be more suitable in South Asia, given the political economy constraints faced by countries in the region, and it would allow more time for adjustment.

Another lesson that emerges is that gains can be reinforced if air services liberalization is accompanied by supporting reforms, such as easing visa constraints. The Sri Lankan government's authorization of visa-on-arrival privileges for Indian tourists complemented and perhaps even gave an impetus to the expansion in bilateral air services.

There are grounds to suggest that, although the liberalization of air services between India and Sri Lanka has had a significant beneficial impact, the gains could have been greater. However, the structural weaknesses faced by the airlines of the two countries constrained their capacity to serve on bilateral routes. In general, the biggest weaknesses usually involve capacity constraints arising from the lack of aircraft and poor service quality; these can be addressed through management contracts and strategic alliances as alternatives to or in conjunction with foreign equity participation. In this context, the Indian government's progressive liberalization of foreign investment policy in the airline sector could offer lessons to other countries in South Asia. In 2012, India allowed foreign airlines to invest up to 49 percent of the equity in Indian airlines; in 2016, it allowed 100 percent ownership for foreign nonairline investors.[18] The policy has paid off through substantial new investments in India since 2012. Since the 2012 policy change, Etihad Airlines has invested in Jet Airways, while AirAsia (Malaysia) and Singapore Airlines have set up joint ventures, namely, AirAsia India and Vistara.[19]

The study highlights that it was in the interest of the government of Sri Lanka to keep pushing for deeper air services liberalization with India, given the relative size of India's market and the potential benefits to Sri Lanka of access to that market, including enhanced tourism and business for its airlines industry. This policy persistence has paid off for Sri Lanka, as documented in this report. Aviation authorities in other countries that still do not have liberal ASAs with India could keep this in mind, especially now that India's National Civil Aviation Policy 2016 offers a reciprocal open skies agreement with the countries of the South Asian Association for Regional Cooperation (SAARC) (India, Ministry of Civil Aviation 2016).

Notes

1. As of October 2016, Mihin Lanka's routes have been taken over by SriLankan Airlines; even though the two airlines continue to exist as separate entities for commercial and legal purposes, Mihin Lanka has ceased to exist for all intents and purposes. However, this chapter refers to Mihin Lanka as a separate entity to highlight the historical developments in civil aviation in India and Sri Lanka and the bilateral ASA between the two countries.

2. Other foreign carriers, especially Gulf-based airlines catering to global markets, became more dominant in subsequent years. According to Directorate General of Civil Aviation of India data, among the foreign airlines during 2016–17, Emirates Airlines carried the

maximum number of passengers (9.9 percent of total passengers) to and from India to international destinations, followed by Etihad Airlines (5.0 percent of total passengers), Qatar Airways (3.9 percent), Air Arabia (3.2 percent), and Oman Air (3.2 percent). The reason for the dominance of these airlines may be the high number of migrant workers flying to and from India to the Gulf region. SriLankan Airlines (combined with Mihin Lanka) stands sixth in this list, carrying 2.9 percent of total passenger traffic in 2016–17.

3. See "Aviation: India Inks Pacts with Sri Lanka, Five Other Countries," *Economic Times*, Mumbai, December 15, 2016, https://economictimes.indiatimes.com/industry/transpor tation/airlines-/-aviation/aviation-india-inks-pacts-with-sri-lanka-five-other-countries /articleshow/56005798.cms.

4. For details on Sri Lankan ASAs with other countries, see "Air Services Agreements between Sri Lanka and Foreign States and Status of Usage," Civil Aviation Authority of Sri Lanka, Katunayake, Sri Lanka, http://www.caa.lk/index.php?option=com_content&view=article &id=601&Itemid=728&lang=en.

5. SriLankan Airlines took over the routes operated by Mihin Lanka on October 1, 2016, and the latter was dissolved.

6. In October 2016, Himalayan Airlines initiated two flights a week between Colombo and Kathmandu (Anurup 2017).

7. A commonly used analytical tool to evaluate the restrictiveness of provisions in an ASA is the air services liberalization index, which is based on the Quantitative Air Services Agreements Review methodology devised by the World Trade Organization in 2006. The index cannot be used to compare regional connectivity within South Asia and ASEAN because the index values have not been updated to reflect the current status of ASAs between, for instance, India and Sri Lanka (index calculated for 1984) or Malaysia and Thailand (index calculated for 1969).

8. ASEAN country pairs also far outpace South Asian country pairs in seating capacity. For example, the annual seating capacity (one way) is about 5.4 million, 5.4 million, and 4.1 million for Indonesia to Malaysia, Singapore to Indonesia, and Singapore to Malaysia flights, respectively, compared with about 1.3 million, 0.7 million, and 0.6 million for India to Sri Lanka, India to Nepal, and India to Bangladesh flights, respectively. See DIIO (Data In, Intelligence Out) (database), Diio, LLC, Reston, VA (accessed August 2017), https://www .diio.net/products/index.html.

9. See "Airlines Serving Sri Lanka," Civil Aviation Authority of Sri Lanka, Katunayake, Sri Lanka, http://www.caa.lk/index.php?option=com_content&view=article&id=599&itemid =311&Itemid=791&lang=en.

10. See DGCA Statistics (database), Directorate General of Civil Aviation, New Delhi, http:// dgca.nic.in/reports/stat-ind.htm.

11. According to 2015–16 data of the DGCA Statistics (database), Directorate General of Civil Aviation, New Delhi, http://dgca.nic.in/reports/stat-ind.htm.

12. See "Destinations," Air India Express, Mumbai, http://airindiaexpress.in/dest.aspx.

13. "Alliance Air," Air India, New Delhi, http://www.airindia.in/alliance-air.htm.

14. DGCA Statistics (database), Directorate General of Civil Aviation, New Delhi, http://dgca .nic.in/reports/stat-ind.htm.

15. Airports Authority of India website: https://www.aai.aero/.

16. Even though the air traffic is similar between Bangladesh–India and India–Sri Lanka, the choice of the control group is critical to any difference in differences estimation. This study also constructed a synthetic control group following the methodology formalized by Abadie, Diamond, and Hainmueller (2010). The methodology involves finding the optimal weighted average between all possible control groups so that the pretreatment period follows a similar trend. This study uses the control pool that contains all of India's destinations in South Asia (Afghanistan, Bangladesh, Bhutan, Maldives, Nepal, and Pakistan). The optimization procedure found that the optimal synthetic group is a weighted average with weight 1 for Bangladesh and zero for the rest. Therefore, Bangladesh is the optimal control group from a synthetic control group perspective.

17. The December 2016 pact between India and Sri Lanka allows unlimited flights from Sri Lanka to six Indian cities.

18. See "Centre Allows 100 per Cent FDI in Airlines, 49 per Cent Cap for Foreign Carriers Stays," *Indian Express* (June 21, 2016), http://indianexpress.com/article/business/aviation/fdi-100 -per-cent-civil-aviation-sector-2865444/.

19. See Lee and Varottil (2017) for an analysis of the foreign investment regime in the Indian airline industry.

References

Abadie, Alberto, Alexis Diamond, and Jens Hainmueller. 2010. "Synthetic Control Methods for Comparative Case Studies: Estimating the Effect of California's Tobacco Control Program." *Journal of the American Statistical Association* 105 (490): 493–505.

Anurup, Pathak. 2017. "Himalayan Airlines Rearranges Flight Schedule to Colombo." *Aviation Nepal*, January 24. https://www.aviationnepal.com/himalayan-airlines/.

Ashenfelter, Orley C., and David Card. 1985. "Using the Longitudinal Structure of Earnings to Estimate the Effect of Training Programs." *Review of Economics and Statistics* 67 (4): 648–60.

Ekanayake, Raveen. 2016. "Opening Up the Skies: Benefits of Air Services Liberalization, What We Can Learn from the India-Sri Lanka Experience." *Talking Economics* (blog), January 19. http://www.ips.lk/talkingeconomics/2016/01/19/opening-up-the-skies-benefits-of-air-ser vices-liberalization-what-we-can-learn-from-the-india-sri-lanka-experience/.

Fu, Xiaowen, Tae Hoon Oum, and Anming Zhang. 2010. "Air Transport Liberalization and Its Impacts on Airline Competition and Air Passenger Traffic." *Transportation Journal* 49 (4): 24–41.

ICAO (International Civil Aviation Organization). 2004. *Manual on the Regulation of International Air Transport*. 2nd ed. Document 9626. Montreal: ICAO.

———. 2012. "Expanding Market Access For International Air Transport (Presented by the Secretariat)." ICAO Working Paper ATConf/6–WP/13 (December 13), ICAO, Montreal.

———. 2013. "Liberalization of Market Access (Presented by the United States of America)." ICAO Working Paper ATConf/6–WP/60 (February 14), ICAO, Montreal.

———. 2016. "Overview of Regulatory and Industry Developments in International Air Transport." September, ICAO, Montreal.

India, Ministry of Civil Aviation. 2005. *Annual Report 2004–2005.* New Delhi: Ministry of Civil Aviation. http://civilaviation.gov.in/sites/default/files/Annual%20Report%20-%202004-2005 %20-%20English.pdf.

———. 2016. "National Civil Aviation Policy 2016." Ministry of Civil Aviation, New Delhi. http:// www.civilaviation.gov.in/sites/default/files/Final_NCAP_2016_15-06-2016-2_1.pdf.

InterVISTAS-EU. 2009. "The Impact of International Air Service Liberalisation on India." July, InterVISTAS-EU Consulting Inc., London.

Kelegama, Saman, and Indra Nath Mukherji. 2007. "India-Sri Lanka Bilateral Free Trade Agreement: Six Years Performance and Beyond." RIS Discussion Paper 119 (February), Research and Information System for Developing Countries, New Delhi. http://ris.org.in /images/RIS_images/pdf/dp119_pap.pdf.

Lee, Jae Woon, and Umakanth Varottil. 2017. "Skies Half Open: Foreign Investment in India's Airline Industry." CALS Working Paper 17/04 (October), Centre for Asian Legal Studies, Faculty of Law, National University of Singapore, Singapore. http://law.nus.edu.sg/cals/pdfs /wps/CALS-WPS-1704.pdf.

Meyer, Bruce D. 1995. "Natural and Quasi-Experiments in Economics." *Journal of Business & Economic Statistics* 13 (2): 151–61.

Morphet, Hayley, and Claudia Bottini. 2014. "Air Connectivity: Why It Matters and How to Support Growth." In *Connectivity and Growth: Directions of Travel for Airport Investments,* edited by Michael Burns, 11–19, London: PwC.

SriLankan Airlines. 2016. "SriLankan Airlines: The Skies Are Clearing, Annual Report 2015/16." SriLankan Airlines, Katunayake, Sri Lanka. http://www.srilankan.com/pdf/annual-report /SriLankan_Airlines_Annual_Report_2015-16_English.pdf.

Wijayasiri, Janaka. 2015. "Should the Sri Lankan Government Be in the Business of Running an Airline?" *Talking Economics* (blog), September 30. http://www.ips.lk/talkingeconomics/2015 /09/30/should-the-government-be-in-the-business-of-running-an-airline/.

Wijesinha, Anushka, and Deshal de Mel. 2012. "Liberalization of Air Services in South Asia: Prospects and Challenges." In *Regional Integration and Economic Development in South Asia,* edited by Sultan Hafeez Rahman, Sridhar Khatri, and Hans-Peter Brunner, 200–49. Manila: Asian Development Bank; Cheltenham, UK: Edward Elgar Publishing.

CHAPTER 5

Bangladesh–India Border Markets: Borders as Meeting Points

MOHINI DATT, PRITHVIRAJ NATH, INDRANIL BOSE, AND
SAYANDEEP CHATTOPADHYAY

Introduction

BACKGROUND

In remote border regions in Bangladesh and India, a government-to-government initiative is changing crossborder relations, shifting the focus from smuggling and skirmishes to mutual economic gains and building a coalition for peace and cooperation.

In 2010, the prime ministers of Bangladesh and India signed a comprehensive framework agreement covering a range of issues, one of which was a memorandum of understanding (MOU) to promote crossborder trade and cooperation through the establishment of border haats. (A haat is a local market that enables small-volume trading among communities.) The MOU documented an agreement to set up 2 haats along Northeast India's border with Bangladesh, on the border between Bangladesh's Sunamganj and Kurigram districts and the Northeast Indian state of Meghalaya. These two border haats were set up in 2011–12. Two more haats were set up on the border between Bangladesh's Brahmanbaria and Feni districts and the Northeast Indian state of Tripura in 2015.[1] These four haats are the subject of this chapter (see annex 5A).

Following a revision of the MOU in April 2017 (an addendum had been signed in 2012), six more haats promised under the agreement are in the pipeline. Both the addition and the revision expanded the scope for trade and economic activity. (See annex 5B for regulations and procedures.)

The border haat initiative recognized the long-standing economic ties in this subregion, where well-established demand and supply structures had been severed by the creation of the border. When the border was fenced and strictly policed, the preexisting trade was continued over informal, hazardous routes. In supplying formal avenues for exchange, the two countries were essentially acknowledging the historical, economic, cultural, and ethnic ties in these contiguous areas. The initiative sought to channel informal trade to a formal route, reduce smuggling-associated conflict, and promote goodwill among the bordering communities, in addition to providing market avenues for less well developed, sometimes remote border regions. On all points, the venture has been successful.

STUDY DESIGN

The India–Bangladesh border haats survey undertaken by the Consumer Unity and Trust Society (CUTS International) with the support of the World Bank has sought to understand the following: (1) the impact of border haats on the livelihoods and incomes of the rural communities participating in these markets, including women; (2) the impact on informal trade in the region, which has historically been high and a source of crossborder tensions; and (3) the impact of haats on crossborder relations.[2] Anecdotal evidence had shown that the border haats were having a positive impact overall. The purpose of the survey was to capture and quantify the impact in these three areas more systematically. The findings reflect a mix of quantitative information based on the survey and the understanding gained from focus group and stakeholder meetings.

The core fieldwork was conducted from December 2015 to February 2016 at the four border haats. People in four key stakeholder groups were interviewed at each haat: 20 vendors (of the total of 50 authorized to work in the haat), 30 buyers (of the 300+ authorized), 8 laborers, and 6 transporters, more or less evenly divided between Bangladeshis and Indians, covering a total of 256 people across all four markets. Annexes 5C and 5D describe the structure of the study. The four groups—vendors, buyers, laborers, and transporters—were identified to have been directly affected by the haats.

The rest of the chapter is organized as follows. The next section draws upon the experiences of border markets elsewhere in the world to highlight that such markets can range widely in scale and ambition, depending on ground realities and supporting policies. The subsequent section underscores that there is ample scope to scale up the border haat initiative without detracting from formal trade. The penultimate section discusses the four main study findings, which pertain to the impact of the border haat initiative on local communities. The final section concludes with recommendations for policy makers. More detailed recommendations on haat design and operations are provided in annex 5E.

Border Markets Elsewhere Range in Size and Degree of Formality

Border trade is often defined as trade destined for markets within 30 kilometers of the border and usually involves nonstandard channels, that is, not through a formal border crossing point, often in small quantities rather than bulk items, and usually unrecorded in trade statistics. Border markets exist throughout the developing and developed world. The markets range widely in scale and ambition and are based on unique local realities and supporting policies. Some of the big national, regional, and international bazaars in Central Asia, which has a centuries-old tradition of bazaars, matched now by a sophisticated logistics infrastructure, are akin to shopping malls in industrialized countries (Kaminski and Mitra 2012).

Khorgos bazaar, a market at the China–Kazakhstan border, was once an important stop along the Silk Road. It is considered a showcase of border trade in Central Asia, characterized by the document-free movement of traders and the duty-free movement of goods and services. The World Bank (2007) documents that 1,300 Kazakh traders—46 percent of whom are women—cross into China daily, purchasing goods to resell in Kazakhstan. Imports from China not exceeding 50 kilograms by weight and $1,000 by value are allowed into Kazakhstan duty-free. If traders wished to import more, up to 10 tons of agricultural goods and up to two tons of industrial products, both not exceeding $10,000 in value, may be brought in for a flat-rate duty of 17 percent. The market and its ancillary services offer employment for 30 percent of the active population in the Kazakh border town of Jarkent (Kaminski and Mitra 2012). The area has become a free trade zone: the Khorgos International Center for Boundary Cooperation opened in December 2011. This expansion has had mixed reviews (Shepard 2016; Trilling 2014).

Amid isolated farming communities at the Indonesia–Malaysia border, the small Malaysian town of Serikin has developed into a weekend hub of semiformal trade, where 180+ traders, mostly Indonesian, sell their wares (Awang et al. 2013). The Indonesian traders bring mostly garments and fabric, food, beverages, furniture and handicrafts, and electrical and household goods, all priced relatively cheaply, but higher than the prices in their home country. The traders feel that Serikin offers secure business opportunities and easy crossborder procedures. Locals trust the traders and have benefited by supplying services such as rentals of stalls, parking slots at homes, and storage space. Ancillary services have sprung up, including room stays, hostels, and restaurants as traders are allowed to stay over weekends. Monthly profits from these services are high. An individual renting business space could net as much as US$500 a month, while a restaurant owner could make US$210. Indonesians also buy domestic consumption items from the locals. Toilets and bathing areas behind the shops are offered on a pay-per-use basis, and the local municipality charges each stall a nominal fee for cleaning up rubbish. Some of the products purchased in Serikin are also sold on by Malaysian women in local markets. Thus, the Indonesians trade in goods, and the Malaysians largely in services.

In contrast, in Africa, crossborder trade in the Great Lakes Region is largely informal, hazardous, and micro in scale (Brenton et al. 2011). At some border crossing points (Goma, the Democratic Republic of Congo–Gisenyi, Rwanda), formal trade takes place along the "grand" barrier at a formal border crossing point. Informal crossborder trade flows through the "petty" barrier adjacent to the grand barrier. Informal traders, mostly women, carry basic foods and commodities through the petty barrier. Informal crossings are reportedly accompanied by a great deal of harassment and extortion.

In South Asia, there are border markets in areas where the border is hard (Bangladesh–India and India–Pakistan) and where the border is de facto open (Bhutan–India and India–Myanmar). Border trade in South Asia reconnects communities that share a common culture and historically traded with each other before the border demarcations and enforcement severed traditional ties. For example, traditional tribes in Northeast India's Mizoram State live in India and in Myanmar. They continue to trade informally along the 400-kilometer open border or at the one formal border crossing point in Zokhawthar, near Champhai (RIS 2011). Border trade between India and Myanmar is allowed on 40 types of products at 5 percent duty, as initially determined by the Border Trade Agreement of 1994.[3] A great deal of informal trade and smuggling continue to take place along the entire open border between Myanmar and Northeast India (De and Majumdar 2014). Recognizing traditional trade links and responding to the demands of communities and political leaders in Mizoram State, the governments have allowed visa-free movement of people within 16 kilometers of the border and for 72 hours; there are calls to return to the freer regime of 60 kilometers and 60 days (Kashyap 2017). However, the free passage of people is not always feasible at all borders and crossing points in South Asia because of problems ranging from insurgency to smuggling and illegal migration.

In designing and operating border markets, governments have needed to balance the gains with the risks. Security and smuggling are core reasons for governments to impose border controls. These controls, however, could also be blunt and expensive instruments, most damaging to the poor, for whom trade has substantial economic benefits (Kaminski and Mitra 2012). Effective policing and risk-based surveillance provide solutions to address the security concerns, while not curtailing economic activity. Indeed, border markets could experiment in the joint delivery of public services, making the most of the experience and strengths of each government: joint health clinics, awareness building among women, centers for information exchange, and so forth. The markets can also be seen as incubators for microtraders who can, with appropriate capacity building, transition into more formal trade.

The Scope for Scaling-Up

Bangladesh–India border markets are critical to local border communities. The haats offer an optimal solution to providing markets for local border communities where there is an inherent demand-supply opportunity. They are optimal, even if there is a seamless formal trade point in the area because formal trade is associated with a cost and distance factor and is often inaccessible to microtraders. For businesses that trade in large volumes, the border markets do not offer sufficient incentives. Bangladesh is already India's largest trading partner in South Asia, and formal trade between the two

TABLE 5.1 Haat Trade Is an Insignificant Share of the Formal Trade between Bangladesh and India

Haat trade potential	Rs. crores[a]	$, millions
Approximate per haat sales per year, at $100 purchase limit[b]	4	0.6
x 2, purchase limit to $200[b]	8	1.2
x 2, haat days per week[b]	16	2.4
Potential trade of 10 haats[b]	160	23.9
Potential value through 50 haats[b]	800	119.4
Total India–Bangladesh formal trade, 2015–16[c]	44,294	6,762.4
Estimated total trade, 2018–19, at 10% CAGR[b,d]	60,305	9,000.8
Haat trade through 50 haats, percent of estimated formal Bangladesh–India trade, 2018–19	1.33	1.33

Source: Calculations based on the data of Export Import Data Bank, Department of Commerce, Ministry of Commerce and Industry, Government of India and Economic Review of Tripura 2015–16, Directorate of Economics and Statistics, Planning Department, Government of Tripura, Agartala.
Note: CAGR = compound annual growth rate.
a. 1 crore = 10 million.
b. Calculated at Rs 67 = US$1.00.
c. The U.S. dollar amounts in this row are calculated at Rs 65.5 = US$1.00, based on the exchange rate in 2015–16.
d. According to export-import data of the Ministry of Commerce of India, the compound annual growth rate (CAGR) between fiscal years 2010/11 and 2015/16 was 21 percent. The table assumes a relatively modest CAGR of 10 percent.

countries has been steadily growing. Formal trade is set to grow further because of deepening trade and economic cooperation and the development of more transport corridors and the associated formal border checkpoints.

Total Bangladesh–India trade reached US$6.8 billion (Rs 44,294 crore or Rs 442.9 billion) in 2015–16. The total trade at each haat is estimated by the state governments at US$600,000 (Rs 4 crore or Rs 40 million) a year.[4] Even if the purchase limit at the haats were doubled to US$200, the number of days of operation raised to two days a week, and many more haats, say 50, were established along the border, these markets could generate total trade of US$120 million (Rs 800 crore or Rs 8 billion) a year, which would still only be slightly more than 1 percent of the total formal trade between Bangladesh and India (table 5.1).[5] Nevertheless, as this study shows, the relatively small amount of trade has improved cross-border relations and is having a positive welfare impact on the communities in the areas near the border markets.

Main Findings

FINDING 1: BORDER HAATS ARE A BOON FOR LOCAL JOBS AND REAL INCOME

The haat gives us an extra source of income, which is very welcome given our generally impoverished condition.

—*Linda Marak, village head and sole woman vendor at Kalaichar haat, Meghalaya, India*

Haats offer a significant supplementary source of income for vendors and create jobs for laborers and transporters (box 5.1). Although many buyers purchase at the haats for personal consumption, especially on the Bangladeshi side, over half those on the Indian side, largely in Meghalaya State, purchase for resale, thereby generating further income from the haats. The biggest beneficiaries have been the vendors and the enterprising buyers, the latter through the resale of goods. Transporters and laborers have also seen

---

BOX 5.1 The Success of Haats

Haats Spur Ancillary Jobs, such as Among Taxi Drivers

Md. Hasem Mia is a transporter who ferries people to the Baliamari haat in Sunamganj, Bangladesh, via motorbike.

"I am not very educated," he said, "but what I see once, I can pick up quite easily." Previously, he had migrated to the Gulf (Dubai) in search of higher-income opportunities.

"I couldn't earn much, as the company deducted a lot from my salary," he said, expressing his disappointment. He came back to Bangladesh disillusioned and seeking what he describes as "a better life, a human life."

"I was frustrated with the opportunities to earn, and then I heard of the border haat," he added. "I heard people came from afar to buy Indian products." He decided to take out a loan on microcredit and buy a motorbike to use as a taxi to and from the haat. He can now earn an extra US$12 to US$14 (Tk 1,000) on a haat day.

"I could pay back the loan on time because the haat provides an income," he said. Hasem Mia is a lucky outlier among the average Bangladeshi transporters.

Border Markets Provide a Lifeline in Marginalized Areas

At the end of the haat day, a young woman in her 20s leaves the market with a bicycle overloaded with packets of biscuits, hurrying home to her 4-year-old son. By her side hobbles her ailing husband. Sahadev Nath and his wife hold buyer cards only. They applied for vendor cards, but have not been successful. Sahadev has undergone a kidney transplant and suffers from glaucoma. The couple comes to Srinagar Haat, Tripura, India, every Tuesday to buy bargain-priced biscuits from Bangladeshi counters, which they then sell in their local market the rest of the week. They also run a small tea stall from their home. Eking out a living in this manner, Sahadev has been able to use the money to travel to Kolkata for treatment for his condition. His brother runs a grocery shop and helps him with the treatment expenses. Given Sahadev's condition, his wife must shoulder the burden of the business. Their story reveals the sore need to create more economic opportunities in remote areas.

On the other side of the border, in East Madugram, Bangladesh, aged Abu Yusuf lives close to the border haat premises.

"I have about 50 decimals of land [about 0.5 acre] in front of the haat," he said, but he was still not able to get a vendor card. Instead, he set up a small, thatched tea stall on the approach road, which earns him US$5 (Tk 400–Tk 500) each haat day. He farms the rest of the time, although he struggles to cultivate his land because of the shortage of water.

"I have to suffer much during boro [spring] season," he admits, "and I am the only earning member in my family, with three school-going children." The border haat has provided a much-needed source of additional income.

an increase in income. Other economic activity that has sprung up includes the food-stalls that line the approach roads to the haats on each side. Although these businesses were not surveyed for this study, some of the stall keepers were interviewed, and their formation was mentioned by locals as one of the positive spillovers of the haats.

Economic Impact on Stakeholders: Vendors

Indian vendors have seen a near fourfold increase in income. Vendors are the biggest beneficiaries among all the players because they are direct beneficiaries and invest the most. For Indian vendors, border haat profits constitute nearly three-quarters of their average monthly income from all sources; total monthly earnings average US$307 (Rs 20,089). Without the haats, the average monthly income among the 40 Indian vendors interviewed would have been US$83 (Rs 5,405). Of these 40 vendors, 35 said the border haats have hugely increased their incomes (by "quite a lot" or "a lot"; figure 5.1).

The extra income still goes for basics, showing the generally impoverished condition of these workers. Most vendors spend a little less than half of their extra incomes on food, which was ranked as the main household expenditure item by 32 vendors, followed by overall household expenses (comprising a little less than a third of the incomes) and children's education (a fifth of the incomes).

> I could never think of spending much for the education of my children. But, due to the haat, I am now able to spend most of my earnings for their education. I want them to have a better life.
>
> —*Asha Nongkhaoi, woman vendor, Balat, Meghalaya. India*

FIGURE 5.1 Ratings of Income Increases from Haat Trade

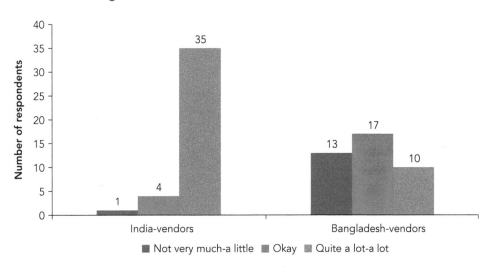

Source: Data from the India-Bangladesh border haats survey conducted by the Centre for International Trade, Economics, and Environment, Consumer Unity and Trust Society, Jaipur, India.

The presence of the haats is thus crucial in providing a boost to incomes in areas where income-earning opportunities are otherwise slim and in securing basic needs such as food. For 49-year-old Swapan Choudhury, the sole breadwinner in his family, the Srinagar haat in Tripura, India, has catapulted his income. When he was selling vegetables in his local market, he earned US$53 (Rs 3,500) a month. With the haat, he makes US$199 (Rs 13,000) a month. Villagers cite his experience as an example of what the haats can do.

Many of the vendors interviewed run local shops or stalls, and a quarter are farmers. At the haats, they mainly sell cosmetics and toiletries, spices, baby food, and vegetables and fruits. Border haats have increased the demand for Indian goods in places where local demand was low. Bangladeshi consumers are reportedly drawn by the quality, the variety, and the cheaper prices that both sides offer in a bid to attract customers. Vendors also purchase at the haats for personal consumption, mainly vegetables, fruits, and processed food items, and also melamine and plastic products.[6] In some cases, the haats are important year-round sources of produce.

> Previously, these products were not available locally, and one had to purchase them either from Shillong [the capital of Meghalaya] or via illegal means.
>
> —*Vendor, Kalaichar, Meghalaya, India*

Bangladeshi vendors experience lower income gains and less draw at the haats compared with Indian vendors. About one-third feel that that the haats have not had a significant impact on their incomes, and over 40 percent felt that the impact was "okay" (see figure 5.1). The majority nonetheless find the supplementary income sufficient to continue to come to the haats regularly, also because of the convenience of the location. Border haat profits top up their regular non-haat monthly earnings by half, less than the gains among Indian vendors but still a sizable increase (figure 5.2). Their total average monthly income is US$261 (Tk 20,745), of which US$84 (Tk 6,675) is from the border haats. The gains are highest among vendors at the Baliamari haat, where incomes almost match the incomes from the primary economic activities of the vendors. However, for vendors in the Tripura-facing haats, haat profits provide a quarter of total monthly income, which is reflected in the many empty vendor stalls in haats in Tarapur.

Bangladeshi vendors invest less in their haat businesses. On average, Bangladeshi vendors spend US$349 (Tk 27,720) on purchasing goods for sale, which is less than one-fifth of the US$2,242 (Rs 148,000) Indian vendors spend (figure 5.3).

The lower demand experienced by Bangladeshi vendors could be driven by a range of factors. They mainly run local trade, and fewer are involved in farming than on the Indian side. Their primary economic activities yield more monthly income than on the Indian side, across all haats. Their average monthly income from other sources is US$177 (Tk 14,070), more than double what Indian vendors make outside the

FIGURE 5.2 Sources of Monthly Vendor Incomes

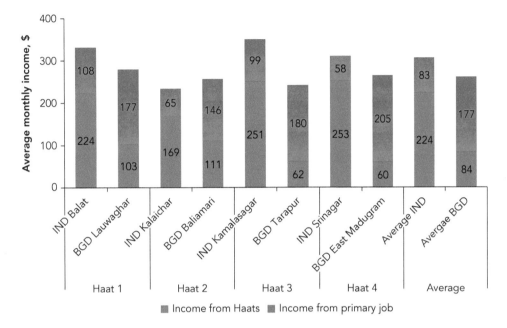

Source: Data from the India–Bangladesh border haats survey conducted by the Centre for International Trade, Economics, and Environment, Consumer Unity and Trust Society, Jaipur, India.
Note: IND = India; BGD = Bangladesh.

haatsl this reduces their incentives to focus on their haat-related activities. In addition, regulatory inconsistencies may be preventing sales of some of the more popular Bangladeshi products (box 5.2).

Despite the demand pattern, the profit margin (profits as a share of sales) of Bangladeshi vendors at the haats is 18 percent, compared with 9 percent among the Indian vendors. This difference may owe partly to the Bangladeshi vendors selling high-value plastic and melamine products. On the other hand, Indian vendors of fruits and vegetables buy these at higher prices from local markets in Northeast India, keeping profit margins lower, except for seasonal, high-quality fruits such as Meghalayan oranges, or the few homegrown items.[7]

The vendors tend to be traders rather than producers. Goods sold at all border haats are not strictly local to the villages. Almost all the vendors on both sides source goods from the nearest towns or state capitals (in the Northeast in the case of India). In addition to large local towns, over half of the Bangladeshi vendors source goods from as far away as Chittagong or Dhaka. Nonetheless, vendors on both sides see themselves as small traders who cannot compete in formal trade, largely because formal trade is difficult and complicated and because they lack the capital investment

FIGURE 5.3 Cost and Profit Components of Average Monthly Sales, by Haat and Country Total

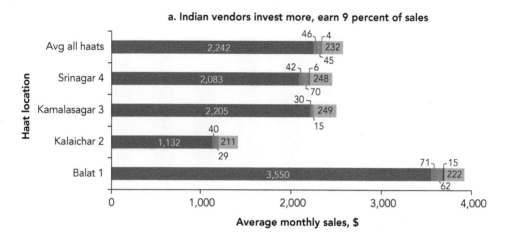

a. Indian vendors invest more, earn 9 percent of sales

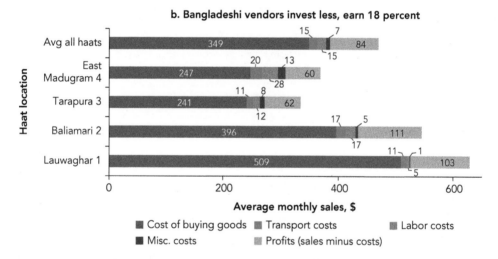

b. Bangladeshi vendors invest less, earn 18 percent

Source: Data from the India–Bangladesh border haats survey conducted by the Centre for International Trade, Economics, and Environment, Consumer Unity and Trust Society, Jaipur, India.

they say is required. The majority would prefer border haat trade even if a formal trade point were to open nearby, although one-quarter of the Bangladeshi vendors said otherwise. Some of the vendors with greater ambitions are interested in receiving training (as in Bangladesh) or are in a position to receive training (as on the Indian side) to scale up operations and start trading at a formal checkpoint. In Balat, India, such training could help some of the women vendors to become small entrepreneurs, who, in time, can become involved in formal crossborder trade. Border haats can therefore be incubators for microtraders.

BOX 5.2 Regulatory and Other Obstacles to Haat Sales

Indian consumer demand is high in certain food products—especially fish (marine, freshwater, and dried)—that are not allowed for sale in the haats. Dried fish is allowed, but this is not clarified or elaborated anywhere in the rules, leading to varying interpretations. The rules prohibiting livestock and related products—the most contentious item in discussions between traders and officials—exist because of the inability to ensure adequate sanitary and phytosanitary standards (SPS) on these products. At the East Madugram haat in Feni, fish is not categorized as livestock and can therefore be sold at the haats. There is also a clamor to allow trade in poultry and eggs.

In other items, such as ready-made garments and saris, there is potential Indian demand, but for high-quality goods, possibly to resell, an issue that can be corrected with greater awareness of sourcing. There is also a need for greater dissemination of the rules. For example, saris are allowed for sale, although many vendors think this is not so. Saris are specifically listed under the cottage industry products category, which includes all handloom products. Additionally, there is demand among Indians for electronics and electrical goods, but such products are supplied through a third country and are therefore prohibited.

Haat regulations are applied inconsistently. In the East Madugram haat in Bangladesh, the purchase of baby food and diapers is now restricted to two or three items per person, and this rule is more strictly enforced by Bangladeshi border guards than earlier. At the same haat, the border guards are said to be strict about the sale of fish on some occasions and not so strict on others.

"Sometimes when I carry fish, they say nothing, and, on my unlucky days, they will not allow entry of even a modest quantity," a vendor lamented. Part of the problem is that while the MOU states that the haat purchases should be for bonafide personal consumption, this may not be uniformly interpreted across haats and haat days, and some fish sellers do indeed try to deal in wholesale trade.

The ad hoc stringency of officials also occurs in some haats on the Indian side. For example, in Kamalasagar, vendors need to prespecify the goods in which they will be dealing and cannot branch out into other products later. In the Kalaichar haat, Indian vendors cannot make personal purchases, but they are allowed to do so at other haats.

Several other concerns are prominent, including poor infrastructure in some places. A difficult approach road to the Baliamari haat in Bangladesh makes the carriage of goods difficult. Since the collapse of a bridge, Bangladeshis have been obliged to travel to the haat by boat.

"I have to carry my goods across a river whose embankments are eroding, and the journey is tiresome," said Tara Mia, a vendor at Baliamari. "Besides, how many goods can you carry in country boats?"

All haats also have a currency exchange problem. The official rate is not well known, and a money exchanger is not always present, a common complaint at haats. In addition, Bangladeshis attribute the lower draw of Indian consumers to the day on which the market is held. It is midweek at most haats, which the vendors feel should be changed to Sunday to draw more consumers, which is agreeable to Indian respondents, but not yet implemented.

Economic Impact on Stakeholders: Buyers

Enterprising Indian buyers claim the largest gains. Although Bangladeshi buyers purchase for personal consumption, two-thirds of the Indian buyers interviewed purchase for resale, especially the Meghalayan buyers, who are mostly women. Many of these buyers are local shopkeepers, and some are farmers. They buy mainly vegetables, food, fruits, and processed food items, as well as plastic and melamine products and garments, which are then sold at local bazaars. One-third of all the buyers said these goods were unavailable in local markets, showing the importance of the border markets for the availability of basic food commodities. Even among the half who said these goods are available in their villages, however, everyone is drawn to the haats because of the lower prices, the convenience of the location (say the enterprising buyers in Meghalaya), and the greater variety on offer (cited by many).

Most of the Indian enterprising buyers who are procuring goods for resale felt the border haats had improved their lives "a lot" or "quite a lot" (figure 5.4). The responses were less enthusiastic among those who purchase for personal consumption only, many of whom do not visit the haat regularly. Thus, local village shops, as reported by half the users, continue to play a role among those people who cannot get to the haats on the days when the market is held.

Bangladeshi buyers are mainly end users who are also drawn to the opportunity to intermingle. Most of the buyers tend to be men, although the survey also interviewed 13 women buyers. Among three-quarters of the buyers, the basic consumption products they obtain at the haats are also available in their villages but are priced more cheaply at the haats. Reaching the haats is typically a half-hour journey, which costs less than US$0.35 (Tk 30); accordingly, it is worth visiting the haat, even if irregularly. Although many buyers are also drawn by the greater variety of goods, a surprising one-third of the

FIGURE 5.4 Perceptions of the Welfare Impact of Haats

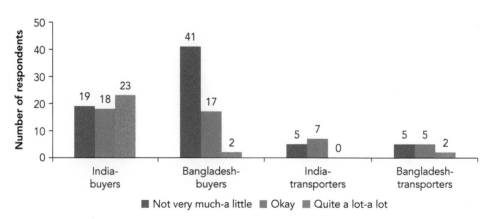

Source: Data from the India–Bangladesh border haats survey conducted by the Centre for International Trade, Economics, and Environment, Consumer Unity and Trust Society, Jaipur, India.

buyers interviewed said they come to socialize. The overwhelming opinion they have of their neighbors is "nice." Therefore, the haats serve an important role in improving crossborder relations.

Economic Impact on Stakeholders: Laborers

Laborers find the haats to be an income boost, but need their collective voices to be heard. Among Indian laborers, one-third of their total average monthly incomes derives from only four days of work at the border haats, approximately US$18–US$19 (Rs 1,200–Rs 1,300) a month. The exception is Kalaichar, where the average is US$47 (Rs 3,060) because of the rough terrain and approach road commanding a higher wage (although the non-haat rate is also high). On non-haat days, the respondents work as laborers, farmers, fruit sellers, and hawkers or in small shops, typically making US$31–US$46 (Rs 2,000–Rs 3,000) the rest of the month (except in Kalaichar, where the laborers make US$105 or Rs 6,900 on average from non-haat work). Although they characterize the work as tedious, the laborers urged that the haat should be held twice a week, which the revised MOU of 2017 offers at the discretion of the border haat management committee (BHMC). The additional income is the main benefit of the haat for the laborers, and the convenience of its location and ease of access greatly help.

> Border haats provide an opportunity to at least earn the basic amenities [and fund my] education.
>
> —*Rajesh Sarkar, 28-year-old student, haat laborer, Srinagar, Tripura, India*

In Tripura, India, laborers sometimes double up as vendors in informal deals with legitimate vendors, showing the extent of local demand for participation in the haats. In Balat, Meghalaya, India, the laborers are often women. Women laborers line the approach to the haat, seeking work from passing vendors. Additionally, all the interviewed laborers in Meghalaya doubled as buyers, making small purchases at the haat for resale locally or to wholesalers. Formally, laborers must enter as buyers because staff cards for laborers do not yet exist.

The average take-home pay for Bangladeshi and Indian laborers is roughly the same, apart from Kalaichar, where the wage rate is much higher. In Bangladesh, labor income from non-haat work is an average US$65 (Tk 5,188) a month, and the haat income is US$17 (Tk 1,343). All the laborers interviewed in Bangladesh were men in small jobs similar to those on the Indian side. The additional income has been a boost.

No laborer on either side belongs to a union or is represented in the BHMC. Some feel the wage does not match the workload. Laborers clamor for representation through inclusion in a union, or for the BHMC to give voice to these key stakeholders. Informal committees have sprung up in some haats on the Indian side, comprising mainly vendors, representing their views to the official BHMC.

Economic Impact on Stakeholders: Transporters

Transporters on both sides earn more by carrying more goods on haat days; Indian transporters make more gains. Indian transporters make an average US$13.50 (Rs 883) on a haat day, compared with US$6.00 (Rs 408) on a non-haat day after deducting costs. The increased income primarily derives from carrying much larger volumes of goods per trip on a haat day (283 kilograms per trip, on average) than on a non-haat day (27 kilograms per trip). Three-quarters of those interviewed owned their own vehicles, and most drive jeeps, cars, or minivans; only two drive auto-rickshaws. However, there is a limit to how many trips each transporter can make to the haat, only two or three each market day, barring Kalaichar, where it is four to six. On nonmarket days, most transporters (except in Balat) make three or four trips. In Kamalasagar, transporters do well: it is only 25 kilometers from the state capital, and the haat is only 300 meters from an ancient temple that draws many tourists.

In Bangladesh, most of the transporters are poorer relative to the Indians. One-half drive auto-rickshaws; some pull cycle-rickshaws; one person even rows a boat (at the Baliamari haat, Kurigram). The transporters own these vehicles. On average, Bangladeshi transporters make US$7 (Tk 573) on haat days, compared with US$4 (Tk 354) on non-haat days. The income of Bangladeshi transporters is lower than that of their Indian counterparts because the volume of goods they transport is smaller; their takeaway per trip is also less. In the haats in Rangpur and Sunamganj, transporters carry an average 153 kilograms of goods per trip on a haat day, compared to only 43 kilograms on average per trip at the haats in Chittagong.

Although haats increase the income of transporters both in Bangladesh and India, the income is deemed insufficient. Most of the transporters on both sides are unable to give high ratings on whether the haat had improved their lives (see figure 5.4). Among beneficiaries such as these, the increased economic activity that border haats can promote is sorely needed.

FINDING 2: WOMEN'S ENTREPRENEURSHIP VARIES BY CONTEXT AND SUPPORT MEASURES

Women are capable of managing everything related to the haat.

—*Woman buyer, Balat, Meghalaya, India*

If we women indulge in border haats or other such activities, who will take care of all our domestic chores?

—*Bengali housewife, Srinagar, Tripura, India*

Women in Bangladesh are no less competent than men, and it is time that they get the highest encouragement and support not only from the government, but also from their families to get involved in business.

—*Sole woman vendor, Baliamari haat, Kurigram, Bangladesh*

Women Vendors and Entrepreneurship: Determined by Sociocultural Context and Policies

Border haats play a role in fostering women's entrepreneurship, but participation is determined by the sociocultural context. Meghalaya differs from Tripura, and rural Bangladesh differs from rural India. Tribal women also differ from nontribal women. Whether they are Hindu or Muslim, nontribal women participate in lower numbers. For example, in Tripura, Hindu Bengali women are expected to play a traditional role, as are Muslim Bengalis on the other side of the border. Gender-emancipated attitudes are largely prevalent among some of the hill tribes of these regions, the Chittagong Hill Tracts in Bangladesh and the Northeast region in India. Meghalaya has a matrilineal structure and sees a lot more participation by women, especially in entrepreneurial roles. The views of all stakeholders in the haats are open and supportive of women's participation, especially in entrepreneurial roles. Of the seven women vendors interviewed in India, all were from Meghalaya. Even the women buyers at these haats come to buy for resale and not solely for consumption, and the labor could also be performed by women.

The proactive efforts of local institutions to encourage women to come forward have been crucial in favoring women's participation in some haats. It was a deliberate decision by the BHMC in Balat to distribute 12 of 25 vendor cards to women, which expanded women's participation. Indeed, in Balat, one-half of all vendors and buyers are women. Elsewhere in Meghalaya, at Kalaichar, where this did not happen, women's participation is not as strong, despite a similar cultural context. There are practically no women vendors in the other haats. Only one woman vendor was found on the Bangladeshi side, and she received a vendor card after persisting with local government and officials for help (box 5.3). In the Tripura haats, men predominate, even as buyers; but, although Indian women are not found as paid labor, they are seen to be helping their men family members at vendor stalls, as unpaid family workers. A gender quota could thus be an important catalyst; in Feni, Bangladesh, haat officials intend to implement such a quota.

Women's participation is deterred not only by the sociocultural environment but also by poor infrastructure. The appalling condition of toilets, the lack of running water, and the poor approach roads exert a larger impact on women vendors, laborers, and buyers. In addition to these obvious constraints, other aspects of inadequate infrastructure also deter women's participation (box 5.4). For example, the vendor stalls are makeshift spaces on a single, shared vending platform, exposed on all sides, with no clear demarcation or division. This means goods must be loaded and unloaded at the stalls each day, and the vendors must be especially vigilant and agile in looking after their goods.

"Vending at a local shop is one thing, but vending at the haat is a different activity altogether," noted a vendor, a man, in Tripura, India. "This is because all kinds of people throng at the haat premises, requiring the vendor to be a lot more active and agile, while conducting business at the haat. Vending at the haat is therefore a lot more strenuous, making it unsuitable for women."

BOX 5.3 Border Haats Provide Avenues for Woman-Led Households

Mazeda Begum is gutsy. She lost her husband in early married life, the sole income earner for her family. With two young children to look after, she was determined to improve her lot. With only a primary-school education, but with some training in tailoring, she decided to set up a tailoring stall in her local village bazaar. Her stall was a tiny tin shed.

"It was very challenging for me to run this small trade, competing with local business people," she recalls.

Sometime later, she learned about a nearby border haat—Baliamari haat in Char Rajibpur Upazila, Kurigram, Bangladesh—and realized there might be an opportunity for her to sell her garments, if only she could get a vendor card. She contacted a member of the BHMC. With time and persistence, they were finally able to elicit the support of the subdistrict administrator to help her get a vending permit.

Now, she sells tailored items, such as bedsheets, pillow cases, and women's wear, and earns US$10 to US$15 (Tk 1,000 to Tk 1,200) on a typical haat day. She is gradually expanding into plastic and melamine goods and can earn as much as US$100 at the haat each month.

"The haat has truly transformed our lives," she says.

Therisia Majau also lost her husband at a young age and brought her children up single-handedly. Now 55, she runs a shoe shop in her local bazaar. Her real break, however, came when the border haat opened (Balat haat, Meghalaya, India). She sells packaged snacks, such as chips, biscuits, and juice, and can make US$100 to US$150 (Rs 7,000–Rs 10,000) on a haat day, which represents 80 percent of her income.

BOX 5.4 Constraints on Entrepreneurship Among Women

An overwhelming response across stakeholder groups on both sides of the border was that the state of the toilets should be improved if women's participation is to be boosted. There is a separate women's toilet, but the lack of water makes it unusable. There is also disagreement across the local level as to which country and agency will fund this infrastructure. The following skeptical comment shows the extent to which decisions by higher authorities may not be adequately relayed to local officials.

"True, we do not have proper urinals inside the haats, but why should the government take these responsibilities?" asked the presiding customs officer in Sunamganj, Bangladesh. "Is the government getting revenue out of border haat trade or making any profit from this kind of informal trading?"

Other small measures would also help. For example, a women-only queue (for vendors, not only buyers) to enter the haats would help women vendors who are more time-constrained than men by morning chores and cannot reach the haats as quickly, as suggested by women vendors in Balat. The difficult access to the market in general—for example, because of the lack of public transport—often typically affects women more because women tend to rely on public transport more than men do (Higgins 2012).

box continues next page

> **BOX 5.4 Constraints on Entrepreneurship Among Women** *(continued)*
>
> Focus group discussions with village women in Meghalaya pointed toward a shortage of investment capital among women entrepreneurs (see the next subsection).
>
> > Getting a vendor card and "maintaining" it for years [in Kalaichar, vendor cards need to be renewed every three years] is difficult, given that we don't have an assured monthly income. We are happy to be participating in this manner (buying a certain number of specific Bangladeshi goods to sell outside via wholesalers or by ourselves), and this does not require a prior commitment or huge capital investment.
> >
> > *—Silne and Bideng, women buyers, Kalaichar, Meghalaya, India*
>
> Capacity building among women to help them take up vendor positions was called for by several vendors and officials across the haats, largely in Meghalaya, India, and in northern Bangladesh. The capacity to run a haat business does not seem to be linked to the level of education among women or men vendors. With training, awareness building, and access to finance, running a haat business could be made more widely accessible.

Women Buyers: Ease of Access to Markets is Critical

Women are more generally expected to be buyers than perform other roles at haats. In India, 18 of the 60 buyers interviewed were women. Most are end consumers, but all 18 women buyers in the Meghalaya haats buy items to sell in local bazaars. The products they buy include vegetables, processed foods such as juices, melamine and plastic products, and garments. The buyers typically run local shops and small businesses. One-half of the 18 women buyers cited constraints that make it difficult to visit the haats freely, such as household chores, looking after children, or working in a primary economic activity. Nine of the 18 women feel the haat has improved their lives significantly ("quite a lot" or "a lot"). The remaining seven, all from Tripura, who visit the haats for consumption only, see less value in the haats and are consequently infrequent visitors.

All 18 women buyers are drawn to the haats by the lower prices of goods, and many (especially the businesswomen) also cited the convenience of the location. The ease of access to the location may help determine whether women buy for consumption or for business. Among the businesswomen, it takes an average of only 15 minutes to reach the haat, and the women typically travel in a shared hired vehicle. For the other women buyers, it takes 45 minutes, whether they come by public transport or hire a vehicle. Where the sociocultural context supports women's entrepreneurship, the ease of access to the location is important in whether women can use markets for business activities.[8] Working women also tend to be more aware of the BHMC. Four women buyers had approached the BHMC with complaints, one even to challenge the officials for being overly strict about the entry of goods. Among the women vendors, only one had relied on the BHMC to discuss problems in the stall infrastructure; the matter was resolved to her satisfaction.

In Bangladesh, of the 60 buyers interviewed, 13 were women, and none of them buy at the haat for resale, only personal consumption, although this is the trend among men buyers, too. Most buyers purchase cosmetics and toiletries, fruits, vegetables, spices, and other foods. They do not visit each time the haat is open, but they are attracted mainly by the cheaper goods. Overall, they feel that women's participation could be boosted, but mainly as buyers rather than vendors. It is unclear why there is an overall lack of entrepreneurship among men and women buyers, but many men wanted more vendor cards to be issued in a fair and transparent manner and by rotation. It may be that aspirations to do business at the haats are held back by the rules and the stringent observation of rules. Focus group discussions with locals at the haat in Baliamari revealed another problem faced by women: items are sold in bulk quantities at this haat, which prevents women from buying in small quantities for personal consumption. As a result, few women visit the haat for provisions.

Crossborder Influence: May Spur Women's Participation

It is possible that the wider participation of women on one side of the border will rub off on the other side of the border.

"Women are much more active on the Indian side in terms of doing business; Bangladeshi women are yet to imbibe this mindset," observed a vendor, a man, at Baliamari haat, Bangladesh.

"Bangladeshi women can also collectively operate as vendors," a woman buyer at the Baliamari haat noted upon learning of the substantial participation of Indian women.

Men's views in Lauwaghar were a little more positive about vendor card quotas in favor of women and their inclusion in the BHMC. Across stakeholder groups in Bangladesh, many of the comments encouraging women's participation, especially in entrepreneurial roles, were expressed by those (especially buyers, and largely men) operating in the northern haats, corresponding with Indian Meghalaya. It is possible that seeing the wider participation of women there on the other side of the border may have influenced these views.

Access to Haats: Skewed Toward Those Who Are Endowed, Disproportionately Impacting Women

Given the few vending opportunities, initially only 25 per country, now increased to 50, competition for the permits must be stiff, begging the question of capture by the local elite. Among the women vendors interviewed, most were in a strong position in their communities. The sole woman vendor in Kalaichar is the village head, and many of the women participants in Balat are relatively higher-income earners. The sole Bangladeshi woman vendor interviewed seemed to be relatively empowered, too, although she was not the most well off.

"Vendors are selected if the family is an owner of land adjacent to the haat premises, . . . and political influence is also a major factor in getting the vendor card," revealed a local resident during discussions in East Madugram, Feni, Bangladesh.

Moreover, the application process appears to be skewed toward those who are endowed with the ability to carry out a year-round business, which requires access to investment capital, valid identity cards, proof of a savings bank account, and the confidence to face an interview panel comprising the BHMC, that is, district magistrates, as well as customs, local government, police, and border agencies. Poorer women tend to be disproportionately affected by requirements such as these (World Bank 2015). Men are more able to meet these requirements despite the stringency: among men vendors in India, several were in a low-income bracket and did not own land of their own (although the pool of men interviewed was also larger).

Women find it more difficult to furnish documents and are often less well connected to banks (World Bank 2015). Moreover, banks in remote localities are often far-flung; thus, the bank nearest to the Srinagar haat is 40 kilometers away. However, Balat—where women participate in large numbers—has a local bank. However, some locals in Balat report that vendors need to show they have at least US$300 (Rs 20,000) in their bank accounts if they want to operate in the haats. This is a large sum for most stakeholders in a border haat context. With regard to women representatives, villagers in haat catchment communities say the BHMCs of most haats include women representatives, although not in Bangladesh, and the formal committee in Balat, India, is reported not to have any women members.

"The vigilance of Ms. Florina Boroh, the extra subcommissioner, Ampati [Meghalaya, India], and Ms. M. T. Sangma, [the] additional district commissioner, Ampati, ensures women's participation in the higher administration concerning the border haat," stated local residents in Kalaichar, India.

Yet, there is only one woman vendor in Kalaichar. Women's BHMC representation does not seem to be sufficient to translate into more women applying for permits to sell their wares in the border haats. More is needed to spur the uptake of women traders, producers, and suppliers. Women's microfinance groups, which respondents said exist only on the Indian side, cannot become suppliers of goods for the haats because their main economic activity tends to be animal husbandry, and livestock is not allowed for sale in the haats. Women could be encouraged to supply not only goods but also services at the haats, such as foodstalls. A Bangladeshi woman tailor at the Baliamari haat, Kurigram (the sole woman vendor), has established a strong Indian clientele for her tailoring services.

Nonetheless, most vendors on both sides of the border, regardless of gender, said it was easy to begin trading at the haats following the required permit procedure. The procedure is therefore transparent once you are in the know, although not necessarily accessible to those less empowered.

"For people like us, who are generally home-bound and illiterate, finding access to border haat trade is not an easy task," said Mazeda Begum at the Baliamari haat, Kurigram, Bangladesh. "I got help from the concerned authorities only when I was able to draw their sympathy after my husband's death."

Men also face challenges stemming from lack of awareness about the opportunities, although they are not home-bound as women often are.

There were not many reports of respondents being harassed by haat officials. This problem disproportionately affects crossborder women traders in some other parts of the world, such as Africa (Brenton, Gamberoni, and Sear 2013). Only one woman buyer on each side of the border rated corruption and harassment as substantial, versus 17 men respondents across the two countries, largely buyers, many in Bangladesh. Of those who were exasperated with how long officials take in checking documents and goods and allowing entry to the haats, nine respondents on the Indian side complained, of whom four were women, and 10 on the Bangladeshi side, none of whom were women. Although two-thirds of the Indian vendors said they were satisfied or very satisfied with the time taken by the haat officials, the higher ratings tended to be those expressed by men. The amount of time taken at entry is a matter of procedure; it reflects the popularity of the haats and highlights that an optimal digital solution for streamlined entry and checking goods is yet to be found.

Safety and security at the haats are not a gendered problem (figure 5.5). Safety was more often cited as a concern by the Indian respondents; 11 women and 31 men complained of this. The main issue cited on both sides of the border is theft, although three or four men respondents in Srinagar, Tripura, India, mentioned smuggling, and one mentioned trafficking. One official in Bangladesh, in Tarapur, also cited trafficking as a cause for concern, although most officials did not feel law and order was a problem. To protect against theft, border forces encourage vendors

FIGURE 5.5 Barring Theft, the Haats Are Largely Safe for Women

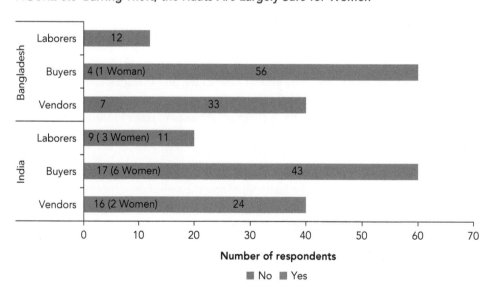

Source: Data from the India–Bangladesh border haats survey conducted by the Centre for International Trade, Economics, and Environment, Consumer Unity and Trust Society, Jaipur, India.

to hire more laborers and support staff and are working with police to ramp up vigilance. Theft is a problem across the haats, but especially in Balat and Srinagar. The latter is a large haat, with as many as 800 registered buyers. Vendor stalls that are more well-built and less makeshift help vendors and their support staff manage the crowds of buyers.

FINDING 3: CROSSBORDER RELATIONS HAVE IMPROVED THROUGH MORE PEOPLE-TO-PEOPLE CONTACTS

"They come here not only for trade, but also to exchange thoughts and establish friendships," said a member of one of the focus groups at the Kamalasagar haat, who added that the border market is a *milan khetra*, a place for meeting up and mingling.

One of the visible benefits of border haat trade is the opportunity it provides people on both sides of the border to connect with each other. In some cases, the haats have brought together families that had been separated for years (box 5.5). Groups of

---

BOX 5.5 Bringing People Together

There have been visibly emotional examples of reconnecting (photo B5.5.1). A woman in Srinagar, Tripura, India, met with her aged mother after a 13-year separation. Mitali was a young girl living in a part of the territory that is in Bangladesh. After she married 15 years ago, she moved to her in-laws who were living in the neighboring area, which is in Indian territory. When the fence came up along the Bangladesh–India border and the border was no longer porous, the requirement of passports and visas stood in the way of Mitali's visits to her parental home and family. The border haat that links East Madugram and Srinagar has given them a place to reconnect.

Mohammad Mosibur Mia from Kasba, Bangladesh, comes to the haat with the additional incentive of meeting with Swapan Debnath. Their association goes back to the time of the Bangladesh Liberation War of 1971, when Mosibur Mia's father sought refuge with his friend across the border, Swapan's father. No cleavage such as caste or class, religion or language could dampen the spirit and strength with which the friendships took root. Mosibur and Swapan look on the border haat not merely as a forum for earning some economic gains but also as a heaven-sent opportunity to rekindle friendship and bonds that were meant to last.

PHOTO B5.5.1 Bonding Across Borders

Source: Photo taken during the India–Bangladesh border haats survey conducted by the Centre for International Trade, Economics, and Environment, Consumer Unity and Trust Society, Jaipur, India.

FIGURE 5.6 The Views on Neighbors

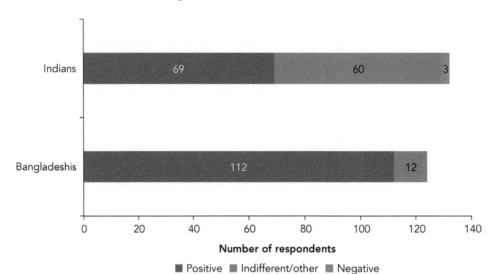

Source: Data from the India–Bangladesh border haats survey conducted by the Centre for International Trade, Economics, and Environment, Consumer Unity and Trust Society, Jaipur, India.

people with a shared history have reconnected; people have recalibrated their opinions of each other; and they have established new connections (figure 5.6). One of the known benefits of border markets is that they allow strangers to trade, rather than relying only on known networks (Kaminski and Mitra 2012).

Over one-half of the Indian respondents have a positive view ("nice") of Bangladeshis, which is especially so in the older haats where weekly contacts at the markets have been cemented over four or five years. In contrast, the Tripura haats were established only six months to a year before the survey was conducted. There, despite the common language (Bengali), the survey ratings are more middle of the range ("okay"), although anecdotal accounts are warm. Across haats and stakeholder groups, the majority of Indians who were interviewed said they have struck up friend-ships with Bangladeshis at the haats. An overwhelming majority of Bangladeshi respondents gave a positive view of Indians at the haats, a view they attributed to their exposure at the haats. Contact at the border market is thus a core source of improved perceptions. Among transporters, who spend less time inside the haats and therefore enjoy less contact, the perceptions of their neighbors veered toward indif-ference. Two-thirds of the Bangladeshi officials interviewed and almost all the Indian officials felt that the border haats faced no safety concerns because crossborder rela-tions were friendly. Officials on both sides of the border said that law and order is fostered because people are business-minded and the economic benefits of the haats are clearly appreciated by all.

Social mixing is a large part of what the haats offer. Women and children gather for picnics and visits, and hawkers sell food items for immediate consumption. One-third of the Bangladeshi buyers said that socializing is a big draw of the haats, as did almost one-fourth of the vendors, all from the haats around Tripura. On the Indian side, one-fourth of the buyers across the haats confirmed this, as did 13 vendors, this time largely at the Meghalayan haats. The survey tried to probe whether the haats had created opportunities for deepening relationships beyond the interaction at the haats, such as in the creation of business relationships. One-fourth of the Indian vendors and buyers felt they had deepened relationships, but the responses focused on the social aspects of relationships rather than new business opportunities. Fewer people on the Bangladeshi side talked of deepened interaction beyond the time at the haats, but those who did also referred largely to the social aspect. Many vendors and buyers described individual cases of the establishment of friendship and intimacy and the exchanges of gifts of homemade delicacies at the border markets on festive occasions.

For people with ties of family or former kinship, but separated by the modern border, the haats offer a place where they can meet, reconnect, and find opportunities to establish new relations with neighbors. The haats help reset sensitivities that arose when the border hardened and was tightly policed. The markets are important in strengthening bilateral relations between Bangladesh and India at the grass roots at places that are the most sensitive, that is, along the border. However, proper infrastructure is needed if the haats are to thrive as places to meet socially. The appalling state of the bathrooms and the lack of water, including drinking water, have a disproportionate impact on women and children. There are no covered areas designated for people to gather and sit, and there are no electricity connections to run fans. In the scorching heat, the officials suffer, too. Additionally, many stakeholders said the haats should be open on weekends to make it easier to visit and attract more buyers.

FINDING 4: INFORMAL AND ILLEGAL TRADE HAS DECREASED IN BORDER HAAT AREAS

> Smuggling and informal border trade have reduced due to the haat, as locals are now involved in different economic activities related to the haat. Previously, people used to go over the barbed wire fence and were seized and punished by the border security agencies.
>
> —*Member of a focus group, Baliamari haat, Kurigram, Bangladesh*

Historic ties along the Bangladesh–India border have meant that goods, especially essential agricultural commodities, have always been traded, including informally, even once the hard border was established, fenced, and strictly policed. Bootleg informal trade is said to have amounted to 41 percent of Bangladesh's US$580 million total imports from India in 2003 over land routes (World Bank 2006). According to state government officials on the Indian side, informal trade was rampant before the border haats were created.

"Previously, 80 percent of the people in this region were involved in informal and illegal trade, but, at present, not more than 1–2 percent are so involved," said residents of Madhavnagar, Tripura, who are vendors at the Srinagar border haat.

Along the Bangladesh–Tripura border, the small amount of informal trade that persists is said to take place through the 10-kilometer unfenced stretch of the 854-kilometer border, in the area of Sonamura. This trade responds to the demand for household products, including saris, clothes, cosmetics, toiletries, diapers, and fish, especially during festivals such as Eid and Durga Puja.

Border haats are simply providing a space that did not exist until now, a space where legitimate trade can replace informal trade. Vendors in Meghalaya and Tripura confessed to having happily abandoned their involvement in informal trade now that there are the haats. Border agencies and state authorities backed this up, confirming that the presence of the border haats has deterred informal trade and smuggling, taking some of the strain off policing the border. Quasi-legal bootleggers who carried small loads or used cycle-rickshaws no longer need to peddle a hazardous, illegal trade. Whereas crackdowns and strict policing of the border once soured crossborder relations, the reduction in crime has helped mend relations.

> "Former black marketers are now earning through a legal trading channel. . . . The dominance of black marketers has reduced drastically, as a result of which the law and order situation has improved on a large scale.
>
> —*Member of a focus group, Lauwaghar, Sunamganj, Bangladesh*

Where there is no haat, anecdotal evidence reveals that smuggling is still taking place. Until the Kalaichar border haat was established in Meghalaya, smuggling occurred through a place called Mankachar, 15–20 kilometers from where the haat is now located. The goods that passed through Mankachar included cattle, imported wine, local cigarettes (*beedi*), spices, saris and garments, sugar, and tea. From Bangladesh, biscuits and baked goods, fruit, vegetables, and fish came through to India. The Kalaichar haat has practically brought this smuggling to an end. According to the Border Security Force, this happened naturally, and no official steps needed to be taken (box 5.6). However, at Dalu, about 60 kilometers to the east of Kalaichar, there is no border haat, and informal trade has always flourished. Dalu and Mankachar have had land customs stations for formal trade for a long time, suggesting that, where there was informal trade in food and agricultural commodities along with a land customs station, formal trade may still have been beyond the capacity of local microtraders.

Members of border agencies said that, after the fencing of the border, the smuggling of drugs and opium decreased by at least two-thirds. But they feel that the border check posts that are still vulnerable to this need more staff and equipment.

> **BOX 5.6 The Views of Border Security Forces**
>
> Inspector Gulzar of the Border Security Force says he is now a happy man. Illegal trade in essential commodities, which the Border Security Force would have to crack down on, has almost completely stopped due to the presence of the border haat, the Kalaichar haat in Meghalaya, India. Moreover, the haat provides a platform for social interaction, and it is gratifying to see friends and family meeting after decades of separation; many of them do not have passports and could have never crossed the border earlier. He also points out other advantages: people can now access the goods each country has to offer, goods that are typically in short supply in local markets.
>
> "There was always demand for these items in our country, but we just couldn't get them locally," he said. Now Bangladeshis sell plastic and melamine products and buy Indian spices and seasonal fruits in exchange.

In addition to Sonamura, informal trade was reported in Chitabari, Harbatoli, Kathulia, and Radhanagar in Tripura, India. If the border haat initiative ramps up substantially, it will reduce smuggling further: the authorities have agreed on establishing six more haats, and there are demands for many more. The initiative will need efficient electronic systems to speed up the checking of goods and entry at the haats, while ensuring security.

Conclusions and Policy Recommendations

In 2011, Bangladesh and India flagged off the first of their border haats, representing an attempt to recapture once thriving economic and cultural relationships that had been truncated by the creation of national borders. Since then, three more haats have been operationalized, and more are in the offing.

Based on detailed fieldwork in the four haats and discussions with all relevant stakeholders, this report shows that border haats have a highly positive impact on bordering communities and crossborder relations, creating economic opportunities among traders, transporters, laborers, and providers of other ancillary services such as foodstall owners. These opportunities are also open to women; although uptake is affected by sociocultural constraints, women's participation can be encouraged by affirmative action, capacity building, and better infrastructure and access to the markets. Border haats help consumers in rural border regions by providing a wider variety of goods at cheaper prices, goods for which there is inherent local demand and supply complementarity. Many of these goods are basic food items, which are otherwise less available throughout the year, and simple household goods. In formalizing informal trade and reducing smuggling, the border haats have contributed to the peace dividend, while providing relief to border agencies from the need for strict policing in these areas. Thus, border enforcement agencies are calling for a large expansion in the number of haats along the border. In offering space for people to meet, reconnect, or establish fresh social and economic ties, the border haats have enhanced crossborder relations. Their welfare impact is highly disproportionate to the small volume of trade that takes place at these markets and thus represents a strong case for the scaling-up of haats in size, number, and ambition. The establishment of more haats and the freeing up of crossborder vendors and products will dispel the premium on scarcity, providing greater accessibility to poorer operators.

The report spells out a few key messages and policy implications, as follows:

- *The haats do not represent a trade-substituting process.* For the mostly small and poor traders, the trade volumes are significant and account for substantial gains in incomes and sales. However, current and future volumes, even if 50 haats are established, will add up to only slightly more than 1 percent of the projected trade flows between Bangladesh and India. Hence, potential government concerns over, for example, the loss of tariff revenue or leakages into formal trade, should not be anticipated.

- *The haats are a story of welfare gains and the building of deepening crossborder relations among communities.* The haats demonstrate the power of low-value trade to affect the lives of the poor. The popular demand for many more haats is further testament. Given the limitations on trade volumes, there is also a strong element of self-selection in haat enterprises. It is unlikely that richer or more well-organized traders will be interested in participating. Moreover, unlike formal trade, border haat trade has a much bigger peace- and relation-building dividend because of the face-to-face contacts involved among vendors, laborers, and buyers from both sides of the border, as well as among officials. This is an important gain and will contribute to the deepening relations between Bangladesh and India.

- *The haats are a valid policy response even if trade were seamless at all formal customs checkpoints.* The number of haats should be increased. Currently, there are 30 existing or planned land customs stations along the 1,880-kilometer land border between Bangladesh and Northeast India.[9] However, haats rely on local operations, often involving exchanges of local fresh produce and low trade volumes. Products that pass through formal customs posts are often more expensive owing to the transaction and transport costs of formal trade and the customs duties. Moreover, there are additional transport costs involved in bringing products to the far-flung communities served by the haats. The face-to-face aspect of haats also enables the delivery of simple services, such as tailoring and foodstall services. Hence, border haats are optimal even in the presence of low formal trade barriers. All of this suggests that there are strong gains to be made from an aggressive expansion of the number and quality of border haats.

- *A focus on value limits rather than limitations on products would help increase welfare gains.* The products currently being traded include fresh fruits and vegetables, as well as manufactured products produced by well-known companies. It has been suggested that the product list should be expanded to encompass more locally made or grown products and then other products that are in high demand. Such products will enhance the gains among both buyers and sellers. The purchase limits for each buyer will ensure that the trade remains low value and outside the mainstream.

- *To maximize welfare gains, the authorities could streamline procedures, improve facilities, and enhance technologies.* Many people who participate in the haats are poor or very poor. Even small gains can therefore be valuable. These people will benefit from facilities that minimize theft, increase productive activities (for example, by minimizing the burden of procedures), cut transport costs, and so on (see annex 5E).

- *Haats provide a strong opportunity for women's participation, with much unexploited potential.* Unlike formal trade in South Asia, where women traders are not especially visible, the haats have enabled women from Meghalaya to participate actively as vendors and also as entrepreneurial buyers. Much more is possible. This has potentially important implications for the welfare of families and women's empowerment (see annex 5E).

With the most recent revisions to the MOU, in April 2017, Bangladesh and India have recognized this positive impact. The MOU has consequently been put on an automatic renewal basis; the purchase limit for buyers has been raised to US$200, and the number of vendors expanded to 50. The remaining six haats planned through the MOU are scheduled for completion soon, and there have been demands for many more, including from local stakeholders, state governments, and the security forces. As the scale-up is planned, several aspects of the haats need to be streamlined and made more efficient. Areas to consider include the following: (1) the design of haats, entailing modifications to the current ones, to ensure the best use of available space; (2) the location of new haats to leverage socioeconomic factors to maximize the benefit along desired dimensions; (3) operational guidelines to streamline and improve the functioning of the current haats; (4) capacity building to ensure greater participation in haats, including by women; (5) haat infrastructure, which suffers from various limitations and has a disproportionately negative impact on women. Suggestions regarding each of these areas are detailed in annex 5E, with gender-sensitive considerations integrated into each category. There is also a suggestion for holding a workshop to bring together all relevant state and central government departments for the purpose of awareness building on border haats and their potential and to build a consensus on future scale-up.

Annex 5A: Market Details

TABLE 5A.1 Haat Market Details

India side	Bangladeshi side	Common issues (infrastructure)
Kalaichar, West Garo Hills, Meghalaya	*Baliamari, Kurigram*	*Opened: August 2011*
Last 200 meters of the approach road is a mud track, forcing the use of carts *Items sold:* spices (in bulk), betel leaf, fruits (seasonal), vegetables, food *Items in demand:* plastic and melamine goods	People come by boat, after a rickety bridge over the river collapsed, which limits how much can be transported *Items sold:* kitchenware (aluminum and melamine), plastic furniture, cotton and low-value garments, and betel nuts (low quality, in bulk) *Items in demand:* betel nuts (high quality)	*Haat day:* Wednesdays 50 vendors, 8–10 laborers allowed per vendor Noncement vending platforms, prone to flooding, tin roofs inadequate during rains, hazardous approach roads, informal foreign exchange service (no kiosk), unusable toilets because of lack of water, nonfunctional tube well for drinking water, no electricity
Balat, East Khasi Hills, Meghalaya	*Lauwaghar, Dalora, Sunamganj*	*Opened: May 2012*
Approach road hazardous during monsoon, not well leveled *Items sold:* cosmetics and toiletries; food, dried fish, spices (in bulk), fruits (seasonal); minor forest products; garments (high quality) *Items in demand:* plastic and melamine goods	*Items sold:* food, dried fish, vegetables; plastic goods (in bulk); melamine ware *Items in demand:* seasonal fruits and winter garments	*Haat day:* Tuesdays 50 vendors, 300 buyers (including laborers) Cemented, but low vending platforms; adequate approach roads; foreign exchange kiosk exists, but not staffed on the Indian side; unusable toilets because of the lack of water; no drinking water facility; single electrical point only
Srinagar, West Tripura	*East Madugram/Sagaria, Feni*	*Opened: January 2015*
Items sold: spices, food, packaged drinks; kitchenware; cotton fabric, saris, woolen garments; cosmetics and toiletries *Items in demand:* fish and plastic and electric goods	*Items sold:* fruits (apples), vegetables (nonseasonal), fish, processed food (snacks, drinks); kitchenware (aluminum and melamine); plastic products (bulk) *Items in demand:* tea, milk powder, baby food	*Haat day:* Tuesdays 54 vendors, 800 registered buyers Raised, cemented vending platforms; good approach road; foreign exchange kiosk exists, but not staffed on the Indian side; unusable unisex toilet (no water); no drinking water facility; no electricity
Kamalasagar, Tripura	*Tarapur, Brahmanbaria*	*Opened: June 2015*
Approach road is usable, but unleveled and rough *Items sold:* fruits, vegetables, spices (bulk); cosmetics and toiletries (bulk); small farm equipment; high-value garments *Items in demand:* fish and plastics	Approach road is too narrow in the last 200 meters; cars cannot enter *Items sold:* fruit (apples, nonseasonal), processed food (snacks); garments; kitchenware *Items in demand:* tea, milk powder, baby food	*Haat day:* Sundays 50 vendors, 1,000 registered buyers Raised, cemented vending platforms; good approach road; no foreign exchange kiosk; unusable toilets (no water); nonfunctional tube well for drinking water; no electricity

Annex 5B: Haat Regulations and Procedures

The border markets are set up on the zero line, that is, at the international border between Bangladesh and India. The haat is wire fenced, with an entry from each country. The older haats (Meghalaya) are less built up than the newer ones, but all have cemented vending platforms with a covering to protect against the sun and rain. Toilets and money exchange facilities exist, but are in a state of disuse and disrepair. Goods and people are checked manually; there are no electronic systems because the haats do not have functioning electricity. Vending permits are issued to 25 vendors per country from catchment villages falling within a 5-kilometer radius; the latest MOU revision has increased the threshold to 50 vendors. Applicants are selected by the BHMC, comprising the district magistrate (the Upazila nirbahi officer in Bangladesh), an additional district magistrate, and local government, customs, local police, and border security agencies (Border Security Force in India, and Border Guards Bangladesh). These administrative and security personnel are also the officials staffing the border haats. The BHMC screens the vendor application forms, followed by a personal interview that asks candidates their objectives and long-term goals. Vendor cards are technically nontransferable and issued for one year (most haats) to three years (Kalaichar haat), after which they are to be rotated to give others a chance. Buyer cards are also distributed (ranging from 150 upward, per side); so buyers are preselected, but there is leeway to accommodate more people on a haat day, on a first-come, first-served basis, as the market perimeter is fixed and can only accommodate so many people. The market is held only once a week, but there is provision in the MOU for the frequency to be increased at the discretion of the BHMC. Many of the administrative decisions regarding the haats have been decentralized to the BHMC. The MOU stipulates what goods can be traded, under broad categories, and there is scope for this to expand by mutual consent, as follows[10]:

- Locally produced vegetables, food items, fruits, and spices

- Minor forest produce, such as bamboo (and grass) and broom stick, but excluding timber

- Cottage industry products (*gamcha* [traditional thin, coarse cotton towel], *lungi* [traditional garment worn around the waist by men], saris, other handloom products, and so forth)

- Small household and agricultural implements (*dao* [kitchenware used for cutting meat, fish, fruits, and vegetables], plows, axes, spades, chisels, and so forth)

- Garments, melamine, plastic and aluminum products, processed food items (including fruit juice), toiletries, cosmetics, kitchenware, and stationery

- Any product of indigenous nature specifically produced in the area of the border haats

Although the locally produced stipulation was removed in a previous addendum when product categories were expanded to allow for more nonseasonal produce, it has been reinserted into the MOU de facto for food products to allow for food produced in a common, contiguous ecological zone to be traded without having to measure for food safety standards because the environmental conditions affecting produce will largely be the same in a local area.

Passports and visas are not needed to enter the border haats, but all vendors and buyers must have photo identity cards, and entry and exit records must be maintained. The per person per haat-day purchase limit was originally fixed at $50, since purchase was meant for "reasonable . . . bona fide personal/family consumption" (MOU), but this later rose to $100 and, as of 2018, stands at $200. Trade can be in cash in Indian rupees or Bangladeshi taka or by barter.

Annex 5C: Study Structure

The study questionnaire examined the income gains from working at the border haat versus the respondent's primary job or sources of income, where goods for sale were sourced, and the time and costs of delivering them to the border markets, how these details compared with accessing local markets, and whether and why border haats were preferred over local markets. There were questions on changes in crossborder relations since the haats had been established, and whether these were business or social in nature. Questions on the impact on informal trade were asked during the survey, focus group discussions, and individual interviews with a range of agencies. The study incorporated a gender-sensitive approach to explore whether and how border haats had affected women's participation and empowerment. It drew on recommended practices in gender-sensitive trade analysis (Higgins 2012) and looked at the following:

- The nature of women's participation and women's roles, whether as microentrepreneurs, producers, or suppliers, mainly consumers, unpaid family workers, or labor
- Mobility among these roles and barriers to entry, which could include any of the following:
  - Access to markets
  - How uptake or profitability is mediated by infrastructure
  - Ability to travel independently and participate freely
  - Autonomy in spending income
  - Experience in interacting with officials
  - Representation at an institutional level and the impact on participation
  - Safety and security at the border markets

Specifically, there were questions on how income from haats was spent, the ease of access and participation in the haats, the experience of interacting with the BHMC and opportunities for representation, and the quality and impact of infrastructure (transport, toilets, water, and power). These questions were relevant to men, too. The survey method especially drew from World Bank studies of crossborder markets in Africa (Brenton, Gamberoni, and Sear 2013). The survey interviewed as many women as possible, to the extent that women participated in the haats. Annex 5D shows how many women respondents were interviewed per category: in total, 34 in India, 14 in Bangladesh (almost all the latter were buyers).

Annex 5D: Number and Type of Respondents

TABLE 5D.1 Number and Type of Respondents, Haat Surveys

Respondents	Meghalaya, India–Sunamganj and Kurigram, Bangladesh								Tripura, India–Feni and Brahmanbaria, Bangladesh								Total	
	IND, Balat		BGD, Lauwaghar		IND, Kalaichar		BGD, Baliamari		IND, Kamalasagar		BGD, Tarapur		IND, Srinagar		BGD, East Madugram		Per haat	All
	M	W	M	W	M	W	M	W	M	W	M	W	M	W	M	W		
Vendors	4	6	10	0	9	1	9	1	10	0	10	0	10	0	10	0	20	80
Buyers	5	10	14	1	14	1	14	1	10	5	9	6	13	2	10	5	30	120
Laborers	2	3	3	0	1	4	3	0	5	0	3	0	5	0	3	0	8	32
Transporters	3	0	3	0	3	0	3	0	3	0	3	0	3	0	3	0	6	24
Officials																		
Border forces	1	0	1	0	0	0	1	0	0	0	1	0	1	0	1	0	0	6
Local government	0	0	3	0	0	0	1	0	0	1	1	0	0	0	1	0	0	7
Customs	0	1	1	0	1	0	1	0	0	0	0	0	1	0	1	0	0	6
Local administration	0	0	2	0	0	0	1	0	1	0	1	0	0	0	1	0	0	6
Police	0	0	1	0	0	0	1	0	0	0	1	0	0	0	1	0	0	4
Other	0	0	0	0	1	0	0	0	0	0	0	0	0	0	1	0	0	2
Total M/W, per haat	15	20	38	1	29	6	34	2	29	6	29	6	33	2	32	5	0	287
Total per country per haat	35		39		35		36		35		35		35		37		0	287

Note: In addition to the four core stakeholder groups, two to eight officials from a range of agencies in each country present at the haat were also interviewed, including customs, border security agencies, police, or members of the border haat management committee (BHMC), who might be with the local government or local administration. In total, 31 officials were interviewed. Separately, focus group discussions were conducted with local villagers from catchment villages (those within the five-kilometer radius of the haats), some of whom fell into the above four categories; in all eight locations, that is, on each side of the border. State officials were also interviewed where possible; this encompassed follow-up interviews during 2016 to delve further into the impact on informal trade. M = man; W = woman; IND = India; BGD = Bangladesh.

Annex 5E: Detailed Suggestions to Improve the Border Haat Initiative

Bangladesh and India both recognize the positive impact of the border haat initiative. As they contemplate scale-up, several areas of improvement need to be considered to maximize benefits. These include the design of haats, the location of new haats, operational guidelines, capacity building, haat infrastructure, and a workshop for building awareness and consensus on the scale-up of the border haat initiative. Suggestions pertaining to each of these areas are detailed below, along with suggestions to improve the participation of women as well as their access to the border haats.

DESIGN

Modifying existing haats and designing new ones so that basic infrastructure is in place and functioning would mean that the use of these common spaces could be maximized now and innovated in the future, when the two countries are ready to scale up their ambition and vision of what the haats could become. For example, if the haats were designed to have a common covered area, the space could be used for occasional cultural or sports activities, designed to enhance the confidence-building aspect of the border haats. If the number of new haats planned increases to as many as 70, it would be worth engaging a specialist in the architecture and design of public spaces to suggest the best layout. For example, the layout could consider placing vendor stalls against the perimeter of the haat, in one or two concentric circles or rectangles, with an open space in the middle. This space could be used for unloading and loading vehicles and as a meeting area at other times and should be adequately roofed. If the haats are to be used for common cultural, educational, or sports activities, this open area would provide the necessary space. Joint sporting events would be a good way to engage youth.

LOCATION

New border haat locations should be identified in such a way that they maximize on certain socioeconomic factors. There is no single predetermined formula, however, and the entire context would have to be considered through discussions with local and state governments. Possible new locations might include the following:

- Areas of poverty and scarce economic opportunity or marginalized communities

- Places where informal trade is known to take place and can be stemmed

- Areas at a certain threshold population density to ensure sufficient uptake at border markets (but not completely excluding areas of low density, as these may be areas of substantial poverty)

- Areas where women's participation can be encouraged (for example, choosing areas where market access points are good)

- Places where local markets are too thinly located

- Places where demand and supply complementarity exists; for example, in Africa, border markets thrive where there is the strong presence of a trading community, a business opportunity on each side that can be maximized, and transport and market infrastructure is good; thus, the location of the market is important for making the most of demand-supply opportunities

- The initiative should also consider how the Bangladesh, Bhutan, India, Nepal Motor Vehicles Agreement might have an impact on the haats, depending on the planned location of formal border crossing points in the Motor Vehicles Agreement; in Africa, some border markets exist along or adjacent to formal crossing points, which may cause fears of leakage in formal duty-bound trade, but would hardly be worth the bother for businesses that trade in large volume; haats adjacent to these crossing points may create other opportunities, with more clientele and the chances to develop transport services and rest stop facilities

- Places that are historical trade points

OPERATIONAL GUIDELINES

Several aspects of the way the haats are currently run need to be streamlined across haats and made more operationally efficient, and the rules need to be clarified and properly disseminated.

The Entry and Exit of Goods and People

Expand the hours of operation to allow for the time it takes to enter and assemble the stalls. The current schedule is typically 9 a.m. to 3 p.m., which is too short.

Demarcate slots. For example, 8 a.m. to 9 a.m. should be only for vendor entry and the entry of vehicles. Because some vendors need more time to get to the haat, an additional slot should be agreed for latecomers.

Similarly, buyers should enter and exit at a set time, for example, 9 a.m. to 4 p.m., and vendors and their teams should be allowed one hour to dismantle their stalls.

There should be a separate queue for women vendors, as there is for women buyers, to ease their access to the haats.

Demarcate tasks among officials more clearly to improve speed and efficiency. At Kamalasagar, the BHMC has appointed *gram rojgar sheboks* to examine entry passes for all entrants, maintain records of goods being traded at the haat, and manage overall activities in the haat premises. The border forces then remain largely responsible for ensuring security and do not need to engage in administrative or procedural work. In all the haats, barring Kalaichar, there is an informal committee, in addition to the BHMC. The members of this informal committee can be designated with facilitating entry and exit, especially of vendors and their goods. A woman security personnel or representative should be present to help with manual checks of women. More staff is needed in the Tripura haats, which draw huge crowds.

Introduce an electronic or information technology system for scanning and recording identification documents and vendor cards, as well as weighing machines and scanners for checking goods.

Criteria for Vendors

Remove ad hoc stipulations in vendor selection, such as the need to show ownership of assets or a bank account with capital, which only leads to elite capture or the need to deal in fixed, preassigned products (as in Kamalasagar). Relay decisions to officials and the BHMC. Currently, there is not enough transparency in the distribution of vendor cards.

Allow for the entry of at least 15 footpath vendors on any given day, including women, and demarcate a space for them. The number should be decided in consultation with the BHMC and local communities. These nonstall vendors should also have a representative on the BHMC.

Mandate a quota for women vendors, at least one-third of total vendors, to encourage women's participation. And mandate women's representation on the BHMC, at least two women from each side of the border.

Vendors need greater predictability in vendor card rotation. A fixed term should be decided by the BHMCs, in consultation with local communities.

Criteria for Other Stakeholders

Provide staff cards for laborers.

A labor representative from each side of the border should be included in the BHMC.

Do away with buyer cards; the market should be freely open to the public. Buyers can still show identification when entering, but do not need to be preselected.

Recording of Goods

Goods may be recorded by weight, type and size of container, or value. A recording format should be developed to supply better approximations. This may be a paper format until an electronic solution is ready. The haats can have their own containers into which items are placed for measurement.

The duty for recording should be clearly assigned to specific, agreed BHMC or informal committee members under the overall supervision of a customs officer.

Clarification on and Dissemination of Rules and Regulations to Ensure Predictability for Vendors

Signboards that are written and, as far as possible, illustrated (to reach the illiterate) should be displayed at the entrance to the haat on both sides. They should show the following: products allowed (not merely broad categories) and prohibited, value limits, that they may be duty and certification free, the number of and criteria for vendor cards, the women's quota, the rotation term for vendor cards, the days and hours of operation of the haat, the number of people allowed to enter, the type of identification accepted for entry, the names of the BHMC representatives and their separate responsibilities (for example, security, recording and checking of goods, and hearing grievances and dispute settlement), and exchange rates. This information will help make all the rules transparent and will assist border forces if they have to replace customs officials in checking goods. A displayed charter of good behavior might spell out appropriate behavior in the haats, including the use of toilets, trash disposal, and punishment for theft.

The rules need to be clarified on issues such as the quantity vendors may sell, the fresh and dry fish trade, the sale of eggs, stall-sharing and subletting (for example, in Kurigram), and so forth. These rules should be discussed with officials, vendors, and the BHMC. For example, vendors spend more on sourcing and transport in the trade in bulk quantities than in the trade on nonbulk items and sell at slightly lower profit margins. Nonetheless, they seem to prefer bulk because the trade is more predictable given that it does not usually involve fresh produce or food, except in the case of fish. Similarly, if the dry fish trade is allowed, this needs to be indicated on the signboard and a decision taken on the status of fresh fish; for example, a volume limit might be stipulated.

The joint BHMC should hold a meeting every month, and a summary of the discussions should be sent to the state governments for their records. Stakeholders at some haats feel the committee does not meet sufficiently frequently to take up their grievances, for instance, on intervendor conflicts, especially in Srinagar and Tarapur. Regular meetings of the BHMC have not been stipulated in the MOU. It may be that, in places where an informal committee has emerged, which has occurred only on the Indian side, at all haats other than Kalaichar, the purpose was to address this gap. (The Kalaichar haat is in a remote location and draws fewer crowds; because of this, officials are less pressured.) The Bangladeshi committees in the Tripura haats are not doing enough to redress grievances objectively, focusing instead on the interests of the more powerful vendors.

A WhatsApp group of all BHMC, state, and central government officials involved in the border haats, as well as people on informal committees, could be established to share views and take decisions collectively. Currently, amendments to the rules do not reach haat officials, and there are discrepancies among the haats, especially on the rules governing tradable products. Some of this is legitimate confusion. For example, should hand sanitizers be categorized as toiletries or medicinal products? But, also, customs authorities are said to use too much discretion in applying the rules of the Director General of Foreign Trade, for example, in Srinagar.

State and central authorities should hold an annual workshop with local officials, all BHMC members, and local community members to clarify the rules and receive feedback.

CAPACITY BUILDING

To encourage wider participation by local communities, awareness and capacity-building workshops should be held in catchment villages. The workshops should include sessions to explain the haat rules, the vendor selection criteria, the duration of the validity of vendor cards, the identity and responsibilities of the members of the BHMC, and the sources of further information. These workshops should be held at hours and locations that allow women to attend, and women's attendance could be encouraged through local governments or community-based associations such as microfinance groups. Women's participation can also be encouraged by developing the capacity of women producers to supply the haats, even if they do not become haat traders.

Some traders have the ability or the interest to scale up their operations. Their capacity to do so should be developed, with a training program on how to trade goods by way of formal land customs stations, the rules and regulations of trade, building market links, and linking local community members with credit and logistics providers and export promotion agencies. Capacity building is clearly needed for financial literacy and linking with banks.

INFRASTRUCTURE

The haats suffer from several common infrastructure problems. The poor infrastructure is having a disproportionally negative impact on women, thus deterring or constraining their participation.

There is no electricity supply to run lights, fans, and electronic goods-monitoring and registering devices, which would improve speed and efficiency. Lights would also allow the haats to run a bit longer during the day. A solar power solution could be devised. In some haats in Tripura, there appear to be power poles, but haat users say electricity is not being supplied.

No drinking water facility is available, and, where there is a tube well supply, it does not work. Drinking water provision is a must. People sell plastic bottles of water, which causes a trash and environmental problem. Taps might also help foodstalls to proliferate, thus increasing the economic benefits of the haats, while enhancing their social role.

Built-up toilets exist, including separate toilets for women (except in Srinagar), but they are unusable because there is no water. A water supply solution must be devised in each location. A rainwater harvesting facility could be part of the solution in the Meghalayan haats; at Kamalasagar, in Tripura, a water pipe extension from adjacent Kamalasagar Lake could be considered. Pit toilets may be appropriate in places where the water supply is constrained. Electricity must be supplied to run the water pumps for the toilets, and a pay-per-use system can be established to finance cleaning and maintenance.

A large part of the success of the haats is the opportunity they offer for meeting and interaction with friends and family across the border. However, there are generally no meeting areas or places where people can sit. This particularly affects women, children, and the elderly, who are the main people congregating at the haats to socialize. Such an area needs to be demarcated, cemented, and covered to protect people from rain and sun, and seats need to be provided. An optimal design should be discussed with local communities.

Theft is a major problem at the haats, more often reported by vendors and buyers in India than in Bangladesh, but at all four haats, though a little less frequently in Kalaichar. A solution would be to make closing up the vendor stalls possible, with physical demarcation between stalls, for example, on three sides, using a low bamboo or wire mesh barrier. Solutions could be discussed with local vendors and the joint BHMC. Currently, a single large platform is shared by several vendors, and each vendor stall is makeshift. The boundaries between stalls are marked by simply tying a cloth. Making the stalls permanent with a proper physical barrier would protect the goods from the elements and theft.

Additional issues include the following: (1) Currency exchange counters exist in most haats, but they are often unstaffed. Links should be established with local banks to designate and secure the presence of a foreign exchange official. Exchange rates need to be displayed. (2) First aid stations should be provided. (3) Storage facilities are not available in any haat. The desirability and feasibility of building simple warehousing could be discussed with local vendors and the joint BHMC. (4) Future haats should be designed to offer much better protection from the sun, including wider roof coverage. The stalls in the Meghalayan haats are exposed to rain.

STAKEHOLDER WORKSHOP

A workshop should be held to bring together the various state, regional, and central ministries and other authorities involved in border haat trade to build awareness about the haats and their potential and to discuss scaling-up. The ministries might include commerce, home affairs, external affairs, finance, and rural development, as well as regional ministries such as the Ministry of Development of North Eastern Region, North East India, and standards, customs, and port authorities. These might be national workshops held jointly by Bangladesh and India. The workshops would represent an opportunity to discuss, for instance, standards in food products; the extent to which the locally produced stipulation should apply to nonvegetarian products in a common ecological zone regardless of the border; whether to allow trade in small household products such as LED bulbs and electronic goods that are made in third countries; and whether border haat trade, if sizably scaled up and fully formalized, would be sufficiently significant to detract from revenue collection. (See the Introduction, which argues that it would not detract.) Global best practices should also be shared at these workshops to calibrate the ambitions about the potential and the future of the border haats.

Notes

1. These four haats are Kalaichar (Meghalaya, India)–Baliamari (Kurigram, Bangladesh), Balat (Meghalaya, India)–Lauwaghar (Sunamganj, Bangladesh), Srinagar (Tripura, India)–East Madugram/Sagaria (Feni, Bangladesh), and Kamalasagar (Tripura, India)–Tarapur (Kasba, Brahmanbaria, Bangladesh).
2. Data gathering in Bangladesh was carried out by Unnayan Shamannay. See also CUTS International (2015).
3. See "Border Trade," Ministry of Development of North Eastern Region, New Delhi, http://www.mdoner.gov.in/content/border-trade.
4. Total sales in the two border haats in Tripura in fiscal year 2015/16 were Rs 7.7 crore (DES-Tripura 2016); 1 crore = 10 million.
5. If we assume that 50 haats could only be set up by 2020–21 instead of by 2018–19, formal trade would have risen to almost $10.9 billion, and the haat trade would stand at 1.1 percent of formal Bangladesh–India trade.
6. The exception is Kalaichar, where vendors are forbidden to make purchases, showing the uneven implementation of rules across haats.
7. This is reflected in relative procurement costs: 74 percent of sales for Bangladeshis versus 87 percent for Indian vendors. The cost share of transport and labor is only 2 percent to 3 percent of sales on both sides. Transport costs are considered irrelevant in border trade, which is driven by the geographical proximity of traders, complementarities of demand and supply, and price differentials (Kaminski and Mitra 2012). Indian vendors spend an average $2,242 (Rs 148,000) on buying goods, some purchased on credit (the survey did not probe sources of funding); average monthly profits from the four days at the haat each month, after expenses, come to $232 (Rs 15,344).
8. Time taken was not asked of vendors; so how this might affect women holding vendor cards is unknown.
9. See "Land Custom Stations," Ministry of Development of North Eastern Region, New Delhi, http://www.mdoner.gov.in/node/1474.
10. From the latest MOU revision, April 2017.

References

Awang, Abd Hair, Junaenah Sulehan, Noor Rahamah Abu Bakar, Mohd Yusof Abdullah, and Ong Puay Liu. 2013. "Informal Cross-Border Trade Sarawak (Malaysia)–Kalimantan (Indonesia): A Catalyst for Border Community's Development." *Asian Social Science* 9 (4): 167–73.

Brenton, Paul, Celestin Bashinge Bucekuderhwa, Caroline Hossein, Shiho Nagaki, and Jean Baptiste Ntagoma. 2011. "Risky Business: Poor Women Cross-Border Traders in the Great Lakes Region of Africa." Africa Trade Policy Notes 11, World Bank, Washington, DC.

Brenton, Paul, Elisa Gamberoni, and Catherine Sear, eds. 2013. *Women and Trade in Africa: Realizing the Potential*. Report 82520. Washington, DC: World Bank.

CUTS International. 2015. "Bangladesh-India Border Haats and Their Impacts on Poverty Reduction." CUTS Project Brief (August), Centre for International Trade, Economics, and Environment, Consumer Unity and Trust Society, Jaipur, India.

De, Prabir, and Manab Majumdar. 2014. "Developing Cross Border Production Networks of North Eastern Region of India, Bangladesh, and Myanmar: A Preliminary Assessment." Research and Information System for Developing Countries, New Delhi.

DES-Tripura (Directorate of Economics and Statistics, Tripura). 2016. *Economic Review of Tripura 2015–16*. Report 17 (March 31). Agartala, India: Directorate of Economics and Statistics, Planning (Statistics) Department, Tripura State, India.

Higgins, Kate. 2012. "Gender Dimensions of Trade Facilitation and Logistics: A Guidance Note." April, International Trade Department, World Bank, Washington, DC.

Kaminski, Bartlomiej, and Saumya Mitra. 2012. *Borderless Bazaars and Regional Integration in Central Asia: Emerging Patterns of Trade and Cross-Border Cooperation*. Directions in Development: Trade Series. Washington, DC: World Bank.

Kashyap, Samudra Gupta. 2017. "Mizoram Wants Open Border, Visa-Free Entry Up to 60 Km." *Indian Express* (June 14), Guwahati, India. http://indianexpress.com/article/india /mizoram-wants-open-border-visa-free-entry-up-to-60-km-4702791/.

RIS (Research and Information System for Developing Countries). 2011. "Expansion of North East India's Trade and Investment with Bangladesh and Myanmar." RIS, New Delhi.

Shepard, Wade. 2016. "An Inside Look at China and Kazakhstan's 'Absurd' Cross-Border Free Trade Zone." *Asia: ForeignAffairs* (blog), July 26. https://www.forbes.com/sites /wadeshepard/2016/07/26/an-inside-look-at-icbc-khorgos-china-and-kazakhstans-cross -border-free-trade-zone/#3b5580d75c8f.

Trilling, David. 2014. "Kazakhstan: On China-Kazakhstan Border Lies a Lopsided Free-Trade Zone." *Eurasianet*, September 5. https://eurasianet.org/node/69856.

World Bank. 2006. "India-Bangladesh Bilateral Trade and Potential Free Trade Agreement." Bangladesh Development Series, Paper 13 (December), World Bank, Dhaka, Bangladesh.

———. 2007. "Border Trade within the Central Asia Regional Economic Cooperation." Interim report (August 20), Central Asia Regional Economic Cooperation, Asian Development Bank, Manila; World Bank, Washington, DC.

———. 2015. *Women, Business, and the Law 2016: Getting to Equal*. Washington, DC: World Bank.